ENLIGHTENED INDIVIDUALISM

LITERATURE, RELIGION, AND POSTSECULAR STUDIES
Lori Branch, Series Editor

ENLIGHTENED INDIVIDUALISM

BUDDHISM AND HINDUISM IN AMERICAN LITERATURE FROM THE BEATS TO THE PRESENT

KYLE GARTON-GUNDLING

THE OHIO STATE UNIVERSITY PRESS
COLUMBUS

Copyright © 2019 by The Ohio State University.
All rights reserved.

Library of Congress Cataloging-in-Publication Data
Names: Garton-Gundling, Kyle, author.
Title: Enlightened individualism : Buddhism and Hinduism in American literature from the Beats to the present / Kyle Garton-Gundling.
Other titles: Literature, religion, and postsecular studies.
Description: Columbus : The Ohio State University Press, [2019] | Series: Literature, religion, and postsecular studies | Includes bibliographical references and index.
Identifiers: LCCN 2018048090 | ISBN 9780814213926 (cloth) | ISBN 0814213928 (cloth)
Subjects: LCSH: American literature—20th century—History and criticism. | Buddhism in literature. | Hinduism in literature. | Beats (Persons) in literature. | Literature and transnationalism.
Classification: LCC PS225 .G38 2019 | DDC 810.9/38294—dc23
LC record available at https://lccn.loc.gov/2018048090

Cover design by Susan Zucker
Text design by Juliet Williams
Type set in Adobe Minion Pro

CONTENTS

Acknowledgments   vii

INTRODUCTION		1
CHAPTER 1	Beat Buddhism and American Freedom: Allen Ginsberg, Gary Snyder, Jack Kerouac, and Tom Robbins	28
CHAPTER 2	Anti-Beat Reactions and Mainstream Mysticism: J. D. Salinger's *Franny and Zooey* and Robert Pirsig's *Zen and the Art of Motorcycle Maintenance*	61
CHAPTER 3	Secret Rituals and American Autonomy: Thomas Pynchon's *Vineland* and Don DeLillo's *Underworld*	87
CHAPTER 4	Asian Religions and African Dreams: Alice Walker and Charles Johnson	118
CHAPTER 5	Buddhist Nonself and Asian American Identity: Lan Cao's *Monkey Bridge* and Maxine Hong Kingston's *The Fifth Book of Peace*	154
POSTSCRIPT		179

Works Cited   189
Index   209

ACKNOWLEDGMENTS

I AM DEEPLY GRATEFUL to all the scholars at the University of Maryland who gave me formative guidance on this project. I thank Linda Kauffman for her help on every aspect of this study, from big ideas to extensive revisions to small edits. I also thank David Wyatt for encouraging me to "rough it up" by being willing to wrestle with the writers whose work I analyze. Additionally, Peter Mallios deserves credit for contributing to my research process his great knowledge of the first half of the twentieth century. I also appreciate Lee Konstantinou's guidance on contemporary literary theory and criticism. And John Caughey warrants thanks for his insights on how people navigate multiple identities in the US. I would also like to thank Mary Helen Washington for her thoughts on Alice Walker and issues of place.

Since this study also has stakes in religious studies as well as in literature, there are many people of varied affiliations whose knowledge of Asian religions informed this project in ways too pervasive to specify. Nevertheless, I wish to especially recognize Chodrung-ma Kunga Chodron, Khenpo Kalsang Gyaltsen, Alexander Mayer, Rajeshwari Pandharipande, and Brian Ruppert.

Several people at the University of Illinois helped refine this project at its later stages. I would like to thank Gordon Hutner for his help in honing the book proposal. I am also indebted to Jamie Jones for her sharp eye for consistency and terminological clarity. And special thanks is due to Vickie Garton-

Gundling, my wife, whose exemplary editing made this book make a lot more sense than it otherwise would.

I also want to thank the people who helped to publish in article form work that found its way into this book. I thank the editors and reviewers at *College Literature* for their extensive feedback on a version of the first chapter, which was published under the title "Beat Buddhism and American Freedom." This article is copyright © 2017 Johns Hopkins University Press and West Chester University of Pennsylvania and first appeared in *College Literature*, volume 44, issue 2, pages 200–230. Thanks are also due the editors and reviewers at the *Journal of Transnational American Studies*, which published a portion of the fourth chapter as "'Ancestors We Didn't Even Know We Had': Alice Walker, Asian Religion, and Ethnic Authenticity," in 2015, volume 6, issue 1.

I am additionally grateful to the always-helpful editorial team at The Ohio State University Press. Lori Branch, Ana Jimenez-Moreno, Lindsay Martin, and Kristen Rowley were all instrumental in seeing this project through to publication. This book is also far richer for the expert feedback of the outside reviewers. And for the concept of the brilliant cover image I thank Laureen Raftopulos, more of whose designs can be found at www.zazzle.com/worldcuprugby.

The contributions of all of these people, and many more I have not named, have helped make this book a fulfilling text to write—and, I hope, enlightening to read.

INTRODUCTION

ON NOVEMBER 6, 2012, Hawaiian voters elected to the US Congress the first Buddhist senator, Mazie Hirono, and the first Hindu representative, Tulsi Gabbard. Their elections were cultural landmarks in a country where, at the time, 73 percent of the adult population—and 90 percent of the members of Congress—identified themselves as Christian ("Faith on the Hill"). To honor their faiths, both Hirono and Gabbard have diverged from the Congressional tradition of taking the oath of office with one's hand on the Bible. In 2007, when Hirono was sworn into the US House of Representatives, she took her oath without any book. Justifying her decision to make her oath without a text, she later said, "I certainly believe in the precepts of Buddhism and that of tolerance of other religions and honesty and integrity" (Camire). Gabbard's religion also played a role in her 2013 swearing-in ceremony, when she took her oath on the Hindu scripture the *Bhagavad-Gita*. Religious scholar Stephen Prothero called Gabbard's groundbreaking gesture "a time to shed some light from Asia onto American politics" ("Hindu Moment"). Prothero further proposed that the *Gita*'s "principle of selfless service" can enrich the "great tradition of reconciliation" of American founders such as Jefferson and Washington and has the potential to counteract the extreme partisanship of current national politics.

Hirono's and Gabbard's elections—and Prothero's response to it—would have been unimaginable for most of US history, given Protestantism's longstanding dominance and the American tendency to view Asian religions and people as inscrutable and incompatible with national ideals. But these historic elections are signs of cultural trends that have long been in the making. As shown in Hirono's and Gabbard's distinctive swearing-in ceremonies, the meeting point between Asian religions and American politics gains particular symbolic force when texts are at issue. To better understand the interplay between Asian religions and American culture, therefore, we should pay attention to these important texts—not only ancient scriptures such as the Bible or the *Gita* but also the religious visions of American literature.

This inquiry helps to flesh out the agendas of postsecular and literary studies. The public viability of stances like Hirono's and Gabbard's are examples of what philosopher Charles Taylor calls the "nova effect," the proliferation of religious and spiritual options in Western societies over the last two centuries, expanding even more rapidly in the second half of the twentieth century (299, 473–76). In his landmark work *A Secular Age,* Taylor mentions that in Western cultures, "Christianity and Judaism [are] now more and more joined by Islam, Hinduism, Buddhism, and other faiths" (676). But the specific ways non-Christian religions shape modern religious landscapes in the West is beyond the scope of Taylor's already extremely expansive study. By exploring US literary adaptations of Buddhism and Hinduism, we can carry Taylor's interest in "new and unprecedented itineraries" of religious exploration further than Taylor does himself (755).

My approach joins postsecular approaches to literature with literary studies' turn toward transnationalism. Although scholarship on Buddhism and Hinduism in American literature has been ongoing for decades, it has gained particular salience in the current climate of transnational American studies, which emphasizes the importance of understanding the many ways American literature reaches out beyond American borders (Appiah; Dimock; Fishkin; Fluck, Pease, Rowe). This book thus builds on developments in transnational American studies with an eye toward giving a bigger, fuller picture of American literature and Buddhism and Hinduism, particularly after 1945. Previous book-length studies on this topic have largely focused on Transcendentalism, Modernism, and single-author studies (Versluis, *American Transcendentalism*; Park; Trigilio). I am indebted to this body of work, which explores the influence of Asian religions on American literature back to the Transcendentalists and even before. However, American literary treatments of Buddhism and Hinduism take on distinctive features in the postwar period, and in this book I seek to understand and explain those features. In a burst of innovative writing and public recognition in the 1950s (Fields 205, Iwamura 5, Seager 40), American writing on Asian religions established unprecedented visibility, concreteness of vision, and a unique combination of countercultural defiance and reformed patriotism. From this point onward, Buddhism and Hinduism have played an increasingly crucial role in shifting understandings of what it means to be an American. The importance of Buddhism and Hinduism to American literature's ongoing engagement with American identity—particularly that identity's rugged, defiant, energetic version of Enlightenment ideals of freedom, individualism, and democracy—is greater and more complex than previous scholarship has acknowledged. This study explores the surprising turn in US literature to synthesize Asian religions and American liberalism rather than to declare incommensurable difference or praise transcendent Asian faiths *against* parochial American liberalism. By engaging with these Buddhist- and Hindu-inspired texts, readers have a fresh opportunity to rethink the limits of American liberalism itself and reexamine what counts as "American."

Along these lines, American literature's adaptations of Buddhism and Hinduism seek to ameliorate the most problematic aspects of American individualism. In his tract *American Individualism* (1922), Herbert Hoover, then Secretary of Commerce, warns of the risks of unfettered individualism and argues that true American individualism is tempered by a dedication to social justice, fairness, and opportunity (8–13). But Hoover's early 1920s optimism looks particularly naive from a post-Depression perspective. More broadly, American individualism has come under heavy criticism for contributing to aggressive territorial expansion (Immerman 25, 106), narrow concentrations of entrenched wealth (Mason 7), shallow consumerism (Archer 9, 18), and racism (J. Turner). These considerations have led one particularly blunt social scientist to conclude that "American individualist ideology facilitates structural injustice" (J. Turner 197). How could an American agree with these critiques while also celebrating how "the novelty of America . . . lay not in the perennially restless pursuit of happiness but in the extension of that pursuit to an entire culture on a scale hitherto unknown" (McMahon 337)? Moving toward an answer, the writers I study seek to challenge common meanings of happiness in the US through ideas of transcendence in Asian religions. These authors believe that American individualism and its attendant pursuit of happiness need not be rejected; instead, these writers strive to reform these ideals by creatively incorporating Buddhist and Hindu notions of freedom into them.

This literary project of cross-cultural synthesis is what I call *enlightened individualism*. The term plays on both the European Enlightenment of democracy and individual rights and the Asian enlightenment of transcendence and nonattachment. As Buddhist studies scholar David L. McMahan points out, when nineteenth-century translators rendered the Pali Buddhist term *bodhi* (literally *awakening*) as *enlightenment,* the word gained a range of European political meanings surrounding representative government and individual rights (4–5, 18). My use of the term *enlightened individualism* has precedent in the work of Arthur Versluis, who coins this phrase in the conclusion of his book *American Gurus: From Transcendentalism to New Age Religion* (243–44). Versluis uses this term to gesture provocatively toward an emerging synthesis between mystical ideas of transcendence and liberal ideas of democracy and individual rights. While I carry on a more sustained exploration related to Versluis's closing thoughts, my sense of the term is more specific: It is a transformation of liberal and American identities through particularly Buddhist and Hindu influences. Furthermore, the kind of enlightened individualism I am concerned with often involves gradual cultivation, not the instant gratification of spiritual "immediatism" that Versluis describes.

The notion that American identity has something to gain from Buddhism and Hinduism may seem far-fetched at first. Given the geographical distance involved, and the marginality of Asian religions for most of US history, it is unsurprising that the best-known tenets of Buddhism and Hinduism appear to be starkly incompatible with long-standing American ideals. What could American individualism and progress gain from Asian transcendence and renunciation? As religion scholar Thomas Tweed observes, these tensions significantly inhibited Buddhism's popularity in late nineteenth- and early twentieth-century America (133). However, post-WWII writers have imagined new ways of walking Asian spiritual paths in the US. Their stories dramatize how the very transcendence that would seem to alienate Asian mysticism from American individualism actually enables a synthesis between the two. If, as Buddhist and Hindu teachings stress, subjects and objects are never truly separate, then there are always ways to build bridges between seemingly incommensurable cultures. Through contemplating Asian religions and cultures, writers have imagined more humane forms of American identity that retain but redefine key American motifs of freedom and individualism.

As positive as this initial description sounds, I want to consider both the admirable and the problematic aspects of what the writers I study are doing. Do the writers I discuss engage effectively with difference, or do they indulge in Orientalism, the Western practice of objectifying Asia (Said)? There are no easy answers. Philosophers Conrad G. Brunk and James O. Young have argued that in spite of America's focus on religious freedom, "there are important moral obligations owed by those who appropriate the religious ideas and practices of others that may place limits on the exercise of these rights" (Brunk and Young 94). But these limits are difficult to define. In the case of Asian religions, scholars have criticized American seekers, past and present, for adopting Asian religions without considering those faiths' cultural context or caring about the voices of Asian practitioners (R. King, *Orientalism* 4; Cheah 20). The authors I examine are conscious of the racist history through which Buddhist and Hindu thought have come to the US. They unsettle ethnocentric assumptions by treating Asian religions not as objects of knowledge, but as socially relevant traditions from which to critique American racism, consumerism, and militarism. However, these writers still participate in the widespread Anglo-American tendency to adapt Asian religions selectively.

More specifically, most Western adaptations of Buddhism and Hinduism emphasize seated meditation and abstract philosophy, whereas the religious lives of most Buddhists and Hindus in Asia traditionally revolve around material rituals and deity devotions, not the rarefied pursuits of meditation or philosophy (Prothero, *White Buddhist*; McMahan; Seager). This selectivity is a consequence of what Charles Taylor, following Max Weber, describes as the West's "disenchantment," the replacement of an "enchanted" world of spirits and sacred objects with a "disenchanted" world of impersonal laws where meanings reside only in minds, not in charged objects (29–30, 553–54). Much of the appeal of Asian religions to American audiences has been that their religious transcendence is supposedly free from the faults of traditional Christianity, such as authoritarianism, "problems of theodicy," and superstitious beliefs in miracles (305). Thus in the case of these transnational adaptations of Asian religions, this disenchantment shapes the terms of what gets transmitted and what gets left out.

The disenchanted lens through which this cross-cultural adaptation has occurred raises complex ethical questions. Given that religions' goals supposedly transcend culture, does one have less of an obligation to engage with a foreign religion's native culture than, for instance, with foreign music or dress? How can writers engage or inhabit Asian religions without exoticizing the cultures these religions come from? What, if anything, do American writers interested in Asian religions "owe" contemporary Asians and Asian Americans? I will not attempt to answer these questions conclusively, but I will show the varied ways American writers creatively respond to them.

My argument that enlightened individualism has flourished in post-1945 American literature supports a more nuanced account of Asian religions in American literature than previous scholarship does. Existing work in this area tends to fall into one of two categories: sympathetic readings that praise texts' investments in Asian philosophy or critical polemics that decry texts' Orientalism. The former type praises writers for bringing assumedly valuable wisdom into a new context, while the latter type scolds writers for complicity in imperialism and stereotyping. Critics doing the first type of work include Todd Giles, John Whalen-Bridge ("Waking Cain"), and Gary Storhoff (*Understanding*). These scholars adopt Buddhist or Hindu metaphysics as their primary theoretical framework, describing ways in which selected American literature uses various elements of craft to convey doctrines such as nonduality [Sanskrit: *advaita*] (Rambachan 43) or emptiness [Sanskrit: *sunyata*] (McMahan 150–51). This body of scholarship occasionally mentions Orientalism but does not dwell on it. For example, Whalen-Bridge and Storhoff acknowledge that Buddhist-inspired writing will "engender suspicions that orientalist writers" are making "a picture of the Other designed especially to flatter the self" (8), but they do not evaluate these suspicions. Their articles' philosophical orientations generate productive readings and are important to our understanding of what these texts do, but this approach tends to leave out crucial political considerations.

By contrast, critics in the second category tend not to discuss Asian religions or spirituality in general (Egan, Eperjesi, Schueller). When religion does come up, these critics mention it only to quickly pull the reader back down to earth. For example, here is Malini Johar Schueller's summary reading of several of Emerson's most famous essays, which were influenced by Asian philosophies: "Although these essays have been read mainly in the light of transcendental aesthetics . . . concerns of the embodiment of the nation remain in them" (162). Elsewhere, Schueller makes a similar point about the poetry of Walt Whitman: "History emerges here as the unavoidable, even as the cadences of the poem attempt to elide it" (192). For Schueller, Emerson's "concerns of . . . the nation" undermine his supposedly "transcendental aesthetics," and Whitman's "unavoidable" embeddedness in the "history" of East-West engagements likewise gives the lie to his pretensions of universalizing holiness. In this view, Orientalism and transcendent spirituality are playing a zero-sum game. If there is more of one, there must be less of the other.

Schueller's critical approach plays an important role in understanding Asian influences on American literature, but it is not the end of the story. Orientalism and religious sentiments are not mutually undermining, as Schueller implies. While Orientalist approaches to spirituality rightly earn suspicion, this dynamic complicates, but does not invalidate, the texts' spiritual dimensions. Religiously concerned literature is always entangled with critically fraught symbols that convey both mystery and insight, and this tension is what makes the texts in this study complex, vexing, and immune to simple dismissals. Whereas previous criticism focuses on either the virtues of Asian philosophies or the ills of stereotyping, my analysis shows how both of these elements are present—and vexingly interconnected—in the same texts.

SCOPE, METHODS, AND KEY TERMS

By focusing on Buddhist and Hindu influences in post-1945 American literature, I am leaving out other Asian traditions, most notably Daoism and Confucianism, that have also influenced American writers. I follow scholars such as Arthur Versluis and, more recently, Jane Naomi Iwamura, in limiting my consideration of "Asian religions" to Buddhism and Hinduism. I have found this boundary useful because enlightened individualism draws from specific ideas in Buddhist and Hindu traditions that are not equally present in Daoism, Confucianism, Shinto, or other Asian religions. By using the term *Asian religions* interchangeably with *Buddhism and Hinduism*, I am not trying to make a strong knowledge claim that Buddhism and Hinduism are the only, or even the most important, religions from Asia. Rather, it is a term of convenience I use to reflect the fact that Buddhism and Hinduism have been the most influential of all Asian religions on American literature, and that these religions' status as Asian has great relevance to how writers contend with these faiths' distant origins and matters of cultural difference.

A more precise term to unify the philosophical systems at issue is *dharma*, a Sanskrit word that refers to teachings in both Hinduism and Buddhism (Iyer 61, 93; Rahula 8; Hiltebeitel 3; R. King, *Indian Philosophy* 171). According to the Dharma Academy of North America, a division of the American Academy of Religion, Hinduism and Buddhism are both "dharmic religions" that share central tenets ("Mission"). The most important of these points are that worldly phenomena are impermanent and illusory (Iyer 68, Deshung Rinpoche 198); ultimate reality is undifferentiated and property-less (Coleman 37–38, Rambachan 43); karma conditions actions and their results (Iyer 89, Rahula 32); and reincarnation is a troubled cycle that one can transcend through meditative insight (Rahula 32, Rambachan 104–5). While Daoism and Confucianism have much common cultural ground with Buddhism and Hinduism, these specific ideas within Buddhist and Hindu intellectual traditions have been distinctively important to American adaptations of Asian religions. The fact that Buddhism grew out of Hinduism makes it unsurprising that there would be many key ideas in common; as Huston Smith writes, "Buddhism drew its lifeblood from Hinduism" (Smith 92). Thus one may refer to the Hindu-Buddhist tradition in the same way that people speak of the Judeo-Christian tradition. Furthermore, these philosophical formulations within Buddhism and Hinduism allow for a transcendence that secular occupants of the West continue to crave (Taylor 727), and they do away with the Christian idea of a personal God who created the universe, a concept many Western spiritual seekers find unpalatable (Campbell). Of course, the very decision to define a religion by a set of beliefs could be said to reflect a Western and specifically Protestant bias (Prothero, *White Buddhist*), and the meanings of this culturally conditioned scope will also occupy my attention. But all of this is to say that this dharmic tradition is the common interest of the writers I study, which is why I focus only on influences from Buddhism and Hinduism.

Given the kinship between Buddhism and Hinduism, it is not surprising that these religions appeal to overlapping audiences. My focus on both Buddhist and Hindu influences reflects these religions' intertwined reception in the US. As Colin Campbell argues, both Hindu and Buddhist practices in the West have become inseparable from Beat, Hippie, and New Age movements; one cannot talk for long about the former without also discussing the latter (191, 112–13, 140). Accordingly, I emphasize that enlightened individualism comes into its own as a countercultural phenomenon, even as it has gradually become more mainstream. The texts I study often mention Buddhism and Hinduism together, although I specify whether a given reference is Buddhist or Hindu where appropriate. But Buddhism and Hinduism have undergone similar adaptations by Western adherents: Both religions have undergone convergent processes of reducing ritual, emphasizing rationality, and focusing on meditation for laypeople, not only monastics (Williamson, McMahan). The texts I discuss both respond and contribute to these ongoing trends.

One can further understand Buddhism's and Hinduism's role in US literature by differentiating between "religion" and "spirituality." Here I follow Alexander Astin, Helen Astin, and Jennifer Lindholm, who specify "religion" as an institutional affiliation with an attendant set of ritual observances and community membership. "Spirituality," on the other hand, is a personal search for transcendent meaning that often involves little or no formal practice (5). This term has a particular American history; Leigh Schmidt explains that what we now call *spirituality* arose in the context of nineteenth-century US progressive religious liberalism (4–7). He further shows that the capacious umbrella of "spirituality" has long been relevant to reforming and revitalizing American individualism in more humane directions (289–90). Keeping this history in mind, I explore how, from the Beats onward, specific influences from Asian religions become increasingly important to countercultural spiritualities and beyond.

Although spirituality may seem vague and difficult to study, it is becoming an increasingly popular term. For example, the US Religious Landscape Survey by the Pew Forum on Religion & Public Life lists "spiritual but not religious" as one of its official categories of religious identification ("Spiritual But Not Religious" 2014). Although the 2014 survey finds that fewer than 1 percent of survey respondents identify with the specific phrase "spiritual but not religious," it also shows that 40 percent of those who identify with no religion say that "spiritual" experience plays a significant role in their lives (Masci and Lipka). This 9 percent of the total population is a significant, but far from the only, constituency of people who are often receptive to Buddhist and Hindu influences.

This distinction between *religion* and *spirituality* allows us to see that Buddhism and Hinduism have influenced many more Americans than those who formally affiliate with these religions. A major factor of these traditions' growing popularity in the US is their tendency to offer American audiences teachings without demanding conversion. For example, the famous Indian guru Maharishi Mahesh Yogi positions his Transcendental Meditation not as a religion but as a form of mental training that can complement any religion one already follows (Griffin). Also, the 14th Dalai Lama writes that people can flourish without religion, but not without a spirituality and ethics based on compassion (Gyatso, *Beyond Religion* xiii–xv). Western-targeted adaptations of Asian religions tend to prioritize spirituality over religion, a trend reflected in the literature in this study. All of the writers I discuss are deeply influenced by Asian religions, but very few claim any religious affiliation, and some explicitly disclaim any affiliation.

Furthermore, the role Buddhism and Hinduism play in post-1945 American literature and culture complicates Charles Taylor's influential notion of the *immanent frame*, a complex concept that has become a widespread point of reference for scholars of contemporary religion and secularity. This immanent frame is a way of viewing the world that is implicitly shared by both religious and nonreligious people in the modern West. Some of the most noteworthy aspects of the immanent frame are the sense that individuals have a "buffered self" impervious to coercive spiritual forces, that time is "pervasively secular" by flowing at the same rate without regard for special occasions, and that "instrumental rationality," not symbolism or mythology, is a definitive method for understanding physical phenomena (37–41, 542). In his response to *A Secular Age*, José Casanova says that non-European religions, including Buddhism and Hinduism, are becoming Americanized in the US, similarly to other previously marginal religions like Catholicism or Mormonism, and thus will not create any significant disruption to the immanent frame as Taylor conceives it (280–81).

And yet what I am calling *enlightened individualism* does not fit neatly into Taylor's understanding of the "cross-pressures" of the immanent frame. For Taylor, the cross-pressures of the immanent frame are toward an openness to transcendence, on the one hand, and toward a closed system of exclusive humanism, on the other (542–44). Taylor identifies this transcendence with

"God," and exclusive humanism with an impersonal order in which humans must create their own flourishing (544, 546–48). But American adaptations of Asian religions rely neither on God nor on a secular impersonal order. The transcendence they offer is not a vertical reverence toward "God, or something ontologically higher" (544), but a horizontal dissolution of all distinctions between subjects and objects. This kind of transcendence involves an embrace of an impersonal order that is also sacred. The limitless, nondual nature of phenomena *is* itself transcendent; therefore, this sacred but nontheistic reality is not experienced as threatening to human fullness. Thus one need not avoid this reality with hedonistic superficiality or make a defiant expression of compensatory self-assertion or courage.

The nonduality of which enlightened individualism partakes further complicates Taylor's immanent frame by eroding the "buffered self" of contemporary individualism. This does not mean the return of a porous self in a world of spirits, but rather a positive vision of compassion based on the interdependence of all phenomena. Furthermore, the formations I am discussing are distinctive to the US because they rework American individualism in terms of ideas from Asian religions, while also changing those imported faiths as well. This synthesis complicates the buffered self in complex ways. Enlightened individualism relies on individualist habits cultivated by the buffered self, such as inner depths, autonomous choices, and philosophical introspection (539–40). But the metaphysical notion of interdependence also changes this individualism into a more relational, embedded model. Enlightened individualism channels Asian ideas of transcendence into a greater openness to others by challenging the idea of a stable, fixed self. This coexistence is remarkable, and we will see in the coming pages how post-1945 writers bring it to life.

By exploring only the development of Asian religions in the US while bracketing their Asian histories, it might seem as though I present Buddhism and Hinduism as fixed systems distorted by transmission to the modern, fast-paced US. Such a portrayal would reproduce the same rarefying tendencies that American literature has problematically practiced, as shown in the work of scholars such as the aforementioned David McMahan, Stephen Prothero, and Thomas Tweed. Indeed, this is not the impression I wish to convey. Rather, I treat Buddhism's and Hinduism's growth in the US as continuous with these traditions' long histories. To view these religions' Asian forms as static would be to repeat the bias of nineteenth-century European scholars of Buddhism, who thought of early Indian and Sri Lankan Buddhism as pure philosophy that later degenerated into superstition as it spread throughout Asia (Seager 29). As Stuart Hall famously declares, "There is always a politics of identity, a politics of position, which has no absolute guarantee in an unproblematic, transcendental 'law of origin'" (226). The Asian religions I reference are no exception. As others have noted, Buddhism underwent significant changes as it spread beyond India and established itself in China, Tibet, Japan, Thailand, and elsewhere (McClure 51, Storhoff and Whalen-Bridge 3). America joins a long series of new homes for Asian religions, one in which American literature plays a unique role.

TRANSCENDENTALISM

The growth of Buddhist- and Hindu-influenced literature after WWII builds on a centuries-old tradition of Anglo-American writing on Asian religions. Although references to Asian cultures in American writing go back to before the Revolutionary War (Schueller 1), the first major wave of American literature that concerns itself with Asian religion is Transcendentalism (Campbell 25–26, Goldberg 7–8). Text-based European scholarship on Asian religions effectively began in the 1780s with Sir William Jones's studies of Sanskrit, but Asian religious texts did not reach a significant audience in the US until the 1840s (Versluis 7). During this decade, Ralph Waldo Emerson's and Henry David Thoreau's "Ethnical Scriptures" column in the Transcendentalist magazine *The Dial* introduced readers to English translations of Asian texts such as the *Baghavad-Gita* or the sayings of Confucius (Versluis 79). Much later, Thoreau's discussion of the *Baghavad-Gita* in *Walden* would help introduce Jack Kerouac to Asian religions (Prothero, Introduction 1–3). While the Beats did not wholly depend on the Transcendentalists for their introductions to Asian religions—D. T. Suzuki and Dwight Goddard were also important transmitters—the Beats were more generally influenced by the Transcendentalist agendas of spiritual innovation and American cultural renewal. In Emerson's best-known writings, direct allusions to Asian religions are rare, but his ideas about spiritual "Unity in Variety" and "universal Spirit" were influenced by the Hindu teaching that all phenomena are fundamentally divine substance (Emerson, "Nature" 506, 507; Goodman 627–28), ideas that Beat writers such as Kerouac would find appealing.

We see more-explicit engagement with Hinduism in the work of Henry David Thoreau. In a well-known passage in *Walden*, Thoreau writes, "In the morning I bathe my intellect in the stupendous and cosmogonal philosophy of the Bhagvat Geeta ... in comparison with which our modern world and its literature seem puny and trivial.... The pure Walden water is mingled with the sacred water of the Ganges" (269). Thoreau's ambitious imagery, which expresses his veneration for Hindu scripture as a fantasy of erasing geographical distances, is noteworthy for its implication that Asian wisdom can emerge in American spaces.

But if American nature can be a place of rebirth for Asian wisdom, it is only because, in Thoreau's view, this wisdom is essentially dead in its lands of origin. In his lesser-known essay "Walking," written shortly before his extended stay at Walden, Thoreau reflects, "The West is preparing to add its fables to those of the East. The valleys of the Ganges, the Nile, and the Shine having yielded their crop, it remains to be seen what the valleys of the Amazon, the Plate, the Orinoco, the St. Lawrence, and the Mississippi will produce. Perchance when, in the course of ages, American liberty has become a fiction of the past—as it is to some extent a fiction of the present—the poets of the world will be inspired by American mythology" (qtd. in Versluis 96). If the future "poets of the world will be inspired by American mythology" only after "American liberty" is extinct, the implication is that poets of the present are similarly inspired by the "fables . . . of the East" whose vital origins now exist only as memories and myth, their crops already harvested. Thoreau treats Asia as a fallen realm whose greatest treasures are static artifacts from the past, not dynamic cultures of the present; he forecasts a parallel course for the New World. The post-1945 writers I discuss build on Thoreau's vision by treating Asian religions as a source of renewal for "American liberty," but they complicate Thoreau's and others' visions of Buddhism and Hinduism as exotic relics.

The writings of Emerson and Thoreau illustrate how Transcendentalists connected Asian religions with projects of questioning authority and discovering personal authenticity. Also important, the Transcendentalists made a crucial modification to the traditional frameworks of Asian religions—probably without fully realizing it—a modification that later American writers follow: They did not fully subscribe to the orthodox Hindu and Buddhist narrative of spiritual development that ends with the complete transcendence of the individual self. Rather, Transcendentalists treated idealized versions of Hinduism and Buddhism as ways of discovering a truer, more authentic individual self. This vision retains elements of a Romantic epiphany in which the self transcends itself in ecstasy but reemerges afterward, revitalized. This vision is in contrast to a Buddhist or Hindu epiphany, after which all clinging to an idea of individual selfhood is gone (Thanissaro, McMahan). Thus Transcendentalist understandings of selfhood create a basis for future writers to preserve a sense of individualism in their American adaptations of Asian religions.

For example, Emerson's *Self-Reliance* describes spiritual growth as a source of creativity and individuality. He writes that for every man [sic], "imitation is suicide. . . . The power which resides in him is new in nature, and none but he knows what that is which he can do, nor does he know until he has tried" (2–3). This rugged, defiant individualism celebrates individual creativity and "power," in contrast to Asian religious texts such as *The Dhammapada*, the sayings of the Buddha. In this text, the Buddha also counsels a certain kind of self-reliance insofar as a realized people should "depart with their thoughts well-collected, they are not happy in their abode; like swans who have left their lake, they leave their house and home" (l.91) But the goal is not achievement; it is renunciation: "There is no suffering for him who has finished his journey, and abandoned grief, who has freed himself on all sides, and thrown off all fetters" (l.90). Emerson celebrates a vigorous individual vitality, whereas the Buddha urges complete detachment and equanimity. With some adaptation—or, less charitably, projection—the Transcendentalists saw Asian religions as ancient but vital ways of finding oneself, expressing individual artistic creativity, and questioning authority, themes that the Beats and their successors would develop further.

While a small number of white spiritual seekers, exemplified by Emerson and Thoreau, explored Asian religions through texts in the first half of the nineteenth century, on the country's opposite coast, immigrants brought Buddhism from China (Fields 72–73), and Hindu immigrants from India would follow a few decades later (Kurien 41–43). These immigrant religions retained the devotional and ritual elements that the white adapters tended to dismiss as mere culturally particular superstition in contrast to the supposedly universal truths that the white adapters could recuperate from sacred texts. West Coast immigrant Buddhists, because of both geographical and attitudinal distance, would almost never interact with the East Coast strain I have just described. This marks the beginning of a deep split between immigrant religions from Asia and primarily white adaptations of them, a chasm that remains up to the present day. This division has profoundly affected enlightened individualism, and I will take up this issue more extensively in my later discussion of Asian American Buddhist writing.

GROWING EXCHANGE AND THE WORLD PARLIAMENT

Cultural exchange between East Asia and the West accelerated in the later nineteenth century in ways that contributed to Asian religions' status in the West as a respectable but distant curiosity. In particular, increased trade between Japan and Europe, which took off in 1853, led to Japanese artistic influences on European and American painters from the 1860s through the 1890s, including Claude Monet, Edgar Degas, Mary Cassatt, and James Whistler (Ives). These painters were not engaged with Asian religions in particular, but they generated an interest in Japanese and Chinese aesthetics that greatly influenced European art. This development set the stage for international figures such as Lafcadio Hearn, Helena Blavatsky, Henry Steel Olcott, Sadakichi Hartmann, and Ernest Fenollosa, many of whom were deeply involved with the visual arts, to further expand the influence of Asian religions among Anglo-American audiences. Some of these writers, such as Olcott and Fenollosa, were also influential contributors to religious and cultural revitalization efforts in Asian countries, particularly Sri Lanka and Japan, respectively. Such transnational circuits contributed to the popularity of Edwin Arnold's epic poem *The Light of Asia*, an instant hit in England when it debuted in 1879. Arnold's admiring narrative of the Buddha's life helped to solidify the Buddha's image in the West as a modern-friendly wisdom teacher who eschewed ritual and superstition, even though the poem presents many traditional miraculous stories (Arnold 10, Clausen).

An expanding interest in Asian cultures, supported by increased international trade, also manifested through Orientalist exoticism. English novels such as Wilkie Collins's *The Moonstone* (1868), Marie Corelli's *A Romance of Two Worlds* (1886), and H. Rider Haggard's *Ayesha: The Return of She* (1905) offered suspenseful plots that centered on mysterious Buddhist or Hindu rituals. American writing on Asian religions at this time included occasional Asian-influenced monographs, such as the Theosophical Society's 1877 *Isis Unveiled, A Master-Key to the Mysteries of Ancient and Modern Science and Theology* (Blavatsky), which lent Asian religions an exoticized air of the occult (Fields 92, Tweed 52–53).

While these various nineteenth-century writings brought gradual growth in American interest in Buddhism and Hinduism, a dramatic turning point came with the World Parliament of Religions in Chicago, a part of the World's Columbian Exposition of 1893. The first event of its kind, the World Parliament of Religions brought together representatives from many faiths from around the world. Through this gathering, numerous Americans in attendance—and many more who read newspapers' accounts—learned about Buddhism and Hinduism for the first time, and from in-person teachers, not translated texts (Goldberg 77, Williamson 27, Seager 35, Snodgrass 1, Tanaka). This event also saw the first known American to convert officially to Buddhism (Fields 129). Asian religions' best-known American adaptations can be traced to this gathering. For instance, modern, fitness-focused American yoga owes its existence to the interest inspired by the Hindu missionary Swami Vivekenanda's charismatic opening address to the Parliament (Goldberg 79–80, Bardach). Additionally, the Parliament's Zen contingent would later send a young D. T. Suzuki, arguably the most influential Buddhist teacher in the early to mid-twentieth century, to continue promoting Japanese Buddhism in the US (Snodgrass 259–60).

Many of the key representatives at the Parliament presented versions of their traditions carefully catered to American audiences. The "Eastern" religions they represented were already influenced by Western-inspired reform movements that sought to emphasize compatibility with rationalism and downplay anything that would look like superstition, such as rituals and deity worship (Snodgrass, Williamson). This disenchanted adaptation was an attempt to cater to American audiences who lived in what Taylor calls an immanent frame of instrumental reason and impersonal order (542). The representatives were sent by their governments to improve their countries' international reputation and promote current modernization movements. The delegates thus attempted to appeal to the progressive spirit that underlay the larger background of the World's Columbian Exposition. A closer look at a couple of key representatives at the World Parliament is warranted, as these figures articulated the basis of enlightened individualism that, while obscure at the time, would be magnified and transformed by countercultural movements a half-century later.

Parliament representatives echoed some Transcendentalist themes of universal brotherhood and Asian religions' relevance to American individualism, but with greater theoretical development and social concreteness. In particular, Swami Vivekananda and Zen Buddhist representative Shaku Soyen are noteworthy examples. Swami Vivekananda's reception at the Parliament was so positive that he used its momentum to launch a speaking tour around the US. In a particularly remarkable lecture in San Francisco in 1900, Vivekananda boldly articulated with unprecedented ambition what would become an influential set of ideas about the compatibility of Asian religions and American democracy:

> You want to be democratic in this country. It is the democratic God that Vedanta teaches.... Its God is not the monarch sitting on a throne, entirely apart.... You are all kings in this country. So with the religion of Vedanta. You are all Gods.... India cannot give up his majesty the king of the earth—that is why Vedanta cannot become the religion of India. There is a chance of Vedanta becoming the religion of your country because of democracy. (*Complete Works* 125–26)

Vivekananda uses the text-based term *Vedanta* instead of the geographical term *Hinduism* both to identify a specific strain within Hinduism [*Advaita Vedanta*, which holds that all phenomena are ultimately undifferentiated divine substance] (Rambachan 43) and to avoid unfavorable cultural associations such as India's caste system. He also boldly inverts Vedanta's foreign status, going so far as to say that the US is actually a better home for Hindu-inspired religion than India itself, which has lapsed into spiritual decline—as manifested in a hierarchical government—and needs modernizing reform. Vivekananda's claim that "you are all kings in this country" is, of course, a flattering exaggeration, but it does effectively appeal to what Thoreau calls the "fiction" of "American liberty."

But the most interesting aspect of this argument is its ambitious—and intriguingly coherent—claim that Indian Vedanta is a better religious basis for democracy than monotheism. A sovereign God "entirely apart" is too monarchical and, by implication, tyrannical. There is no surer way, Vivekananda must have thought, to critique something to Americans than by labeling it as *monarchical*. By contrast, the Vedantic belief that all beings are ultimately at one with the universal Divine is more consistent with democratic commitments to individual rights and representative government—in short, that there are certain ways in which each person always matters. Vedanta's "democratic God" is immanent, impersonal, and nonhierarchical. But in a sophisticated appeal to American sensibilities, Vivekananda still uses this belief to celebrate individual sovereignty over oneself rather than Vedanta's traditional ideal of a total erasure of individuality. Vivekananda's ideas also influenced William James, whose decision to focus his groundbreaking treatise *The Varieties of Religious Experience* on private religious experiences rather than religions' social and ritualistic aspects further reinforced American literature's tendency to focus on Asian religious philosophy at the expense of culture.

At the World Parliament of Religions, these building blocks of enlightened individualism emerged from Buddhism as well as Hinduism, as seen in the thought of Zen Buddhist representative Shaku Soyen. Like Vivekananda, he parlayed his Parliament appearance into a US speaking tour, and his talks were compiled into a book, translated into English by D. T. Suzuki and published in 1906 as *Sermons of a Buddhist Abbot*. More reserved and less outspoken than Vivekananda, Soyen is eager to show that Buddhism has much in common with Western traditions more familiar to his American audience. He declares that the "moral law" that leads to "enlightenment" and "Buddhahood . . . was incarnated not only in Gautama-Buddha, but also in all great men in a higher or lesser degree, foremost among them in Jesus Christ, and, allow me to add, in George Washington, Abraham Lincoln, and other great men of your country" (71). This is an odd juxtaposition. Many Americans greatly revere Washington, but if they could have dinner with him, it would probably not occur to them to ask him what the meaning of life is. It is also incongruous to place the Buddha, who taught and lived nonviolence, alongside statesmen who presided over momentous wars. It appears, then, that appealing to

American patriotism is more important to Soyen than engaging in nuanced cross-cultural comparisons.

A particularly troubling aspect of Soyen's efforts to reach American audiences is his reliance on Orientalist stereotypes. As I mentioned, the few late nineteenth- and early twentieth-century Americans who knew about Buddhism mostly viewed it as passive and therefore incompatible with American industriousness and political activism (Tweed). In response, Soyen defends Buddhism against accusations of passivity not by refuting the charge but by conceding the point and shifting the blame elsewhere: to the Asian race. He says, "If there is anything passive in Eastern culture, which is often no more than tolerance or indifference or self-restraint, it is not due to Buddhism but to the racial idiosyncrasy of Asiatic peoples" (43). While admitting that there are always exceptions, Soyen reinforces the stereotype that "generally speaking . . . the West is energetic, and the East mystical" (89).

Nevertheless, Soyen argues that Buddhism has important contributions to make to American life. In particular, he promotes meditation as a valuable tool for relaxation "in these days of industrial and commercial civilization" (104–5). In a remarkable anticipation of later secular meditation trends such as Mindfulness-Based Stress Reduction (MBSR), Soyen proposes that Buddhist meditation, "whatever its religious merits, is not devoid of its practical utilities and *even for this reason alone* its exercise is universally to be recommended" (92, emphasis added). This is the basic rationale for using Buddhist meditation for secular purposes—articulated more than seventy years before the emergence of the contemporary mindfulness movement in the 1970s (Kabat-Zinn, Wilson). Overall, Soyen's cross-cultural adaptations focus more on bending Buddhism into an American shape than on using Buddhist teachings to critique American society.

The World Parliament of Religions gave Asian religions unprecedented exposure in the US and yielded some ambitious frameworks for synthesizing Asian religions and American liberalism. But these ideas did not gain much traction in the immediate aftermath of this historic event, except among small numbers of bookish white sympathizers. And in the late nineteenth and early twentieth centuries, American literary treatments of Hinduism and Buddhism, while often sympathetic to abstract doctrines in these religions, still depicted the people who practice these religions as incommensurably foreign, a symptom of the strong anti-Asian immigrant beliefs and policies in the US during this period. For example, late nineteenth- and early twentieth-century American fiction showed varying degrees of admiration for Chinese religion, but it generally suggested that Chinese people could not successfully integrate into the US. Stories of this type include Mary Austin's "The Conversion of Ah

Lew Sing" (1897), Willa Cather's "The Conversion of Sum Loo" (1900), Katherine Anne Porter's *My Chinese Marriage* (1902), and Joseph Hergesheimer's *Java Head* (1918). During the same period, English novels also continued to combine admiration for Asian faiths with stereotypes of foreignness and antiquity. Noteworthy instances include Rudyard Kipling's *Kim* (1902), E. M. Forster's *A Passage to India* (1924), and James Hilton's *Lost Horizon* (1933). Just as the age-defying properties of Shangri-la disappear as soon as one leaves, *Lost Horizon*, along with many other texts of this period, conveys the sense that Westerners can learn from, but not truly inhabit, Asian religions. However, a remarkable outlier in this period is W. E. B. Du Bois's little-known novel *Dark Princess* (1928), which weaves a plot that spans Hindu mysticism and Chicago machine politics. The novel's African American protagonist meets an Indian princess who seeks to organize a revolutionary uplift of dark-skinned peoples around the world, citing Hindu teachings as the source of her perseverance. This novel is an early example of dramatizing how Asian religious teaching can be a resource for American—and even global—political reform.

MODERNISM

The view of Asian religions as exotic counterparts to Western corruption continued largely unchanged in Anglo-American Modernism. Major Modernist writers integrated established tropes of Asian religions into their ambitious aesthetic agendas of capturing experiences with maximum vividness. Many figures were crucial in Modernist engagements with Asian religions, including Ernest Fenollosa, T. S. Eliot, Ezra Pound, and Amy Lowell. In the words of literary scholar Josephine Park, "modernist Orientalism rendered the Asiatic sign as a silent figure" and not as a pathway into living traditions (3; see also Stalling 147–48, Sielke and Kloeckner 9–12). Modernist treatments of Buddhism and Hinduism were Orientalist in the sense that they positioned the authenticity and ancient purity of Asian religions against the contemporary soulless corruption of Europe. For example, R. John Williams and Jonathan Stalling have persuasively argued that Ernest Fenollosa was deeply influenced by Buddhist ideas, such as emptiness and interdependence, in forming his aesthetic principle that good art involves interacting elements without separate foregrounds and backgrounds. He came to think that this method is best exemplified in East Asian art as opposed to sterile, rigid, fixed-perspective European art, and that European artists should learn lessons from these East Asian styles (Williams 95–100, Stalling 34–38).

American literature's interest in Asian religions as bygone glory, well established by the early twentieth century, takes a particularly poignant turn in the high Modernism of the post-WWI period, when the reaction to the devastation of the Great War was a dominant theme, and when Asian teachings on emptiness and impermanence took on even greater social timeliness. An especially important example of Modernist Orientalism is T. S. Eliot's *The Waste Land*. The poem's third section, "The Fire Sermon," is named after an important Buddhist text of that title (Rainey 99–100). In the scripture, the Buddha describes desires as like fire, extending this analogy to argue that the greatest achievement is to extinguish all craving just as one would put out a dangerous and painful fire. Eliot alludes to this text to critique Western decadence, implying that the fires of nationalism are responsible for the devastation caused by the Great War, and that postarmistice entertainments are vain, superficial distractions that perpetuate the underlying fires of desire. (See chapter 5 for a related discussion of *The Waste Land*'s influence on novelist Lan Cao.) Additionally, the poem's last thirty-eight lines repeatedly allude to the Hindu *Upanishads* (Rainey 74n401, n433), giving the poem's end a distinctive turn toward Asia. The "fragments I have shored against my ruins" include artifacts from Asia, not just Europe (l. 430) In particular, the poem's last words, *Shantih, Shantih, Shantih* (l. 433), are the Sanskrit word for *peace*, a yearning especially salient in the uneasy peace of Eliot's immediate historical context. Eliot's allusions express a concluding desperation for mystical Oriental transcendence. If Europe is a Waste Land, fragments from ancient Asian texts are a resource through which to yearn for something better. Eliot thus positions Asian religions as an idealized but unattainable answer to the *wasteland* that post-WWI Europe has become; these faiths are beautiful but ultimately too distant to grasp.

WORLD WAR II AND AFTER

During the 1920s and 1930s, readers continued to flirt with Asian religions in texts such as Hilton's *Lost Horizon*, and more serious seekers gathered with small organizations such as the Vedanta Society in New York or the Zen Mission in Los Angeles. During this time, Asian religions in the US remained mostly obscure. The 1930s and 1940s saw the emergence of several important writers adapting Buddhism to English-speaking audiences, including D. T. Suzuki, Alan Watts, Dwight Goddard, and Walter Evans-Wentz, all of whom who would later influence the Beats and subsequent authors.

However, the Second World War hindered Asian religions' already modest growth in the US, especially Buddhism. Although Japan's official religion during the war was Shinto, Buddhist centers in America came under suspicion by their assumed association with the Japanese enemy. During the war, D. T. Suzuki stayed out of the public eye (Fields 195), and several important Japanese American Buddhist teachers were interred by Executive Order 9066 (Fields 192–94, Seager 57). After the war ended, Japanese Buddhist teachers resumed teaching, this time free from political suspicion, but they had lost ground they needed to make up for.

The end of WWII also brought some noteworthy—and divergent—allusions to Hinduism. For instance, J. Robert Oppenheimer invoked the *Bhagavad-Gita*'s emphasis on national duty to justify the Manhattan Project, and he famously quoted the text's cosmic imagery to capture the destructive power of the bomb: "I am Shiva, destroyer of worlds" (Hijiya 123–24). In contrast, in Theodore Dreiser's 1947 novel *The Stoic*, a character's discovery of Hinduism inspires philanthropy. The protagonist's widow travels to India and, alarmed by the poverty there, returns to America and learns to attend to the squalor in her own midst, donating money to build hospitals in New York.

Given these varied treatments, it was unclear in the 1940s what shape Asian religions would take in American literature and culture. Emblematic of this uncertainty, W. F. C. Northrop's ambitious study *The Meeting of East and West* (1946) attempted a postwar framework for helping previously disparate cultures to relate harmoniously. The book sought to help citizens and leaders of the world navigate the still-emerging postwar world order in ways that would lead to greater peace and understanding. Although the book gained immediate attention and acclaim, especially in academic circles (Williams 209–10, 305n32), it did not retain a significant readership in succeeding decades. I think the reason is that the book pinned its exigency to a number of specific geopolitical situations that dramatically changed shortly after the book was published in 1946, as evidenced by the establishment of Israel, the independence of India, the victory of Communism in China, and the start of the Korean War. Nevertheless, the book's basic argument is influential in its ambitious but ultimately oversimplifying argument for cross-cultural synthesis. Northrop sees the roots of international conflict as arising from incompatibilities between cultures, and he tendentiously identifies these cultural characteristics in representative works of literature, philosophy, and art. His main argument is that bridging the mainly "theoretic" nature of "Western civilization" and the primarily "aesthetic" character of "Eastern civilization" is crucial in building a more peaceful world (375–77; see also 434, 443). This book was also a significant influence on Robert Pirsig (Williams 209), whose work I will discuss in chapter 2.

Having briefly overviewed some of the most noteworthy Anglo-American literatures on Asian religions before the Beats, the general stage I want to set is this: Prior to the mid-1950s, American literature about Asian religions had a distinctly genteel and polite character, an assessment that the contrast of exuberant and irreverent Beat writing will soon make even clearer. These pre-Beat texts were read by a small number of sympathizers who largely viewed Asian religions as beautiful threads in their ecumenical tapestry rather than traditions with unique ideas and practices to offer American identities. There was no meaningful interaction between white spiritual seekers who read Thoreau, Vivekananda, and others, and West Coast Asian Americans who practiced Buddhism. Pre-Beat American literature on Asian religions also followed patterns of Orientalist stereotyping that, contrary to what much scholarship argues, was actually disrupted by Beat Buddhism.

What changed from the Beats onward is that Buddhism and Hinduism in the US became countercultural. I treat this change not as the definitive beginning of enlightened individualism but as a meaningful maturation of it. Once the Beat Generation adapted Asian religions into a resource for American anticonformism, Asian religions took on countercultural associations that influenced American treatments of Buddhism and Hinduism from that point onward. This development drove countercultural seekers to explore Asian religions more extensively to escape from what they saw as the hypocrisy, corruption, and complacency of mainstream US culture. Some of these engagements have included reenvisioning US individualism through specific Buddhist and Hindu mantras, receiving spiritual tutelage from Asian teachers, and giving closer consideration to specific Buddhist and Hindu metaphysical theories of emptiness, nonduality, and transcendence. Paradoxically, this countercultural impulse itself turned into a kind of devotion to American ideals of the Enlightenment because of the revolutionary nature of the American founding. As a result, appeals to the revolutionary spirit of individualism played a role in Buddhist- and Hindu-inspired countercultures, even as these movements defied contemporary national norms. Beat and hippie engagements with Asian religions showed an unprecedented openness to the details and depths of Buddhism and Hinduism as traditions that could transform the US.

One noteworthy consequence of this shift is that enlightened individualism was characterized by a more uneven relationship to Christianity than to its antecedents. Pre-WWII promoters of Buddhism and Hinduism, such as Swami Vivekananda, Shaku Soyen, and Paul Carus, tended to go out of their way to say positive things about Jesus Christ, presumably to build bridges to their mostly Christian audiences. Since American identity has been largely bound up with Christianity (Ahlstrom, Taylor 447–48), pre-WWII efforts to cater to American audiences mostly strove not to threaten this alliance. But enlightened individualism from the Beats onward often had a greater willingness to break from Christianity. Writers of enlightened individualism are devoted to disruptively renewing American identity through Asian religions, but the extent to which this enlightened identity has a place for Christian identities and motifs varies greatly from one writer to the next. As the following pages will show, the writers I study have, for all their commonalities, very different relationships to Christianity that range from friendly (Salinger) to indifferent (Snyder) to hostile (Walker).

As a result of Asian religions' counterculrural turn in post-WWII US literature, whether viewed positively or negatively, it became increasingly difficult for Americans to see Asian religions as passive in their American versions. Ironically, for the last sixty years Asian religions have seemed cool and hip in the US, even though their reputation in Asia is one of stuffy and old-fashioned establishment. The popularity of Beat literature and bemused coverage of Beats and Buddhism by the mainstream press gave Asian religions unprecedented visibility in the US, to the point that scholars describe the late 1950s as a "Zen Boom" (Fields, Seager).

Starting with the Beats, the texts I focus on vividly dramatize what American conversion to Buddhism and Hinduism can look like and how these faiths can confront—and be confronted by—specifically American racial and economic histories. I will focus especially on how these narratives create cross-cultural syntheses in elements of literary craft such as plot, character, metaphor, and imagery. As I will show, these texts have an ambivalent relationship to Orientalism: On the one hand, they shatter Orientalism by presenting Asian religions not as strangely foreign but as just what America needs, and with a far greater attention to the specifics of these religions than their predecessors. On the other hand, these writings selectively transmit and adapt some aspects of Buddhism and Hinduism but not others, often ignoring the lived religion of Asians and Asian Americans and indulging in visions of Asian religions as relics to be revived. Still, by creatively rewriting Asian religions into the fabric of American life, these writers explore what it means to be American in tandem with what it means to be spiritual.

CHAPTER SUMMARIES

While American writing since the Transcendentalists has explored what enlightened individualism might mean, I start with the Beats in chapter 1 because their countercultural turn decisively shapes subsequent adaptations of Buddhism and Hinduism in American literature. I first show how disruptive Buddhist *crazy wisdom*—a Buddhist pedagogy of deviance designed to disrupt conventional thought—animates the anticonformist, anticonsumerist Beat visions of Allen Ginsberg, Gary Snyder, Jack Kerouac, and Tom Robbins. In response, as the second chapter explores, countervailing appeals to mystical equanimity govern the anti-Beat responses of J. D. Salinger and Robert Pirsig. The third chapter shows how secret Asian rituals inform reflections on the faded countercultures and inspire a renewed sense of American freedom in texts by Thomas Pynchon and Don DeLillo. In chapter 4, I turn to how Asian metaphysics of ultimate unity inspire unique visions of African American spiritual ancestry in the works of Alice Walker and Charles Johnson. Finally, the fifth chapter examines how Buddhist doctrines of nonself enrich Asian American identities in novels by Lan Cao and Maxine Hong Kingston.

The Beats resisted the conformism of American middle-class norms that emerged in the 1950s, which involved jingoistic patriotism, the nuclear family, suburban living, and some version of monotheism, whether Catholic, Protestant, or Jewish. For many of the Beats, Buddhism offered an ecstatic liberation from America's vapid consumer culture and alienating monotheism, and this veneration led them to emphasize both Buddhism's spiritual transcendence and its cultural difference from the American mainstream. This tendency creates a uniquely American approach to Buddhism, an approach that downplays traditional teacher-disciple lineages and celebrates individual spontaneity. This dynamic is the theme of the first chapter, "Beat Buddhism and American Freedom: Allen Ginsberg, Gary Snyder, Jack Kerouac, and Tom Robbins." Each of these writers appeals to *crazy wisdom* as inspiration for their contemporary nonconformism. Beat Buddhism, I argue, synthesizes Buddhist and American ideas of freedom in original ways. It envisions an enlightened individualism that uses Buddhist disruptions of conventional thought to critique contemporary American decadence. In its place, Buddhist emptiness informs a more authentically American individualism that frees one from social oppression— and one's own sense of clinging to a fixed self. Within this common vision, Beat Buddhism shows considerable diversity. Ginsberg establishes influential links between Buddhist emptiness, countercultural critique, and the American Revolution. Snyder sees a harmonious synthesis of Buddhism and American freedom, while Kerouac struggles with unresolved tensions. A half-generation later, the relatively overlooked Tom Robbins, a standard-bearer of Beat aesthetics and motifs, develops a cautious stance that is more reserved than Snyder's but more optimistic and realized than Kerouac's. This view of Beat Buddhism complicates current scholarly debates on Beat engagements with Asian religions. In a reflection of larger trends in American literary criticism, scholars of the Beats are split into opposing camps that see the Beats as either shallow Orientalists or sincere devotees of Asian faiths (He; Griswold; C. Jackson; Prothero, "Holy Road"; Giamo; Giles). I argue that a more complex understanding is necessary, one that accounts for both the Beats' selective adoption of Buddhist thought and their receptivity to the new ideas of American identity that these philosophies inspire.

This Americanized Buddhism of the Beat movement, or "Beat Buddhism" for short, was the most visible expression of Asian religions in the US until well after its heyday. Thus Beat Buddhism has inescapably shaped subsequent American adaptations of Asian religions. One of Beat Buddhism's most noteworthy legacies is inspiring counter-countercultural writing that takes exception to alleged Beat, and later hippie, frivolity and superficiality. Two of Beat Buddhism's foremost detractors are J. D. Salinger and Robert Pirsig, whose key works I examine in the second chapter, "Anti-Beat Reactions and Mainstream Mysticism: J. D. Salinger's *Franny and Zooey* and Robert Pirsig's *Zen and the Art of Motorcycle Maintenance*." Like the Beats, Salinger and Pirsig adapt Asian religions for American audiences by synthesizing American and Asian notions of freedom, thus continuing the tradition of enlightened individualism. But countering Beat narratives of disruption, Salinger and Pirsig portray Asian religions as nonthreatening and mainstream, compatible with the postwar status quo. Whereas the countercultural literature of the first chapter focuses on freewheeling adventure, Salinger's and Pirsig's narratives prioritize healing fractured nuclear families with the help of Asian-inspired spirituality. Salinger and Pirsig disparage countercultural nonconformism as too adversarial to convey the Asian equanimity that Americans truly need. Their cross-cultural syntheses offer harmony, not heresy; reassurance, not provocation. They attempt to show that Asian ideals are compatible with normative middle-class American life. However, although Salinger and Pirsig critique the Beats, they still use Beat-inspired rhetoric, repurposing a radical tone to steer readers toward mainstream modes of living. Crucially, Salinger and Pirsig view the American mainstream as not necessarily conformist; in their texts, Buddhist and Hindu philosophies offers ways to live authentically as unique individuals without disrupting the larger social status quo.

Both the Beats of the first chapter and the anti-Beats of the second enthusiastically advocate for adapted Asian religions as solutions to the challenges of contemporary American life. They are, in short, believers. The faith expressed in their fiction comes under fire by postmodern writers who refuse the ultimate promises of religion, patriotism, and absolute truth in general. But even these skeptical writers reveal investments in enlightened individualism. This persistence comes about, surprisingly, by giving up on transcendence instead of celebrating it. I explore this development in the third chapter, "Secret Rituals and American Autonomy: Thomas Pynchon's *Vineland* and Don DeLillo's *Underworld*." Pynchon and DeLillo adapt Asian religions in ways that offer modest spiritual resources for addressing American problems, particularly an oppressive and opaque government and the paranoia that results. I show how Pynchon and DeLillo empower readers to overcome reactionary paranoia—and even recuperate American ideals of freedom and autonomy—by adapting earthbound versions of Buddhist and Hindu traditions of secret transmission, not these religions' philosophies of transcendence. Pynchon's *Vineland* (1990) imagines a form of ninjutsu that is influenced by both Buddhism and consumer capitalism and gives political radicals tools to resist, not simply fear, governmental oppression. Furthermore, *Vineland* critiques the shortcomings of 1960s infatuations with Asian religions, dramatizing both followers' naive zeal and these religions' tendency to prioritize metaphysical transcendence over political change. For Pynchon, ninjutsu offers a model of resistance that responds to sinister conspiracies by fashioning underground practices of Buddhist-inspired empowerment.

Whereas *Vineland* focuses on countercultural engagements with Asian religions, DeLillo's *Underworld* (1997) foregrounds mainstream mistrust of them. *Underworld*'s characters repeatedly encounter Hindu and Buddhist mantras, but they dismiss them as foreign, thus keeping Asian religious insights secret through socially reinforced dismissal. However, by juxtaposing these supposedly exotic Asian practices with more familiar Christian chants, the novel's form shows the reader hidden kinships between East and West that its characters fail to acknowledge. The novel invites the reader to uncover how Asian religions can redeem American individualism, thus obtaining the secrets hidden from the novel's own characters. *Underworld* is charged with religious language and symbolism, but it does not valorize any one religion. Rather, the novel suggests that paranoia, whether against foreign religions or domestic institutions, inhibits one's ability to form an adequate picture of the varied influences that shape our lives. Pynchon and DeLillo, the consummate postmodernists, are skeptical of everything, including both Asian enlightenment transcendence and liberal enlightenment governance. But even so, they still adapt Asian ideas and practices in ways that promise to advance something like American freedom. Furthermore, their metaphysical skepticism leads their adaptations of Asian religions to make more room for the materiality of ritual, offering an interesting exception to enlightened individualism's tendency to privilege abstract ideas over specific, often culturally marked, practices.

This selection of writers thus far reflects the fact that most of the American literary voices exploring Asian religions have been white. However, recent years have seen the emergence of noteworthy minority American literatures about Asian religions. Crucial examples have appeared within African American literature, which is the focus of the fourth chapter, "Asian Religions and African Dreams: Alice Walker and Charles Johnson." Walker's and Johnson's novels allegorize Asian religions' relevance for African Americans by reimagining Asian-style sages as African Americans' ancestors. For both writers, Buddhist and Hindu teachings of nonduality—the idea that ultimate reality is undifferentiated—enable this complex, imaginative move. Walker's and Johnson's fiction suggests that the universal insights of Asian religions allow African Americans to claim Asian religions as their own. Their protagonists develop connections to Asian traditions that do not strictly depend on heredity; but in a complex bid to legitimate Asian religions for African American spiritual seekers, the texts still rely on ancestry as a metaphor for this connection. Walker and Johnson further propose how Buddhist and Hindu nonduality can uniquely critique racism and enrich African American identity. As I will show, both writers' bold adaptations raise complicated issues about cultural authenticity, the ethics of cross-cultural adaptation, and the relevance of Asian religions to American liberal activism.

In the developments I am tracing within enlightened individualism, one striking feature has been the relative lack of contributions from Asian Americans, the very people for whom Asian religions would be an inheritance rather than an import. Curiously, since the flowering of enlightened individualism in the 1950s, religiously themed prose narratives by Asian Americans have been rare. But that has recently changed, as I show in the fifth chapter, "Buddhist Nonself and Asian American Identity: Lan Cao's *Monkey Bridge* and Maxine Hong Kingston's *The Fifth Book of Peace*." Here I explore reasons why Asian American Buddhist fiction has emerged only recently. For one thing, there has been a steady increase of Asian American immigrants after liberalized policies in 1965, along with the maturation of a second generation of immigrants. Another significant consideration is Asian American studies' theoretical shift, c. 1990, toward questioning the concept of coherent Asian American identity that previously gave rise to the label *Asian American*. The last of these developments is especially important, I argue, as this theoretical move allows Asian American novelists to reflect on Asian American identity in terms of Buddhist teachings of nonself. My case studies are Lan Cao's *Monkey Bridge* and Maxine Hong Kingston's *The Fifth Book of Peace* (1997, 2003). Whereas the other writers in this study explore Asian philosophies largely without representing Asian people and practices, Cao and Kingston put readers up close to Buddhist materials: colorful shrines, shiny statues, food offerings, gritty pilgrimages, loud bells. Cao and Kingston use the novel form to bring Asian Buddhism into an American context and attest to previously undernarrated varieties of Buddhist experience. Furthermore, by engaging with Buddhist teachings on the illusory nature of both individual and collective identity, Cao's and Kingston's texts open up a space for fluid identity that can be both Asian and American, valuing Asian Buddhist tradition while also integrating American individualism and future-oriented thinking. Cao and Kingston begin to fill a gap left by non-Asian novelists who neglect Asian American religious life. By concluding with Cao and Kingston, I show how enlightened individualism has taken a long journey back to a greater consideration of Asian cultures and histories. Cao's and Kingston's contributions raise intriguing possibilities for an enlightened individualism that balances multicultural identities, abstract philosophy, and religious materiality.

CHAPTER 1

Beat Buddhism and American Freedom

*Allen Ginsberg, Gary Snyder,
Jack Kerouac, and Tom Robbins*

THE AFTERMATH of the Second World War led to an increasingly consolidated middle-class ideal that included religious elements. During this time America saw an upsurge in church membership, church attendance, and religious identification. In a landmark midcentury study of American religion, Will Herberg cites a survey in which 95 percent of Americans identified as Protestant, Catholic, or Jewish, the three groupings that Herberg identifies as the contemporary American religious mainstream (46). Factors behind this religious revival included a wish to feel and appear patriotic, an impulse to affirm a religious bulwark against Godless communism, and a yearning for spiritual consolation against the uncertainties of the nuclear age (Ahlstrom 949–52).

This increasingly consolidated religious mainstream inspired a countertrend. As many scholars have recognized, religion and spirituality played an important role in the rift between the bourgeois mainstream and the bohemian Beat and, later, hippie countercultures (Roszak). For many of those disaffected by the religion of their upbringing, Asian religions were appealing because of their cultural distance from the perceived vices of the US (Campbell 128, 190; Masatsugu 425). Charles Taylor nicely captures the religious mainstream the Beats rebelled against by describing American civic religion of the 1950s as a "bland religion of American conformity" (506). The denominationalist consensus of the 1950s somehow managed to seem both wishy-washy and oppressive at the same time. This description indicates two ways in which the Beats wanted to rebel from the status quo. One is that midcentury Christianity was a sign of bourgeois social conformity, as shown, for example, by the decision to add the phrase "under God" to the pledge of allegiance in 1954 (Lipka).

A second factor is that this religion seemed watered-down and did not actually deliver satisfactory transcendence. This kind of midcentury Christianity emphasized the "social function" of religion over the importance of specific beliefs (Hungerford 2). Taylor writes that when a society makes "an identification of Christian faith and civilization order . . . [we] lose sight of the full transformation that Christians are called to" (743). This sort of impression contributed to the Beat interest in Buddhism, a faith many Beats thought of as a fresh, radical way to experience transcendence and go against the stifling order of the time. In this context, literature played a crucial role in Asian religions' growing popularity, as shown in Buddhism's emergence in the 1950s. Influential documents included teachings by Japanese teachers such as D. T. Susuki and Nyogen Senzaki, reflections by Western students of Buddhism such as Alan Watts and Eugen Herrigel, and creative works by Beat writers and their literary descendants.

The Beats stand out for their inventive contributions to Buddhism's rapid emergence in the US. They defined themselves against the American religious mainstream of the 1950s, which promoted conformity to seemingly triumphant middle-class norms. In spite of its lack of doctrinal rigor or devotional intensity, this religious consensus still bore the history of belief in a paternalistic God separate from and superior to humanity, a hierarchical theology that irreverent and freedom-loving Beats tended to find unpalatable. In contrast, Beat writers such as Gary Snyder, Jack Kerouac, Allen Ginsberg, Philip Whalen, and others praised Buddhism for its perceived nondualistic view of reality and criticism of established institutions (Prothero, "Holy Road" 208, 216; Seager 46–61). Buddhism's religion of origin, Hinduism, would also become a major point of interest for Allen Ginsberg, and it also plays a role in Snyder's religious explorations.

A central element of Buddhism's appeal for the Beats was its perceived exotic difference from the US. As Beat critic Jonathan Eburne points out, by defining themselves as exiles from the American mainstream, the Beats made otherness into a hip commodity. This countercultural credential depended on the marginal status of the various groups with whom the Beats claimed affinities (55). Accordingly, the Beats tended to valorize Buddhism, and, by extension, Asian Buddhists, as an exotic other. But they also presented Buddhism as uniquely suited to America, often by appealing to traditional notions of American freedom. How, then, could the Beats both exoticize Buddhism as different from the US—even to the point of emphasizing a distance from the mainstream Christianity bound up with American prosperity—and also identify with Buddhism as a fulfillment of American values at the same time?

Previous accounts of Buddhism and the Beat Generation have not answered this question fully, for they engaged with only limited facets of relevant texts. Beat studies tend to split into unfavorable and favorable camps, each side focusing on a different aspect of Beat texts. The first camp views the Beats as appropriative distorters of Buddhism, a view pioneered by influential Zen popularizer Alan Watts. In 1958, Watts famously derided "Beat Zen" as too adversarial and agenda-driven to convey the equanimity of mere "Zen" (7–8). Watts contends that practitioners of Beat Zen are still unconsciously governed by the very Western culture they think Buddhism helps them to resist, and thus these practitioners are not successful at cross-cultural adaptation (6–7). Given this critique, it is ironic how much the Beats had depended on Watts's writings for their understanding of Zen and Buddhism more generally (Roszak 132, Coupe). One of Beat Buddhism's most important resources became its most influential critic.

While Zen is only one of many forms of Buddhism that drew the interest of Beat writers, scholars have often agreed with Watts that Beat writers were too invested in their own anticonformist agenda to engage with Buddhism on its own terms. For example, Carl Jackson ambivalently writes, "The way in which the Beats utilized and distorted Asian conceptions reveal[s] both the rewards and dangers of turning to non-European sources" (53). Similar, or harsher, criticisms have issued from Jonathan Eburne, Jerry Griswold, and Yuemin He, who agree that the Beats distorted Asian religions and exoticized Asia in the process. They argue, with significant justification, that Beat Buddhism is guilty of Orientalism. This criticism fits easily within the larger judgment that the Beats failed in their treatments of racial, sexual, and cultural difference, far more often celebrating stereotypes than questioning them (Martinez, Panish). However, members of this unfavorable camp often ignored the seriousness with which many Beat writers engaged with Buddhist philosophy.

Conversely, critics who judge Beat Buddhism more favorably admire how Beat writers incorporate Buddhism's abstract philosophical doctrines, but they do not give sustained attention to the question of cultural appropriation. They view the Beats as faithful transmitters of Buddhism. Deshae Lott, for instance, writes approvingly of how Kerouac, "like a Buddhist, uses concepts or language to transcend concepts" (179). For Lott, Buddhism is a static system against which to measure Kerouac, one which Kerouac strove but failed "to understand completely or *apply* fully" (182, my emphasis). Similar analyses admiring Beat writers' philosophical complexity have occurred in the work of Stephen Prothero, Benedict Giamo, Nancy Grace, and Tony Trigilio. These scholars praise the Beats for applying authentic Buddhist ideas, but for the most part they do not wrestle with the often stereotyped cultural images at work in these texts.

Both of these views rest on problematic assumptions about authenticity that treat Buddhism as a fixed object. Furthermore, both camps talk past one another; that is, they focus on different aspects of the texts in question. In light of this situation, I want to promote a view of the Beats as neither merely inauthentic nor strictly authentic but as creative agents of cross-cultural adaptation. This perspective is influenced by scholars of religion such as Jeff Wilson who argue that while American adaptations of Buddhism involve novel engagements with Western individualism, they are also continuous with Buddhism's long history of cross-cultural adaptation as it spread throughout Asia (Wilson 4–6).

To bridge these views, I argue that Beat Buddhism marks the decisive emergence of enlightened individualism in American literature. Beat Buddhism makes a significant and innovative cross-cultural adaptation by attempting to harmonize Buddhist and American views of freedom, a process that relies on both abstract Buddhist philosophy and culturally specific images of Asia. At first these two types of freedom seem to be incompatible. The American freedom of "the pursuit of happiness" has largely come to mean the freedom *to obtain* what one desires (Foner 28, Taylor 484–85), whereas the Buddhist (and Hindu) freedom of *moksa* (Sanskrit, *liberation*) is a freedom *from* the constraining pull of desires themselves (McMahan 17). Beat Buddhism attempts to stretch the meaning of American freedom to include liberation from consumerism and celebration of the downtrodden, while also shifting Buddhist freedom to be more open to individual pleasure. Furthermore, this effort to harmonize Buddhist and American freedom has allowed Beat Buddhism to remain influential well beyond the Beat period, even to the point of somewhat transcending the countercultural associations of the Beat Generation. Beat Buddhism is a historically significant strain of cross-cultural adaptation that has influenced subsequent generations of American writers, readers, and spiritual seekers, offering novel ideas about how Buddhism can inhabit—and change—the US. The legacy of the Beats thus carries through all the chapters that follow.

As I showed in the introduction, many of the themes of Beat Buddhism were already percolating through previous movements and events, especially Transcendentalism and the 1893 World Parliament of Religions. The history of enlightened individualism certainly begins well before the Beats. Nevertheless, the Beats mark a turning point that I treat as the decisive emergence of enlightened individualism. Relative to the Transcendentalists to which they are most often compared, the Beats are significantly more reliant on an aesthetic of raucousness and disruption, openly supportive of profanity and sexual liberation, engaged with specific content from Buddhist and Hindu traditions, detailed and concrete in their vision of what Asian religious practices in America can look like, and capable of challenging stereotypes about Asia. Furthermore, the media environment in which these adaptations occur also allows the Beats to make Asian religions highly visible to American popular culture for the first time. Moreover, the distinctively countercultural character of enlightened individualism from the Beats onward paradoxically enriches its connection to Enlightenment liberalism because the counterculture's political dissent often ties itself to the rights-based defiance of the American Revolution, even as it refracts these ideals through Asian religions. It may be true, as literary scholar Lee Konstantinou points out, that "midcentury . . . countercultural heroes . . . were never so completely oppositional as they were commonly imagined to be" (275). But then again, as the Beats' creative adaptations suggest, neither must defining American values be as conformist as people often believe.

To explore the significance of Beat Buddhism, I will first consider how Allen Ginsberg attempted to transform the spiritual patriotism of Walt Whitman into a countercultural movement in which Asian religions fostered post-1945 American renewal. Ginsberg's creative vision sets the stage for my subsequent focus on three key figures who offer a revealing window into the long life of Beat Buddhism: Gary Snyder, Jack Kerouac, and Tom Robbins, the last of whom postdates the Beat period but influentially carries on Beat values, aesthetics, and motifs. I will briefly touch on how Ginsberg is relevant to each of these three writers, specifically in terms of Snyder's mantra-based activism, Kerouac's self-criticism, and Robbins's use of crazy wisdom. My examples are not comprehensive and should not lead to overgeneralizations about all Beat and Beat-influenced writers, but they point toward a fuller understanding of Beat adaptations of Buddhism in America. While there are too many contributors to Beat Buddhism to discuss at length here—Diane di Prima, Kenneth Rexroth, Lew Welch, Anne Waldman, and Philip Whalen are also important—the three writers I discuss here provide especially revealing syntheses between Buddhist and American notions of freedom. Within this shared Beat commitment to shaping American Buddhism, there is diversity. Ginsberg's synthesis of Whitmanian vitality and Buddhist emptiness becomes an ambiguous, evolving prophecy. Snyder optimistically envisions a harmonious merging of Eastern and Western cultures. Kerouac, by contrast, hopes for such a synthesis but struggles with unresolved conflicts. Robbins ambivalently hovers between Snyder's synthesis and Kerouac's conflict, combining cross-cultural openness with ethnically sensitive caution.

GINSBERG'S BUDDHIST REVOLUTION

Snyder, Kerouac, and Robbins are all significantly connected to Allen Ginsberg. His poetic influence, enduring celebrity, and famous tutelage under the eccentric Tibetan Buddhist teacher Chögyam Trungpa Rinpoche qualify him as the Beat Buddhist *par excellence*. As Ginsberg specialist Tony Trigilio has extensively discussed, Ginsberg's progressively more serious Buddhist practice was a complex, always evolving struggle to integrate Romantic individualism and Buddhist nonself (61, 88, 99, 104–5, 112, 154–55, 178–79, 184–85, 193). While there is no need to recapitulate Trigilio's excellent work on Ginsberg's Buddhist poetics, what is worth adding to Trigilio's perspective is that Ginsberg's body of work reveals a meaningful investment in distinctively American ideals of democratic individualism.

Ginsberg's commitment to American democracy is not always obvious. He mostly invokes American ideals to ironically call out hypocrisy, as when he sarcastically describes the American "Freedom to assemble & get gassed or shot" ("Industrial Waves" 1981, 847; all Ginsberg poems are from *Collected Poems*). But Ginsberg's investments in American notions of freedom and individualism can be best understood by reading him through his hero, Walt Whitman. Whitman's 1871 essay *Democratic Vistas* was of particular importance to Ginsberg, as direct references in Ginsberg's poetry show ("Wichita" 1966, 408; "Salutations" 1988, 976). In this text Whitman issues a call for American writers to create a "prophetic literature of these States," declaring that "a new Literature, perhaps a new Metaphysics, certainly a new Poetry, are to be, in my opinion, the only sure and worthy supports and expressions of the American Democracy" (70). This literary expression of American democracy must be both individualist and religious. One of the nation's core principles, Whitman says, is "individuality, the pride and centripetal isolation of a human being in himself," which he deems "of utmost importance" to American democracy (38). Whitman further asserts that "at the core of democracy, finally, is the religious element. All the religions, old and new, are there" (27).

Whitman prophetically urges that "In the future of these States must arise poets immenser far" than those who have come before (76), and Ginsberg's poetry positions himself as one of those "immenser" poets who answers Whitman's call. Even though Ginsberg does not fully share Whitman's optimism about the trajectory of American society, Whitman's influence indicates that when Ginsberg is being prophetic, individualistic, and religious, he is attempting to carry on Whitman's project of promoting American democratic individualism. The fulfillment of this ideal would mean a US that lives up to its liberal promise. Whitman, citing John Stuart Mill, defines the purpose of the US as using its individualist-religious culture of government by the people to allow "full play of human nature to expand itself in numberless and even conflicting directions" (1). For Whitman, true progress is both the "Daughter of a physical revolution—[and the] mother of the true revolutions, which are of the interior life, and of the arts" (62). Accordingly, in Ginsberg's 1957 poem "Death to Van Gogh's Ear!" which decries American hubris, Ginsberg says, "The day of the publication of the true literature of the American body will / be day of Revolution." Ginsberg echoes Whitman's connections between the revolutionary spirit and American art and literature, thus showing his wish to carry out Whitman's patriotic agenda in spite of Ginsberg's stinging political critiques.

Ginsberg's investments in American individualism relate complexly to his interest in Asian religions; his early exoticism changes as his career goes on. Ginsberg's early Buddhist poetry exoticizes Asia, as with "Angkor Wat," written at the famous Cambodian Buddhist temple complex. Here Ginsberg's poetic speaker explicitly takes refuge in the Buddha for the first time in Ginsberg's poems (314, 317). But this refuge is still mysterious; the speaker compares the Bodhisattva Avalokitesvara to the inscrutable Sphinx, describing the images in the compound as "Sphinx-Avalokitesvara, all mixed up" (324). Ginsberg's sense of exotic distance decreases as time goes on, especially after 1972, the year Ginsberg took Buddhist vows from Chögyam Trungpa. Ginsberg dedicates his 1978 poem "Plutonian Ode" "to you O Poets and Orators to come, you father Whitman as I join your side, you Congress and American people" (713). If Whitman says that American democracy needs a "religious element," for Ginsberg the religion it most needs is Buddhism. In the close of "Plutonian Ode," Ginsberg exhorts these future poets, politicians, and citizens, to "Take this wheel of syllables in hand [. . .] thus empower this Mind-guard spirit gone out, gone out, gone beyond, gone beyond me, Wake space, so Ah!"

This concluding line synthesizes the institutions and citizenry of American democracy—"Congress and American people"—with Buddhist emptiness that has "gone beyond" conventional ideas of subject and object. What Ginsberg presents in this last line is a translation of a famous mantra from the Prajnaparamita Heart Sutra, one of Ginsberg's favorite scriptures and one of the most famous of all Buddhist texts. Ginsberg also makes a drawing of this mantra in *Cosmopolitan Greetings Poems* with the Sanskrit transliteration and Ginsberg's own earlier translation: "*Gate gate paratage parasamgate bodhi svaha*" [All gone, all gone, all overgone, all gone sky high now old mind so ah!] (975). This mantra is used to understand and meditate on the words in this sutra, whose most pivotal passage is usually translated as "form is emptiness, emptiness is form" (Lopez). That is, the mind that understands emptiness still sees the appearance of forms, but that mind is "gone" from the suffering of ordinary existence. "Plutonian Ode" sees this Buddhist sutra as holding the key to transforming America. Here Ginsberg brings the American frontier, which offers the "full play of human nature," to a Buddhist fulfillment in a field of infinite possibilities. This vision of transcendence is empty of any fixed essence—and thus free from the dualistic thinking that leads to violence. Ginsberg's Buddhist transformation of Whitman's ideas exemplifies how Beat Buddhism takes Transcendentalist influences in a new direction, one that is both more invested in the specifics of Asian religions and more pointedly countercultural than Transcendentalist engagements with Asian religions. As I will show, Ginsberg's imprint on enlightened individualism remains relevant to the three writers I discuss in this chapter.

The popularity of these writers across many decades, as well as their collective breadth of genres including poetry, fiction, and essays, indicates a resonance with larger cultural trends. The issues Ginsberg, Snyder, Kerouac, and Robbins wrestle with—Asian religions' relevance to a politics of dissent, the ethics of borrowing across cultures, and the compatibility of Buddhist and American freedom—have shaped American engagements with Asian religions and given Beat Buddhism cultural relevance well beyond the Beat period. Beat Buddhism thus makes a significant contribution to American receptivity to Asian religions that is not reducible to appropriation. It has influenced American institutions (e.g., Naropa University's Jack Kerouac School of Disembodied Poetics; Spirit Rock Meditation Center; and San Francisco Zen Center), American lexica (many American Buddhists now call themselves *Dharma Bums*, after Kerouac's coinage), and the writers I examine in the chapters that follow.

SNYDER'S SYNTHESIS

Gary Snyder is noteworthy for his pioneering Beat approach to Buddhism that changes along with the advancing century. Snyder (b. 1930) became involved with Buddhism in his early twenties, attending services at a Japanese Buddhist center in San Francisco in the early 1950s (Snyder, *Mountains and Rivers* 154). His interest in Asian religions and cultures deepened, and he spent most of

1956 to 1968 in Japan, receiving traditional Zen training in Kyoto (Murphy 7–9). Snyder's time in Asia also included travels through India with Ginsberg from 1961 to 1963, during which they both became more invested in Asian religions and in helping the disadvantaged (Sweet 247–62). Since his return to the US, Snyder's Buddhist faith has continued to animate his poetry and prose. His work consistently bears Zen emphases of concentration on the present moment, spontaneous realization, and reverence for nature. No American writer of his generation has matched Snyder's combination of dedicated Buddhist practice, international experience, and prolific creative output. In fact, Snyder is one of the few Beat Buddhists that Alan Watts, one of Snyder's early teachers of Buddhism, consistently approved of (Coupe 30, 44–45).

Previous critics have examined the role of Buddhist philosophy in Snyder's writing (Gray, Huang, Johnston, Kern), but they focus on how Snyder uses Buddhist ideals to critique US violence and pollution. This critical pattern has prevented literary scholars from seeing in Snyder's work important affinities between Buddhist and American concerns. The only exception, as far as I know, comes from American Studies scholar James Brown, who writes that "the very freedom in Zen that Suzuki had promised . . . was connected, in Snyder's thought, to American republican traditions of individualism and self-reliance" (224). I take Brown's idea a step further: Snyder's writing does not stop at seeing connections; it actually combines features of Buddhist and American freedom. Snyder's career is an evolving effort to harmonize Beat wildness with Buddhist calm. He defends Beat Buddhism by praising its subversion and, later in his career, by redefining its rebelliousness as responsibility. Every level of Snyder's writing reflects this complexity. In his work, East meets West by weaving American content into Buddhist forms, and vice versa.

Snyder's early work was strongly influenced by the ninth-century Chinese poet Han Shan, known in Chinese lore, along with his friend Shih-te, as "poor but happy recluses, bordering on the crazy, who constantly do and say nonsensical things" (Henricks 7). Snyder's first published work, *Cold Mountain Poems*, is a translation of twenty-four of some three hundred of Han Shan's poems. Snyder's translations of Han Shan have a more complex relationship to the Beat Generation than scholars have recognized. It is certainly true that Snyder represents Han Shan as a "countercultural role model" for the Beat Generation (J. Tan 228), and that this portrayal involves "appropriating [Han Shan's] Chinese texts for purposes other than those of the texts themselves" (Kern 234). And by portraying Han Shan as a "mountain madman in an old Chinese line of ragged hermits" (Snyder, *Riprap* 35), Snyder invokes the stereotype of the Oriental Monk who is inscrutable, otherworldly, and Asian (Iwamura 6).

But Snyder does not simply force Han Shan into a Beat mold. While he emphasizes parallels between Han Shan's social commentary and Beat critiques of American consumerism, Snyder's Han Shan models a different mode of living than a prototypical Beat adventure. In poem sixteen, Snyder translates: "I've got no use for the kulak / With his big barn and pasture / He just sets up a prison for himself." This ridicule of the superficial status of land ownership strongly evokes Beat criticisms of stultifying American middle-class conformism. But Snyder's Han Shan does not exemplify a positive American freedom *to* go on adventures, a freedom the Beats thought of themselves as reclaiming. Instead, he embodies a more negative Buddhist freedom *from* the hassles of worldly life. In poem seventeen, the speaker muses, "Go ahead and let the world change— / I'm happy to sit among these cliffs" (55). Likewise, in poem five, the speaker wants to "settle" and find a place that is "safe" (43). Snyder's Han Shan speaks not of Beat restlessness but of the contentment valorized in Buddhism. Snyder challenges the Beat Generation by presenting Han Shan as a role model for Beat irreverence, a role model who is nevertheless not straightforwardly assimilable into Beat culture.

Snyder's efforts to synthesize Buddhist and American freedom develop more fully in his original poems. In *Riprap*, Snyder's earliest publication of original poems, Snyder relies on Buddhist concepts of emptiness and impermanence that owe much to Han Shan. But Snyder innovatively presents Beat adventurism as a liberating expression of this underlying Buddhist vision. Buddhist emptiness comes across strongly in "Piute Creek," where the speaker, upon seeing "Sky over endless mountains," rhapsodizes that "All the junk that goes with being human / Drops away" (8). In this expansive vision, "A clear, attentive mind / Has no meaning but that / Which sees is truly seen" (8). Snyder's title suggests that the same Buddhist sense of meditative expansiveness that Han Shan experiences in China is available in America.

But Snyder also gives voice to a more rambunctious spirit in *Riprap* than in *Cold Mountain Poems*. For example, in "All Through the Rains," the speaker tries to grab onto a moving horse to go bareback riding, a stunt the unassuming Han Shan would probably not have attempted. Also, the poem "Toji," written at Shingon temple at Kyoto, conveys a distinctively Beat combination of reverence and irreverence. A statue of Avalokitesvara, the Buddha of compassion, has "An ancient hip smile / Tingling of India and Tibet." It is a fine piece of venerable craftsmanship, "haloed in snake-hood gold," but it is also "cool" and "hip." Thus the speaker solicits the reader's Orientalist curiosity about Avalokitesvara's "ancient hip smile"; the hope is that one will pursue the inner peace from which the expression presumably arises. Furthermore, Avalokitesvara is "Bisexual and tried it all." This line refers to the fact that the Indian and

Tibetan version of this Buddha is male, while the Chinese and Japanese version is female (Yü). But Snyder's gloss of Avalokitesvara as "Bisexual and tried it all" carries a sense of sexual experimentation and free love absent from traditional Buddhist contexts. "Toji" exemplifies how *Riprap* creatively combines Buddhist calm with Beat wildness. Snyder's Buddhist American freedom is its own kind of Zen riddle, a paradox of individualism and nonself.

Just as Snyder helped shape the politically alienated Beat Buddhism of the 1950s, he also tied Buddhism to the more activist hippie counterculture of the 1960s. This project is exemplified in Snyder's short prose piece "Smokey the Bear Sutra" (1969), which rewrites a Buddhist scriptural genre for a hippie audience. While in his 1986 commentary on the essay, Snyder is right that it "follows the structure of a Mahayana sutra fairly faithfully" (244), its innovative appeals to American values and institutions are significant. The essay replaces traditional Asian Buddhist tropes with American counterparts and mixes Buddhist formality with countercultural irreverence.

The text's central conceit is that Smokey the Bear is a Buddha. This conflation sets up Buddhist critiques of environmental destruction. The Great Sun Buddha, speaking "in the Jurassic, about 150 million years ago," prophesied that "the human race in [Snyder's] era will get into troubles all over its head and practically wreck everything in spite of its own strong intelligent Buddha-nature" (242). In Mahayana Buddhism, every being has Buddha-nature, the inherent potential to become enlightened (H. Smith 2, 388). This potential is heavily obscured by ignorance, especially, according to Snyder, the ignorance of those who pollute. One must carelessly objectify nature in order to abuse it. Later, the narrator calls forest fires a symptom of "the stupidity of those who think things can be gained and lost whereas in truth all is contained vast and free in the Blue Sky and Green Earth of One Mind" (242). This admonition seems to misattribute accidental fires started by careless campers to corporate greed. But the larger point stands that environmental degradation is caused by those who objectify nature. The Buddhist implication here is that a more insightful attitude would emerge from the doctrine of nonduality (Suzuki, *Essays* xxix), such that one's self and nature are inseparable.

Snyder makes these points speak to contemporary America by inserting American place names into Buddhist figures of speech. The Buddha prophecies that a future "continent called America . . . will have great centers of power such as Pyramid Lake, Walden Pond, Mount Rainier, Big Sur, Everglades, and so forth; and powerful nerves and channels such as Columbia River, Mississippi River, and Grand Canyon" (242). In this vision America has sacred spaces just as India has the Ganges River. The narrator later says, "Those who recite this Sutra and then try to put it into practice will accumulate merit as countless as the sands of Arizona and Nevada" (243). Snyder tweaks a common Buddhist hyperbole which describes immense quantities "as there are grains of sand in the river Ganges" or "as high as Mount Sumeru" (Goddard 95, 91). By rewriting Buddhist expressions with American instead of Asian place names, "Smokey the Bear Sutra" appeals to an exotic, mystic East while also suggesting that sacred places are not confined to Asia; they are in America as well, right in its readers' backyards.

Snyder's substitutions give "Smokey the Bear Sutra" a tone different from that of canonical Buddhist texts. Whereas Buddhist sutras are rigorously formal, "Smokey the Bear Sutra" is irreverently playful. By deifying Smokey the Bear, the sutra plays on the comical tension between the Buddha's mystical dignity and Smokey the Bear's status as a mass-media cartoon mascot. Accordingly, Smokey is "austere but comic." He holds a "vajra shovel" and raises "his left paw in the Mudra of Comradely Display" (Snyder 242). *Vajra* is a Sanskrit word for *diamond,* conveying clarity and strength; a *mudra* is a ritual gesture (Seager 29–30). The text thus describes Smokey's signature pose in Buddhist terms, a move that simultaneously makes light of Buddhist decorum and valorizes Smokey's appearance.

This essay is thus an act of synthesis that combines Buddhist and hippie concerns. But it also offers another, even less expected, meeting point. "Smokey the Bear Sutra" actually merges a broad critique of industrial civilization with an indebtedness to the institutions of the US. The text criticizes modern pollution as the result of "a civilization that claims to save but only destroys." And yet the essay's central figure is a production of the US Forest Service, which is funded by the federal government. Therefore, American "civilization" does not only destroy nature; it protects it too. Snyder resists this point in his 1986 commentary to the essay by saying that the Forest Service was unaware "that it was serving as a vehicle for this magical reemergence" (244). He works hard to avoid acknowledging the US government as the source of something good. Even so, Smokey wears "the broad-brimmed hat of the West, symbolic of the forces that guard the Wilderness." Again, the West does not simply destroy the wilderness; it can protect it as well.

Although Snyder's implicit affirmation of the West may seem surprising, it makes Buddhist sense that Snyder would find merit, if only unconsciously, even in US institutions. If Snyder is serious about Buddhist nonduality, then he cannot treat the US as a monolithic evil. Buddha-nature can be obscured, but never lost. Therefore even a degraded civilization must still be capable of manifesting wisdom. For Snyder, Smokey the Bear is a rare touchstone of holism in a culture increasingly alienated from nature. Snyder's imagery does not simply denigrate the West, of which the modern US is a major part. It also makes room for productive engagements between Asian and North American traditions.

This synthesis also occurs through elements of mantra that blend American activism with Buddhist incantation. Snyder writes that "if anyone is threatened by advertising, air pollution, television, or the police, they should chant SMOKEY THE BEAR'S WAR SPELL: DROWN THEIR BUTTS / CRUSH THEIR BUTTS / DROWN THEIR BUTTS / CRUSH THEIR BUTTS, / And Smokey the Bear will surely appear to put the enemy out with his vajra-shovel" (243). This is a playful version of Buddhist mantras and rituals that invoke wrathful powers to destroy one's enemies both symbolically and, sometimes, literally (Samuel 7–9; see also Oppert 10). Snyder thus combines Buddhist mantras with the repetitive chanting of protest slogans. Snyder's combination of mantras and American activism has a significant parallel in Ginsberg's use of Americanized mantras. When Ginsberg famously writes in "Wichita Vortex Sutra" (1966), "I lift my voice aloud, / make Mantra of American language now, / I declare the end of the War!" (415), he is using "American language" like a Buddhist or Hindu "mantra" whose utterance brings about the state it declares through the vibrations of the sound itself (Hungerford 38–41).

Ginsberg and Snyder put these ideas into practice at the 1967 Human Be-In in San Francisco. This was an antiwar protest, but it had a festive air of pageantry and even goodwill (Roszak 65–66, Trigilio 2–3), an ethos further suggested by the name *Be-In*, an irreverent riff on *sit-in*. Although it is not apparent who coined the name *Be-In*, it clearly captured the attitude of the event's participants and its countercultural ringleaders. In this event Ginsberg and Snyder adapted Buddhist and Hindu techniques to lend American protest a kind rather than a predominantly angry energy. Ginsberg and Snyder sought to "make mantra of American language now" in ways that combined Western-style activism with Asian mantras about transcendence. This technique was also on display in the 1967 attempt to levitate the Pentagon (Hungerford 32, Roszak 124–25). While Ginsberg was not directly involved with that spectacle, his poem "Pentagon Exorcism," written less than a month before the protest, supports its methods of chanting Sanskrit mantras in order to make the "Pentagon wake from planet-sleep!" (491). Such an inclusion of transcendence and positivity in protest activism envisions, and attempts to enact, a reality in which the rifts that spur the activism are overcome, just as Buddhist and Hindu practice seeks to transcend subject-object duality in general.

This emerging synthesis between Buddhist-inspired activism and American ideals became even more nuanced later in Snyder's career. Earlier texts such as "Smokey the Bear Sutra" transmit the raucous energy of countercultural movements. These texts capture the mood of Beat Buddhism, which defined itself against an American mainstream it sought to subvert. From the mid-1970s onward, however, the tenor of Snyder's writing shifts from revolution to reconciliation while retaining its basic commitments to spirituality and environmentalism. Snyder's evolution, and the ambiguous place of Beat Buddhism in American culture more broadly, gain particular illumination in his 1990 essay "The Etiquette of Freedom." While *Riprap / Cold Mountain Poems* (frequently published as a single volume, as indicated) is consciously derivative of Han Shan, and "Smokey the Bear Sutra" inhabits a Buddhist literary genre, Snyder's later essays are less dependent on Buddhist role models, having more in common with the essays of Thoreau.

"The Etiquette of Freedom" has broad significance for the life and afterlife of the countercultures with which Snyder was involved. Here Snyder proposes an alternative understanding of the word *wild* that replaces negative connotations of chaos with positive resonances of naturalness. Snyder is aware of how the term *wild* is not merely an epithet against general unruliness; it is a historically specific criticism of the Beat and hippie countercultures. Popular culture of the time saw Beats and beatniks as "delinquent" and "ridiculous," views somewhat encouraged by Beat writers but also caricatured by journalists covering them (Petrus 5, 9; see also Lawlor 233). The hippies also bore a "stigmatized identity" often associated with filth and delinquency (Hoffman and Steffensmeier). In "The Etiquette of Freedom," Snyder implicitly writes against these unfavorable perceptions, even though time has reduced their intensity.

Snyder poses his central question: "Where do we start to resolve the dichotomy of the civilized and the wild?" (15). He works toward an answer by defining "the wild" as a type of order, a counterintuitive move that nevertheless makes sense within Snyder's body of work. In his straw-man definition, a wild society is "uncivilized, rude, resisting constituted government." But in his favored definition, a wild society is one "whose order has grown from within and is maintained by the force of consensus and custom rather than explicit legislation" (10). Here, *wild* and *order* are complementary. In sum, Snyder asserts that "to speak of wildness is to speak of wholeness" (12). The wild is not brute savagery but a healthy balance, a self-regulating system. Snyder attributes these positive definitions to Buddhism and Daoism, emphasizing that his understanding of the wild "is not far from the Buddhist term *Dharma* with its original senses of forming and firming" (11, emphasis in original).

By recuperating the word *wild,* Snyder echoes Thoreau's essay "Walking," in which Thoreau declares, "I wish to speak a word for Nature, for absolute freedom and wildness, as contrasted with a freedom and culture merely civil." Thoreau's paean to the spiritually vital "art of Walking," not for transportation but for its own sake, seems almost to anticipate the "rucksack revolution" of

Beat Buddhist pilgrims. But Snyder develops a much more intricate synthesis of American and Asian ideals than Thoreau did, one based on both Buddhist philosophy and a countercultural motivation to create new kinds of communities, a synthesis that is in contrast to Thoreau's inward and solitary purview.

Snyder argues that *impermanence*—a word Westerners usually associate with fear and instability—is actually crucial to liberation, writing that "in a fixed universe there would be no freedom. With that freedom we improve the campsite, teach children, oust tyrants. The world is nature, and in the long run inevitably wild, because the wild, as the essence and process of nature, is also an ordering of impermanence" (5). This positive treatment of impermanence echoes the preeminent Buddhist philosopher Nagarjuna, who made a similar claim using the related concept of emptiness. In the second century, Nagarjuna influentially declared, "All is possible when emptiness is possible" (Siderits and Katsura 276). In an exemplification of enlightened individualism, Snyder's synthesis uses Buddhist thought to encourage American social activism, relying on both the concept of impermanence and the classically American imperative toward "freedom."

Snyder's discussion implicitly reflects on his entire career. In his early writing, Snyder is "wild" with an exuberance that Alan Watts criticizes as "Beat Zen." Snyder's later definition of the wild does not contradict his early Beat enthusiasm but recontextualizes it. The energy and irreverence in "Smokey the Bear Sutra" have faded and are tempered with calm. In his 1960 address "Notes on the Beat Generation," Snyder speaks approvingly of Beat "revolution" (11). In 1990, Snyder writes instead of "The Etiquette of Freedom." Snyder's terms of choice change from subversion to politeness. A young Snyder fondly called Han Shan "a mountain madman" (*Riprap* 33). But the Snyder of the 1990s and beyond would surely not use *madman* as a term of praise. Snyder's ongoing adaptations of American Buddhism speak to the mood of his times, while always retaining the spiritual imperative to defy oppressive forces and honor the natural world. Snyder's later work marks an important development in Beat Buddhism that continues its process of cross-cultural adaptation. Ironically, Snyder's capacious "Etiquette of Freedom" creates a conceptual framework for audiences to understand Beat Buddhism as increasingly compatible with nonrebellious American middle-class life.

KEROUAC'S CONFLICT

Gary Snyder was central to the Buddhist explorations of the Beat Generation's most programmatic spokesperson: Jack Kerouac. Kerouac met Snyder in San

Francisco in 1955, and the two quickly became close friends (Tan 231). Snyder's presence in Kerouac's writing quickly grows from two brief mentions in *Some of the Dharma* to, in the fictionalized persona of Japhy Ryder, the central figure of *The Dharma Bums* (Kerouac, *Some* 346, 408). Kerouac, like Snyder, offers Buddhist critiques of American consumerism and an injection of American restlessness into Buddhism. But whereas Snyder's long career evolves toward a greater synthesis of Buddhist and American values, Kerouac's writing reveals a hope for synthesis that it cannot fully realize. Kerouac's Buddhist period, which peaked from 1954 to 1957 (Giamo 180), is characterized by intensity, hope, pain, and conflict. Kerouac's Buddhism came exclusively from reading texts and conversing with Beat colleagues; he met D. T. Suzuki once but never studied under an in-person Buddhist teacher (Lott 172–73). Buddhism did not become a stable spiritual home for Kerouac, and after 1960, he gave it up, reverting in the following years to a preoccupation with Christian imagery derived from his Catholic background (Aronowitz 83; Maher 384). But during his fleeting engagement with Buddhism, Kerouac produced important reflections on how Buddhism was emerging in the US.

Kerouac's Buddhist period yielded several works of poetry and prose; my discussion will focus on the latter. Kerouac's Buddhist poetry, comprised of *Mexico City Blues* and *The Scripture of the Golden Eternity* (1959, 1960), tends to be highly abstract, dreaming, for instance, of "the knowledge that sees the golden eternity in all things" (Kerouac, *Scripture*). Kerouac's Buddhist prose more fully envisions what an American Buddhism might look like; therefore, I will examine *Some of the Dharma* (1956, but published posthumously in 1997) and *The Dharma Bums* (1958). Furthermore, by reading *Some of the Dharma* in tandem with *The Dharma Bums*, we can newly appreciate the latter as a dramatized outgrowth of the tensions presented in the former.

In the leading reading of *Some of the Dharma*, Nancy Grace convincingly argues that Kerouac's "Buddhism was more than Beat whim" by showing, among other things, how Kerouac "combines Buddhist and Christian concepts" and develops a "distinctly American" Buddhism that emphasizes individualism (134, 156, 158). But this adaptation does not only occur on the level of concepts; it also happens on the level of images. These images involve Orientalist resonances that Grace does not address, and the critics who do address such Orientalism view it as mutually exclusive with a serious commitment to Buddhism. My reading of *Some of the Dharma* explores how Kerouac appeals to abstract but salutary philosophy and concrete but stereotyped images at the same time.

Some of the Dharma develops Kerouac's conflicted commitment to spreading Buddhism in the US. Even though the text reads much like a freewheeling private journal, it is an essentially missionary work Kerouac intended to publish, although it was not published until nearly thirty years after his death. Kerouac was convinced that Buddhist nonattachment and nonself are crucial antidotes to American consumerism and technocracy. He laments, "In America only the silent Buddhahood may be possible. . . . The clinging here is so intense and widespread (democracy) the populace is literally unteachable and sees not life as sorrow" (61). Thus the very reason that America needs Buddhism is also the reason Buddhism is difficult to establish.

Therefore, Kerouac's efforts at cross-cultural adaptation remain fundamentally conflicted throughout the text. Kerouac cannot decide how compatible American and Western culture are with Buddhism, and he reads Buddhism both into and against Western traditions. Kerouac regards "even great thinkers" in the West as "ignorant compared" to Asian sages who "understand everything" (288). He wants to write "AN AMERICAN DHARMA" that contrasts from the Western literature of "Proust, Emily Dickinson, Joyce, etc." (255). Accordingly, Kerouac dismisses Shakespeare's poetic brilliance as "just a shining technique in the darkness, and goes out" (103). But later Kerouac cites Shakespeare's phrase "waste of shame" as a gloss on Buddhist understandings of the dangers of sexuality (239), and he likens Buddhist concepts of emptiness to "the first pages of Dostoevsky's 'Eternal Husband'" (117). While these links are provocative, Kerouac does not present a fully formed idea of what enlightened individualism could look like, a problem deepened by Kerouac's nostalgia for a mystic Orient of the past.

This longing expresses itself as a fantasy of geographical transposition. Kerouac, eager to feel "connected with Asia" (278), imagines North America *as* Asia, declaring that "West is East" (319). For instance, Kerouac asserts that "My India / Is right in this house" (78); "Mexico is like old India" (124); and, writing in San Francisco, "It's Saturday morning in China" (241). Encompassing people as well as places, Kerouac imagines "In America, real wandering Taoist bums going around the country" (115), here using "Taoist" as closely aligned with "Buddhist" in an anticipation of his coinage of the influential term *Dharma Bums*. Rather than considering how Buddhism could change America, and vice versa, these transpositions convey the escapist wish that Buddhist Asia replace America.

To try to bridge this gap, Kerouac envisions distinctive forms Buddhism can take in America, creatively reapplying Eastern terms to Western situations. He encourages hermetic living in vehicles: "Get an old panel truck for $95 and be your own Monastery in it" (117). With this image, Kerouac innovatively combines tropes of monasticism and the Asian hermetic sage with Beat motifs of motorized road trips. Kerouac also applies the language of Western political activism to the Buddhist path to overcome spiritual blindness by calling upon the reader to "BOYCOTT IGNORANCE" (166). He further recommends explaining Buddhism to Americans by retranslating the Buddhist term *Mind Essence*, Dwight Goddard's influential translation of the Sanskrit term *tathata* (roughly *suchness*, or the unelaborated nature of reality) (Goddard 518–19, Giles 194), as the "Mind of God" (198). This proposed translation prioritizes the use of theistic terminology recognizable to Westerners over philosophical accuracy. These efforts at cross-cultural adaptation coexist with lamentations that Americans are unteachable and Western civilization is too spiritually impoverished to understand Buddhism, demonstrating Kerouac's conflicted combination of hope for and frustration with American Buddhism.

In the midst of this tension, Kerouac struggles with whether to abandon literature as a self-aggrandizing, worldly fetter or to embrace it as a skillful means of teaching others. As other readers have observed, Kerouac wants to spread Buddhism through his writing, but he also develops hubris from imagining this missionary role (Grace 150–51, Smithers). Kerouac is ambivalently aware that he is "using Buddhist images for [my] own advantage, instead of for spreading the Law" (169). Although he aspires to be "THE WRITING BUDDHA" (312), Kerouac "realized I should perhaps not write a Buddhist novel for fear it will re-attach me to self-attainment" (188). This ambivalence makes it difficult for Kerouac to decide whether to continue writing at all (159, 310) and, if so, what Buddhist literary projects he should take up. Kerouac sees his attempt to spread enlightened individualism as continually threatened by his own impulses of unenlightened, self-important individualism.

Kerouac's self-awareness about his ulterior motives makes for an interesting comparison to Ginsberg. One of Kerouac's great contributions to Beat Buddhism was to introduce Ginsberg to Buddhism (Trigilio xii, 36–37); this influence became, in a sense, Kerouac's Buddhist legacy well after Kerouac's own involvement with Buddhism ended. Much later, Ginsberg named the Naropa University poetry program the Jack Kerouac School of Disembodied Poetics, a dark riff on Kerouac's death. But it might have discouraged Kerouac's ghost to know that Ginsberg, even after decades of Buddhist practice, still felt acute conflict over ego and fame much as Kerouac did. In a poignant example, Ginsberg's 1992 poem "After Lalon" conveys regret at his own spiritual inadequacy:

> How'd I get into this fix,
> this workaholic show-
>   biz meditation market?
> If I had a soul I sold it

>   for pretty words
> If I had a body I used
>   it up spurting my essence
> [...]
> If I had speech it was
>   all about boast (1020)

Ginsberg was more involved with Buddhism than Kerouac was, but Ginsberg's longer life and extended fame made the temptations of egotism correspondingly greater as well. Later, in 1996, struggling with illness and feeling death upon him, Ginsberg scolds himself in "Bowel Song": "Your master gives good advice, you listen, follow it couple weeks / then lapse into old habits" (1097).

And yet Ginsberg's Buddhist self-analysis allows him to engage in more kinds of self-criticism than Kerouac, not only in terms of writerly ego but also in terms of sexual desire. Ginsberg exposed himself to Buddhist and Hindu teachings on renunciation that problematize sex in general, regardless of orientation (Trigilio 46, 55). This understanding is different from the stigmatization of homosexuality prominent in the 1950s US religious mainstream. So Ginsberg feels conflicted about his attachment to sex, saying in late illness that when he dies, "What good, half dozen gay porno films them?" (1097). The openly gay Ginsberg questions his attachment to sex far more than Kerouac ever does, but not because Ginsberg internalized antigay beliefs; on the contrary, Asian religions help Ginsberg accept his own homosexuality (Trigilio 46). But Ginsberg gradually takes Buddhist and Hindu critiques of sexual desire more seriously than Kerouac does.

Whereas Ginsberg brought Buddhism into his activism and formal religious affiliation, Kerouac's engagement with Buddhism remained primarily literary. Kerouac imagines "BUDDHIST MOVIES" and "BUDDHIST STORIES" as effective teaching tools for Westerners (Kerouac 199) and also considers writing a "Historical Novel of Buddhist India" (04). Kerouac's sense of conflict is productive, spurring him to continuously develop new ideas. But rather than write Buddhist movies, short stories, or a novel of ancient India, Kerouac decided to write *The Dharma Bums*, which is closely based on his own life during 1955 and 1956 (Miles 95). Here the reader encounters many of the leading lights of Beat Buddhism in fictional form. In addition to Kerouac as Ray Smith and Snyder as Japhy Ryder, readers will also recognize Allen Ginsberg in Alvah Goldbrook, among other playfully transparent references. *The Dharma Bums* attempts to harmonize Kerouac's conflicted Buddhist literary aspirations by dramatizing Buddhist content in a prose narrative set in America. It is Kerouac's most detailed vision of what American Buddhism could look like, and his most famous and influential contribution to American Buddhism—and, for my purposes, to enlightened individualism. It is true, as critics have held, that Ray and Japhy distort Buddhist teaching and indulge in Asian stereotypes. But Ray's failings are not simply Kerouac's; they are conscious exhibitions of the problems of Orientalism that impede Ray's spiritual progress. *The Dharma Bums* thus contains a sincere hope for cross-cultural synthesis that it cannot fully envision.

The Dharma Bums is the first novel set in America with a Buddhist protagonist. Ray seeks to adopt the altruistic motivation of a Mahayana Bodhisattva, one who delays entry into nirvana in order to teach other beings the path of liberation from cyclic existence (H. Smith 124). The novel further exemplifies Beat Buddhism as a whole by linking Asian religion to countercultural critiques of capitalist consumerism. This move is evident in the novel's title, which connects Westerners who adopt bohemian lifestyles—"Bums"—to Buddhism—"Dharma." For Japhy, the mythic realm of ancient East Asian Buddhism contrasts with a degenerate modern America. Accordingly, Japhy describes the novel's Beat Buddhists as "Dharma Bums refusing to subscribe to the general demand that they consume production and therefore have to work for the privilege of consuming" (Kerouac, *Bums* 73). The logic here seems to be that if one is against American capitalism, then one should be for something as far away from America in both time and space as possible. Thus, in order for Buddhism to remain relevant to Ray's counterculture, "Eastern" religions must remain exotic relative to mainstream culture. Later writers attempt to resolve, and Kerouac seriously wrestles with, this tension in Beat Buddhism.

Ray and Japhy begin to deal with this tension by cultivating a version of Beat Buddhism that valorizes ancient role models for contemporary rebellion. They discuss Japhy's in-progress translations of Han Shan, whom Japhy describes as "a poet, a mountain man, a Buddhist . . . who could take off by himself" (22). Even though Ray (and Kerouac) turn away from Zen in favor of a more eclectic Mahayana Buddhism (Giles 180, 203n6), Ray speaks affectionately of the "Zen Lunatics of China and Japan" and listens to Japhy Ryder tell "anecdotes about the Zen Lunatics of the Orient" (6, 11). This description exoticizes Buddhism because the content of the lunacy is not clear at first, apart from Ray's repeated emphasis that the "Zen Lunatics" are Oriental.

This Orientalist Zen lunacy turns out to be, for Ray and Japhy, a way of rediscovering American freedom. Alvah Goldbrook calls Japhy "a great new hero of American culture," even though Japhy "didn't feel that I was an American at all" because "nobody has any fun or believes in anything, especially freedom" (22–23). Buddhism, with its perceived lack of repression, is an antidote to America's "general dreary newspaper gray censorship of all our real human values" (22). Japhy's Buddhism models an exotic freedom of spontaneous action that is truer to the American revolutionary spirit than the conformity into which American "freedom" has deteriorated.

But Ray's and Japhy's stereotyping gives credence to Alan Watts's complaints against "Beat Zen." The novel often presents Beat Buddhism with too great a point to prove in order to effectively evoke Buddhist nonattachment. But *The Dharma Bums* is not merely a symptom of this appropriation; it is also a conflicted engagement with it. The novel recognizes the faults of Orientalism even as it acknowledges that exoticism is a large part of what draws many Americans to Buddhism. More broadly, the novel expresses the vague hope that Buddhist ideals can spread across America and transform US individualism into enlightened wisdom. But Ray cannot envision how American society at large could integrate Buddhist teachings. Instead, he nurtures the escapist fantasy that an ancient Buddhist paradise would replace contemporary America altogether, a vision that began in *Some of the Dharma*.

Japhy's cultural openness arouses Ray's admiration, but the novel does not wholly endorse it. This fact represents the ambivalence of Beat Buddhism as it struggles to integrate that which it reveres. Japhy says, "East'll meet West anyway. Think what a great world revolution will take place when East meets West finally, and it'll be guys like us that can start the thing" (*Dharma* 155). For Japhy, the Westernization of Asia is one side of a growing, positive exchange between two hemispheres. He has a "vision of a great rucksack revolution [of] thousands or even millions of young Americans wandering around with rucksacks, going up to mountains to pray, making children laugh and old men glad making young girls happy and old girls happier, all of 'em Zen Lunatics" (73–74). Japhy eagerly hopes for reviving America with Buddhism: "Just think how truly great and wise America will be, with all this energy and exuberance and space focused into the Dharma" (74). Ray is not on-board with this social vision, reflecting that he "didn't want to have anything to do . . . with Japhy's ideas about society" (80), but he still admires the optimism in Japhy, whom he memorializes as "the number one Dharma Bum of them all" (5).

The tensions between Ray and Japhy also illustrate larger ambivalences in the relationship of Christianity, a prominent aspect of American identity for many, to Beat Buddhism, and to enlightened individualism more broadly. Ray thinks Christianity is compatible with Beat Buddhism while Japhy does not. Japhy says, "'I don't like all that Jesus stuff,'" whereas Ray "'felt suppressed by this schism we have about separating Buddhism and Christianity, East from West, what the hell difference does it make?'" (86). While it is unknown if a conversation like this historically took place between Kerouac and Snyder, the fact that Snyder does not mention Christianity in his own work does suggest that he wishes to distance himself from it. Kerouac, on the other hand, reaches out to Christianity, inspired by his Catholic background.

Kerouac, then, is engaged in a "religious pluralism" that seeks "to articulate a blend of Christian and Buddhist truths" (Ferretter 410, Grace 79). There seems to be a particular resonance for Kerouac, however implicit, between the suffering of Christ, which Catholic iconography particularly emphasizes, and the Buddhist truth that "All Life Is Sorrowful" (Kerouac, *Some* 3). Kerouac's preoccupation with suffering, and his sense of personal fallenness, is further reinforced by his older brother's death when Kerouac was four, as well as Kerouac's entanglement in self-destructive behavior such as alcoholism (Kerouac, Foreword viii; Maher 419–20). Ironically, Kerouac's ambivalent Buddhism is more open to Christian influences than Snyder's more optimistic Buddhist synthesis, which incorporates Native American, but not Christian, elements.

But Ray is ultimately too tied to a rarefied exotic vision of Buddhism to experience a Buddhist transcendence of all conditions. He tries but fails to transcend his Beat Buddhism as a fire lookout on Desolation Peak, where he lives alone for two months. Peering out from his secluded cabin, Ray muses, "The clouds were distant and frilly and like ancient remote cities of Buddha-land splendor" (180). Ray directly compares his surroundings to a Buddhist pure land, a heavenly realm in Mahayana Buddhism. The implicitly Asian "ancient remote cities" exist in a celestial "Buddhaland," which replaces Desolation Peak. In this vision, the exotic is heavenly.

This spatial imaginary also includes a spiritual description of Japhy:

> I saw that unimaginable little Chinese bum standing there, in the fog, with that expressionless humor on his seamed face. It wasn't the real-life Japhy of rucksacks and Buddhism studies and big mad parties at Corte Madera, it was the realer-than-life Japhy of my dreams, and he stood there saying nothing. 'Go away, thieves of the mind!' he cried down the hollows of the unbelievable Cascades. (186)

Here, not only does Japhy appear as unequivocally Chinese; he also takes on a mythic dimension. Ray's description is saturated with paradoxes. Japhy is both clearly visible and "unimaginable." His face shows "humor" and is yet "expressionless." The Japhy of his dreams is "realer-than-life." He is silent, "saying nothing," yet he shouts. These paradoxes show that Ray thinks in terms of Zen koans, unanswerable riddles that are designed to propel the mind beyond conventional, intellectual thought (H. Smith 133–36). This moment illustrates how much Japhy has taught him. Earlier, when mountain climbing with Japhy, Ray is not yet comfortable with koans: "With horror I remembered the famous Zen saying, 'when you get to the top of a mountain, keep climbing'" (Kerouac, *Bums* 63). At the time, Ray takes Japhy's remark too literally; but when Ray sees dream-Japhy on Desolation Peak, he has learned how to let koans work on his mind without intellectual resistance. This is the moment at which Ray is supposedly enlightened (Miles 103), and the stylistic imitation of Zen koans is impressive evidence in Ray's favor.

But Ray's vision is still shaped by Orientalism, and as a result his apparent epiphany lasts only as long as his peaceful, hermetic circumstances. Although Ray feels exalted in the moment, he also remains bound to concerns of time and space and feels the "'sadness of coming back to cities'" (Kerouac, *Bums* 186). It may seem as though Ray is tranquil when he "turned and went on down the trail back to this world" (187). But given Ray's apprehension about his return—and the opening retrospective in which Ray admits to having become "a little tired and cynical" (2)—we know that going back to the world means going back to more problems. If Ray were really enlightened, he would not feel sad at the prospect of reentering cities, given the Mahayana Buddhist doctrine of the nondifferentiation of samsara and nirvana (Fauré 39–40). True enlightenment would be impervious to circumstance; but by fixating on an image of exotic Asia, Ray is not using the relative truth of appearances to guide himself toward the ultimate truth of emptiness. Instead, he mistakes relative truth for ultimate truth. Ray's realizations do not transcend changing conditions because of his attachment to Orientalist fantasies.

Kerouac's Buddhism was a bright flame that burned out quickly; he did not live long enough to reflect on his Buddhist period from a great distance of many years. But Kerouac's Buddhist output has much to teach us about American receptions of Buddhism. The cultural associations Buddhism carries have made Orientalism an unavoidable aspect of Buddhism's growth in the US. In this context *The Dharma Bums* does not portray a successful fusion of East and West, but it sympathetically dramatizes the obstacles that enlightened individualism must deal with. As a groundbreaking work of American Buddhist fiction, *The Dharma Bums* juxtaposes the appeal of Buddhist transcendence with the risks of cross-cultural appropriation. Kerouac's portrayal is largely aware of Beat Buddhism's limitations; he was dedicated to making American individualism more enlightened, but he did not figure out how. The novel's unfulfilled hope has remained influential in later generations, as writers continue to wrestle with how to go beyond admiring Buddhism to being truly changed by it. As it evolves, this search will lead to new ideas of what it means to be an American and what goals Americans should pursue.

ROBBINS'S AMBIVALENCE

Kerouac directly influenced a prolific but overlooked contributor to Beat Buddhism: Tom Robbins (b. 1932). Because he did not travel in Beat circles at the generation's peak, and his first novel did not appear until 1971, Robbins is not considered a Beat writer, even though he is only two years younger than Gary Snyder and he befriended Allen Ginsberg in the 1960s (Robbins, *Tibetan* 222–24). But Robbins deserves attention for extending Beat themes and motifs well beyond the Beat—and hippie—periods, especially through his investments in Beat Buddhism. A recent collection of interviews calls Robbins "the principal voice of American countercultural fiction" (Purdon and Torrey, *Conversations*, back cover), an alignment Robbins inched toward early in life. Robbins's experiences of hitchhiking around the country and taking LSD are typical of Beats and hippies, respectively (Purdon and Torrey, Introduction xxi; Rentilly 125–26; Miller 154). Robbins also lived in Korea and Japan as a weather observation instructor for the Air Force, where he developed an interest in Asian religions; upon his return, he took master's coursework in Eastern religions (Purdon and Torrey, Introduction xxiii). However, Robbins has not done extensive, rigorous meditation training, so his study of Asian religions and extensive travels throughout Asia indicate a level of involvement with Buddhism that is greater than Kerouac's but less than Snyder's.

In spite of his wide readership and skillful artistry, Robbins has received very little critical attention. Except for a handful of articles and one critical book in a series on "popular writers" (Hoyser and Stokey), most publications about Robbins are interviews. However, Robbins is an important artist thoughtfully engaged with what it means for Asian religions to become popular in the US. References to Asian religions can be found in all of his eight novels, and Asian religions are a particularly conspicuous theme in *Even Cowgirls Get the Blues* (1977) and *Villa Incognito* (2003). I will show how these novels indicate Robbins's movement toward greater receptivity to Western practitioners of Asian religions, and I will touch on how he further refines his thoughts in his memoir, *Tibetan Peach Pie* (2014). Robbins's vision lies in between Snyder's one of union and Kerouac's one of incommensurability. Robbins's early work combines a fascination with Asian religions with a skepticism toward all Western attempts to practice them, suggesting that cultural—and, troublingly, racial—differences prevent Westerners from doing anything other than merely appropriating Buddhism and Hinduism. Robbins's later work signals a progressively greater openness to cross-cultural adaptation and the hope that Asian ideals can transform American freedom, although he still retains a strong touch of humility about Westerners' ability to understand Asian faiths such as Buddhism.

Robbins achieved literary success during the 1970s when the countercultures with which he identified were fading. During this time, as R. John Williams explains, many texts engaged in "postcountercultural" reflection on the supposed excesses of the 1960s (174). Robbins's *Even Cowgirls Get the Blues* is a noteworthy reflection on this situation. The novel admonishes its readers of the risks of adapting foreign religions, but it also further develops Beat Buddhism's hope that Buddhism can renew and transform American freedom. *Cowgirls*'s spiritual vision directly engages with Kerouac's. Like *The Dharma Bums*, *Cowgirls* is a road novel with strong debts to Asian mysticism. The novel attempts to carry on Beat Buddhism's zeal for subversion and enlightenment while envisioning a more complete cross-cultural synthesis than what *The Dharma Bums* presents. *Cowgirls*'s heroine, Sissy Hankshaw, is the greatest hitchhiker in the world because of her exceptionally large thumbs. This fact makes Jack Kerouac, whom Robbins fancifully imagines as having briefly dated Sissy, deeply envious (47). Also, throughout her travels, the "rucksack" Sissy wears is evocative of the "'rucksack revolution'" that Japhy prophesies in *The Dharma Bums* (170; Kerouac, *Bums* 351).

Sissy's better hitchhiking is not just a funny allusion; it also reflects her better insight. She improves upon Ray Smith's Beat Buddhism by pursuing spiritual liberation without resorting to Asiatic fantasies. Paradoxically, the novel promotes the transmission of Buddhist (and Hindu) teachings even as it admonishes Westerners against believing they can understand and practice a religion from a distant culture. This allows Robbins's Beat Buddhism to be more sensitive and informed than Kerouac's while maintaining more cultural distance than Snyder's. Robbins shares Kerouac's and Snyder's Beat Buddhist irreverence and commitment to mystical liberation as an alternative to Western consumerism. But whereas early Snyder and Kerouac ambivalently use images of the exotic East as both obstacle and lure, Robbins is especially emphatic about ironizing Orientalist stereotypes, and even slurs, allowing him to form an especially complex and daring synthesis between East and West.

Sissy's main spiritual teacher, the Chink, is a deliberately outrageous caricature of old Asian wise men. For all his wild behavior, his most alarming feature is Robbins's exclusive use of a slur as the character's name. I will not try to argue whether this choice is ethically justified, but it is a deliberate and provocative tactic. The narrative seeks to satirize and defuse the slur's offensiveness through nonemphatic overuse. Furthermore, it draws attention to the indignity of ethnic conflation as well. The Chink, who is actually Japanese American, claims that a group of Native Americans misnamed him with the wrong slur (Robbins, *Cowgirls* 197). The Chink has chosen to riff on his marginal status by ironically reclaiming a label that is doubly offensive as both an insult and a sloppy misidentification.

The Chink's appearance and behavior are almost as extreme as his name. When Sissy first sees him, we learn that his "problem was that he looked like the Little Man who had the Big Answers. . . . He looked as if he had rolled out of a Zen scroll, as if he said 'presto' a lot, knew the meaning of lightning and the origin of dreams. He looked as if he drank dew and fucked snakes. He looked like the cape that rustles on the backstairs of paradise" (163). The Chink is a mysterious guru, but he relishes in sexual libertinism, vulgar speech, and teachings that focus more on appreciating one's present life than dissolving into a property-less transcendence.

These traits make the Chink an exemplar of Tibetan *crazy wisdom*, a term profoundly linked to Kerouac's earlier coinage, *Zen lunacy* (*Bums* 73). The term, coined by Chögyam Trungpa Rinpoche as a translation of the Tibetan term *drubnyon*, refers to the "disruptive holiness" of eccentric saints. These teachers' outrageous actions—including drunkenness, fornication, and pranks—serve to jolt their students out of conventional dualistic thought. By flouting distinctions between sacred and secular, pure and impure, "crazy wisdom" is supposed to help students realize the innate emptiness of all phenomena (S. Bell 59). Echoing the anticonformism of the Beat and hippie countercultures, Robbins has repeatedly emphasized the influence of crazy wisdom on his fiction (Miller 151–52), defining it as "the opposite of conventional wisdom. It is wisdom that deliberately swims against the current in order to avoid being swept along in the numbing wake of bourgeois compromise" (Robbins, "Defiance" 180).

Although the Chink never uses the term *crazy wisdom*, it is likely that the Chink is based on Trungpa himself, given the latter's exceptional and well-earned reputation for extensive drinking and sexual relations with students (Trigilio x). Furthermore, Robbins was friends with Ginsberg, Trungpa's most famous student, in the years before *Cowgirls*'s publication (Robbins, *Tibetan* 207, 222–24), giving further circumstantial evidence of Robbins's indebtedness to crazy wisdom. Robbins, who praised Ginsberg as "a Vedantic versifier" with "the capacity to cast a net of enchantment around nearly everything" (223–24), was likely an admiring onlooker of Ginsberg's forays into Trungpa's crazy wisdom in the early 1970s. Robbins's crazy wisdom shares the countercultural values of Ginsberg's, Snyder's, and Kerouac's Beat Buddhism, even though *Cowgirls* makes jokes at Kerouac's expense.

Like *The Dharma Bums*, *Cowgirls* showcases a myopic perspective on Asian religions that the novel as a whole calls into question. In *The Dharma*

Bums, Ray fails to effectively practice an Asian religion because he cannot see Buddhism outside of his Orientalism. In *Cowgirls* the Chink argues that Westerners cannot practice Eastern religion at all, a claim the novel refutes through Sissy's own spiritual journey. The Chink declares:

> Throughout the Western world, I see people huddled around little fires, warming themselves with Buddhism and Taoism and Hinduism and Zen. And that's the most they ever can do with those philosophies. Warm their hands and feet. They can't make full use of Hinduism because they aren't Hindu; they can't really take advantage of the Tao because they aren't Chinese; Zen will abandon them after a while—its fire will go out—because they aren't Japs like me. To turn to Oriental religious philosophies may temporarily illuminate experience for them, but ultimately it's futile, because they're denying their own history, they're lying about their heritage. (230)

According to the Chink, when Westerners try to get light, or insight, from Eastern religions, what meager light they can get from it will only "temporarily illuminate experience." Westerners should instead follow their ancestral pagan lineage: "The United States of America is the logical place for the fires of paganism to be rebuilt—and transformed into light" (234). Not only does this passage react to Asian religions' growing popularity in the US in the preceding two decades; it also implicitly criticizes Kerouac himself, given his eventual abandonment of Buddhism and his susceptibility to the criticism that his Buddhism is shallow and under- or misinformed. But the Chink troublingly indicates that Kerouac's limitation is not one of understanding but of race. Cross-cultural adaptation is impossible; spiritual seekers should restrict themselves to whatever the religion of their "heritage" happens to be. The Chink's admonition to avoid appropriation ends up positing gaps between cultures so unbridgeable that it starts to sound like racial determinism. In this context, the Chink's self-directed use of the slur *Jap* is especially noteworthy. His casual reappropriation of this slur suggests that he is immune to feeling ashamed by others' racism, reinforcing his teaching that "freedom . . . is largely an internal condition" (183). Furthermore, the Chink ironically redeploys this racist insult as a marker of superiority, positioning him in a privileged position of authentically understanding Eastern wisdom in ways Europeans cannot.

Significantly, the Chink also defines Christianity as an "'*Eastern* religion'" because it teaches "truths that are universal" (231, emphasis in original). This universalism is connected to a religious transcendence that the Chink contrasts to the worldliness of Celtic paganism, which the Chink believes "put pleasure ahead of asceticism" (231). The difference the Chink posits between worldly Western paganism and transcendent Eastern religions corresponds to Charles Taylor's distinction between Pre-Axial and Axial faiths, respectively. Pre-Axial religion dealt with ordinary human flourishing, whereas Axial religions such as Christianity, Buddhism, and Daoism teach transcendent goals that go beyond human flourishing (Taylor 147–51). The fact that the Chink acknowledges this, and links Buddhism and Christianity along these lines, suggests that Robbins sees more possibilities to connect Buddhism with Christianity than Snyder does, although he is less ultimately invested in this avenue than Kerouac. Overall, according to the Chink, Axial faiths do not properly belong in the US.

And yet, against his own words, the Chink transmits Buddhist insight to the Westerner Sissy by inspiring her spiritual awakening. This suggests that Eastern wisdom is available to Westerners after all, as long as they stumble onto it through crazy wisdom rather than seeking it in a doctrinaire system. The Chink helps Sissy realize what she already knows (174), which is that "one can change things by the manner in which one looks at them" (72). The Chink's method resonates with Zen Buddhist pedagogy, which focuses not on believing in propositions but on realizing one's innate wisdom (Kapleau 55). His message also fits the Buddhist notion that external reality is an illusory projection of one's own mind (Seager 30–31).

The Chink further adopts Zen methods by using koan-like enigmas to teach Sissy, a pedagogy Robbins sees as aligned with crazy wisdom (Robbins, "Defiance" 182, 186). The Chink gives Sissy paradoxical or nonsensical statements that force the mind to abandon familiar logical categories. While not strictly Zen koans, they employ similar tactics of contradiction and surprise. For example, the Chink explains to Sissy that the world needs "magic and poetry" to permeate all levels of society, including stereotypically prosaic enterprises such as politics and journalism (Robbins, *Cowgirls* 333). When Sissy asks if such a poetic sensibility could ever prevail on a mass scale, the Chink replies, "If you understood poetry and magic, you'd know that it doesn't matter" (333). This statement may seem to be a dangerous retreat from politics, but the Chink does not mean to generalize that one should care about "poetry and magic" and not bother with the world at large. His comment has a more immediate purpose: He tells Sissy what she needs to hear at that exact moment. The Chink's apparent negation mysteriously resolves Sissy's uncertainties. This moment is expressed by the convergence of several events: "The moon rose. / The clockworks struck. / A crane whooped. / She understood" (333). The novel expresses Sissy's new understanding in a seemingly abrupt, non-narrative digression that defines poetry as "an intensification or illumination of common objects and everyday events until they shine with their singular nature" (333). In this Buddhist-inspired epiphany, objects and events, although distinct, occur within a background of transcendent "illumination" that permeates everything. Furthermore, by presenting this realization without direct segues, the novel's form imitates the sudden enlightenment of Asian spiritual practitioners (Cheng 595–600). *Cowgirls* seeks to transmit Asian wisdom in the US without explicitly calling it as such, thus skirting the issue of Orientalism in its use of Asian philosophies even as it parodies cultural Orientalism in its characters and motifs.

The novel further casts this sort of Asian wisdom as the fulfillment of American freedom, particularly by depicting a migration of American whooping cranes to Tibet. In so doing, Robbins uses animal symbolism to place American values in the service of an Asian vision. The cranes symbolize courageous, individualistic American freedom, an ideal the novel both values and complicates. Earlier in the novel, the narrator emphasizes that the cranes evolved in North America and are paragons of "majestic beauty" that habitat loss has driven to the edge of extinction (*Cowgirls* 251–52). The narrator rhapsodizes, "Unlike those integrity-short teemers, including man, the whooper opted for quality instead of quantity. . . . It would survive on its own terms or not at all" (252). Near the novel's end, the cranes change their migratory pattern and leave the country altogether. Observing this journey, the narrator rhetorically asks, "Is the most splendid and sizable American bird searching for a new home, scouring the globe in quest of a place where it can be private and free?" (360). The novel thus underscores the birds' Americanness by emphasizing a desire for privacy and freedom.

Although the novel positions these birds as quintessentially American, their quest for life, liberty, and the pursuit of whooping crane happiness ironically leads them out of the US into Tibet (360). In this provocative vision of enlightened individualism, the novel suggests that the American aspiration for individual freedom is most fully realized in Buddhist-inspired teachings. In this view, the Buddhist freedom of spiritual liberation is more profound than the debased version of American freedom responsible for an "industrialized, urbanized, herding" society that the narrator identifies as the "one wrong way" to live (192). By imagining Tibet as the whooping cranes' best new home, the novel nudges its American readers toward Buddhist wisdom as well. The novel is not saying that Americans should literally move to Tibet as the cranes do; a more credible reading is that Americans should follow the cranes symbolically by exploring Asian religious insights as a new spiritual frontier. This move seeks to integrate Buddhist liberation into American life in a way that Kerouac hoped for but failed to envision. It also celebrates its particular sense of freedom *as* American more explicitly than Snyder's work does.

Robbins evolves his hopes for Asian inspiration in America in *Villa Incognito,* which shows an increased, but still qualified, openness to Caucasians practicing Asian religions. Whereas *Cowgirls* highlights an Asian guru who settles in the US, *Villa Incognito* portrays an American-born guru who settles in Asia. In this novel, Mars Stubblefield, a former US soldier lost while helicoptering over Laos in 1973, is declared missing in action and presumed dead. But he survives the crash and settles in a remote village in Laos, choosing to remain there even after the Vietnam War ends. Although technically a prisoner at first, he quickly charms his way into a position of prominence as a local spiritual authority, combining his Western philosophical training with his accumulation of experiences with local Buddhism and shamanism. Like the Chink, he is unkempt, sexually promiscuous, intellectually independent, given to didactic speeches, and self-deprecating.

Ironically, Stubblefield remains invested in American ideals even though he chooses to live in permanent exile (142–43). His frayed relationship to his home country is tied to his history of insubordination and antiwar sentiment, and even to his intentional botching of missions to avoid "inflicting collateral damage" (119–20). Nevertheless, Stubblefield's conflicted experiences as a soldier have led him not to reject American freedom as a ruse but to critique contemporary American politics as a corruption of worthy ideals. At one point, he muses, "What bouncy, enterprising weirdness is leaking out around the edges of [America's] disguise? *That's* the real America. That's what justifies its existence" (114, original emphasis). The novel leaves the question open. But the question's prominence suggests that the American "enterprising" spirit can find its justification in "bouncy, enterprising weirdness," the freedom of joyful, disruptive spontaneity that carries on the *crazy wisdom* discussed above. America has a "disguise" of bourgeois conformity, but a "real" American spirit can be revealed underneath this superficial layer. Crucially, Stubblefield's notions of what it means to be American arise because of his spiritual development in Asia.

Furthermore, Stubblefield's crazy wisdom relies on tropes from the Beat generation. He describes the soul as "a long, lonesome freight train rumbling from generation to generation on an eternally rainy morning: its boxcars are loaded with sighs and laughter, its hobos are angels, its engineer is the queen of spades—and the queen of spades is wild" (78). This passage is steeped in Beat imagery, style, and themes, including a focus on boxcars, a Kerouac-like freewheeling and run-on syntax, and a veneration of the derelict. Here the word *generation* invokes both the Beats and the Asian doctrine of reincarnation. Stubblefield is also self-deprecating, saying that the speech he just gave "might be high wisdom, it could be pure bullshit" (79).

The fact that Stubblefield is a white European demonstrates that one does not have to be Asian to gain crazy wisdom. But Stubblefield must settle in Asia to attain it, suggesting that what matters is not ancestry but immersion in a particular culture. That is, in order to realize a religion's wisdom, one must live where the religion is effectively indigenous. It is troublingly ironic that a necessary precondition for this immersion, in Stubblefield's case, is the gruesome escalation of the Vietnam War. But Stubblefield distances himself from the war to the extent that he can and thus embodies a cross-cultural intersection that suggests new relationships between Americans and Asian religions. In the novel's opening section, which takes place in late nineteenth-century Japan, a Zen monk says, "The blue-eyed ones can attain neither wisdom nor tranquility . . . because they're too busy clapping their hands in glee over the suffering of the damned" (20). Generations later, Stubblefield's example refutes this overgeneralization. But the "blue-eyed ones" must leave Western territory to overcome their ethnic disadvantage, as Stubblefield does.

The views of cross-cultural adaptation in *Villa Incognito* gain additional development in Robbins's more recent writings and interviews. In a 2009 interview, Robbins echoes the Chink's hope for a pagan "revival of mystical nature worship" in the US (Miller 154). But he does not repeat the Chink's insistence that Westerners take a spiritual detour around Asian religions altogether. Instead, his caution is more understated: Robbins says that "Americans may hold Buddhist ideals in our hearts and minds, but they're not yet in our genes" (Miller 154). In an apparent continuation of the racial-religious boundaries the Chink posits in *Cowgirls*, Robbins implies that one must have a particular religion in one's "genes" to practice it effectively. But by saying that Buddhist teachings are "not *yet* in our genes" (emphasis added), he suggests that Buddhism can work its way into Westerners' genes with enough time and, presumably, practice. With these remarks, Robbins's post-*Cowgirls* perspective moves closer to Japhy Ryder's vision that "East'll meet West" after all (Kerouac, *Bums* 430).

However, Robbins also thinks that the US is not yet a suitable place for realizing Eastern wisdom, establishing something of a spiritual Catch-22. In his autobiographical book *Tibetan Peach Pie*, Robbins reports an experience of *satori*, or Zen insight, in 1966 in which he "was witness to an indissolvable totality of reality" (89). What is especially interesting is how Robbins assesses the aftermath:

> Had I been Asian and of a certain temperament, I suppose I would have repaired to a Zendo, an ashram, or a wilderness cave to meditate on my neon

golfball satori for the rest of my life, striving to integrate it somehow into my daily existence. Instead, although shaken, galvanized, and fairly splish-splashing in a fading aura of awe, I just motored on through the subsiding snow squall and went to a Hollywood movie. (89–90)

In this account, Asians have culturally supported opportunities to develop spiritually, opportunities that Westerners such as Robbins lack. Of course there are far more retreat centers in the US now than there were in 1966. But Robbins, writing about this memory in the present day, gives no indication that he thinks the cultural gap he posits has disappeared. He also opines that the risk of culturally shaped misinterpretations is so great that "Asian spiritual texts were probably best left to spiritual Asians" (215). However, one does not necessarily have to be an ethnic Asian to be a "spiritual [Asian]," so Robbins subtly leaves a door open. While Robbins envisions a fuller synthesis than Kerouac does, he gives more weight to the persistence of cultural difference than Snyder does.

Ginsberg, Snyder, Kerouac, and Robbins indicate the variety of visions within Beat Buddhism. But within this variation, these writers are similarly devoted to synthesizing Buddhist and American notions of freedom through creative cross-cultural adaptations. The complexity of Beat Buddhism has been fruitful for American literature and culture. This rich area of study shows how cross-cultural adaptations cause notions of American freedom to evolve, compete, and coexist. Kerouac's enduring popularity, as well as the long careers of Ginsberg, Snyder, and Robbins, shows that Beat Buddhism has outlived the Beat moment. These four writers were instrumental in a cultural breakthrough: They raised Buddhism's profile by linking it with a counterculture whose public recognition surpassed its strength in raw numbers. American perceptions of Buddhism, and other Asian religions, would never be the same.

The potential relationship between Beat Buddhism and American cultural history comes across especially vividly in Ginsberg's 1994 poem "City Lights City" (*Collected Poems*). Ginsberg imagines a fictional American city in 2025 with Beat-based place names, including "Via Ferlinghetti & Kerouac Alley," "Bob Kaufman Street," "McClure Plaza," "Snyder Bridge," and "Neal Cassady R.R. Station." In this vision of the near future, not only is the Beat legacy countercultural; the Beat impulses of enlightened individualism are embedded in city infrastructure, a vision of an American culture renewed, not overthrown, by countercultural exuberance, creating a place where "international surrealist tourists climb to see the view." While this future has yet to arrive, it remains clear that the issues Ginsberg, Kerouac, Robbins, and Snyder wrestle with—Asian religions' relevance to a politics of dissent, the ethics of borrowing across cultures, and the compatibility of Buddhist liberation with American freedom—have set the stage for succeeding engagements with Asian religions. As I will show, these themes continue to evolve in anti-Beat, postmodern, African American, and Asian American expressions of enlightened individualism.

CHAPTER 2

Anti-Beat Reactions and Mainstream Mysticism

J. D. Salinger's Franny and Zooey *and Robert Pirsig's* Zen and the Art of Motorcycle Maintenance

BEAT BUDDHISM was a decisive influence on Asian religions in the US, lending Buddhism and Hinduism distinctly countercultural associations. This development provoked a variety of responses. As I mentioned in the previous chapter, mainstream society dismissed the Beats as delinquents and viewed their dabblings in exotic religions as a facet of an immature rejection of an orderly and well-functioning society. But it is also important to note that the strains of Asian religions in the US that preceded the Beats, many of which trace directly to the World Parliament of Religions, did not go away with the advent of the Beat Generation. Some Asian religious organizations more or less ignored Beat Buddhism, such as the Ramakrishna-Vivekananda Society. Other parties, such as D. T. Suzuki and the Buddhist Churches of America, had only fleeting encounters with the Beats (Masatsugu). (Although Suzuki largely inspired the Zen Boom of the late 1950s, his lone meeting with Kerouac was reputed to be an awkward and ambivalent affair [Maher 384–85].) Some figures, for example, Alan Watts, chided Beat Buddhists for their trying-too-hard-to-be-transgressive Beat Zen but still remained in the Beat orbit. Whether approving or disapproving of Asian religions in general, these views of Beat Buddhism relied on rejecting or at least not using the Beat rhetoric of radicalism.

But in literary terms, I contend that the most influential dissents from Beat Buddhism were those that critiqued countercultural defiance while still bearing its imprint. This argument further underscores the depth of the Beats' influence on Asian religions in the US. The anti-Beat perspective I explore in this chapter co-opts and privatizes countercultural rhetoric. This vision has in common with Beat Buddhism a critique of square society. But it instead promotes a version of Asian religions that is compatible with a mainstream existence. Whereas countercultural Beat Buddhists endorse flamboyantly outrageous behavior, these anti-Beats present a version of Asian religions that focuses on private introspection. This adaptation rejects crazy wisdom or Zen Lunacy in favor of a nonconfrontational inwardness that does not react to, or even depend on, outside conditions. These writers' basic instinct is to mollify, not provoke, to exist better within existing structures rather than rebel against them. This version of enlightened individualism positions Asian religions as tools for living bourgeois, middle-class, mainstream American lives in a way that is nonthreatening to existing institutions and religions (e.g., Christianity). It is a view that Alan Watts, if he was in an ungenerous mood, might have placed under the heading of "square Zen," a stuffy form of practice that, while still "more imaginative" than mainstream midcentury Christianity, gives a lot of weight to decorum and restraint (Watts 8–9).

Two champions of this vision are J. D. Salinger and Robert Pirsig. In this chapter, I focus on Salinger's *Franny and Zooey* (1961), written at the height of the Beat movement, and Pirsig's *Zen and the Art of Motorcycle Maintenance* (1974), composed after the hippie counterculture had passed its late-1960s peak. These texts bookend and contrast with the countercultures of the 1960s. This is not to say that Salinger and Pirsig wished only to affirm American conformity; rather, they looked beyond social structures to a transcendent truth that includes and surpasses all divisions between mainstream and counterculture. But for their part, Salinger and Pirsig mostly opposed the counterculture, whereas the later work of Gary Snyder, for instance, sought in its own way to revise Beat motifs into mainstream acceptability. Also, whereas Snyder's later redefinitions of Beat wildness still involve an active environmentalism, Salinger and Pirsig are not politically engaged.

The nonthreatening, mainstream-friendly stance of Salinger and Pirsig depends on a strategy of emphasizing commonalities rather than differences across cultures and religions. Thus, whereas the Beats contrasted Asian religions with the supposedly corrupt American culture that midcentury Christianity helped solidify, Salinger and Pirsig presented Asian religions as a harmonious complement to Christianity. Accordingly, there is an ecumenicalism in Salinger's and Pirsig's work that can be considered a mode of Perennialism. This is the view, popularized by Aldous Huxley's tract *The Perennial Philosophy*, that all religions point toward the same ultimate truth. I am not arguing that Huxley was a direct influence on Salinger or Pirsig, but there are enough similarities between Huxley's spiritual framework and theirs to make such an association meaningful. Salinger was at least aware of Huxley's ideas; Huxley wrote the preface to the 1942 edition of *The Gospel of Sri Ramakrishna*, one of Salinger's most cherished books (Letter to S. Adiswarananda). As for Pirsig, although there isn't direct evidence that he read *The Perennial Philosophy*, his conflation of the divine ideals of diverse religions is similar to Huxley's. While Huxley's term *Perennialism* has stuck, it is a part of a larger current, with antecedents going back at least to the Transcendentalists and certainly on display at the World Parliament of Religions. As Vivekananda famously said in his address to the Parliament, "We accept all religions as true" ("Speech Delivered"). Versions of this idea can also be seen in the work of William James, Joseph Campbell, and, more recently, John Hick and Huston Smith.

Furthermore, the type of Vedantic Hinduism championed by Vivekananda, which has come to represent the essence of Hinduism in the eyes of the Western world (R. King 98–99), supports a version of Perennialism, emphasizing a quote from the Rg Veda that "God is one but men call him by many names" (Radhakrishnan and Moore, qtd. in Junghare 17). It is ironic that the belief that all religions are true has strong roots in a specific culture. In fact, the claim that all religions are true is incoherent when pushed far enough, because such a claim denies the validity of highly exclusivist and triumphalist religions. This point means that the Ramakrishna-Vivekananda strain of universalism turns out to be quite particular. Indeed, some have complained that the statement "all religions are one" really means "all religions are Hinduism" (Buswell and Lopez). This type of Perennialism finds expression in the writings of Salinger and Pirsig, who propose a magnanimous openness to all perspectives, even though such a position is difficult to maintain with logical consistency.

And yet Salinger and Pirsig also rely on a kind of repurposed countercultural language. They promote a rhetoric of authenticity against phony and corrupt superficial consumerism. The protagonists of *Franny and Zooey* and *Zen* come across as incisive critics of a stultifying social order. But the right response, for Salinger and Pirsig, is not a countercultural devotion to alternative lifestyles of itinerancy, escapism, or activism. The more overtly countercultural writers, and their heirs such as Pynchon and Walker, use a synergy between countercultural and Asian religious rhetoric, the common point of which is to free the mind from delusion, whether it be the delusion of subject-object duality or the delusion that the dominant society is a benevolent one. But Salinger and Pirsig count the appeal of the counterculture as yet another myopic delusion. Whereas the counterculture urges people not to be a sucker of mainstream conformity, Salinger and Pirsig want their readers not to be a sucker of any excessively limited perspectives, *including* those of the counterculture. Instead of adhering to a particular social vision, Salinger and Pirsig call for a more absolute transcendence, one that withdraws from social vices rather than trying to change them.

J. D. SALINGER'S ANTI-BEAT INWARDNESS

Salinger has become, ironically, a countercultural hero who disdained the counterculture. Salinger shared with the Beats a distaste for stuffiness and conformity—that is, squareness—but his response was to turn inward rather than to inspire alternative social movements. As Salinger scholar Stephen Whitfield puts it, "Salinger's own sensibility was definitively pre- (or anti-) 1960s" (585). Whereas the Beats critiqued bourgeois capitalism and the hippies engaged in significant social protest, Salinger's defining achievement, *The Catcher in the Rye*, is "utterly apolitical," and there is an "aura of passivity that pervades the novel" (587, 585). *Catcher* has appealed to many young and disaffected people because it portrays a relatable alienation from "snobbery, privilege, . . . stunted human possibility" and the like (Ohmann, qtd. in Whitfield 582). But another important factor in the novel's historical popularity was how much censorship it provoked because of paranoid and superficial reactions to its use of profanity and criticism of authority (Whitfield 574–82). The novel thus gained social significance as "a catalyst for revolt . . . [and] a threshold text to the decade of the sixties" due more to its aura as a banned book than to attentive readings of the text (Seelye, qtd. in Whitfield 583). As I will show, Salinger promoted neither Beat bohemianism nor hippie activism, but rather a quiet, intensely individual authenticity through nondisruptive mysticism.

Salinger's interest in this sort of mysticism shows that he did at least share with many Beats a deep interest in Asian religions. Salinger's affinities with Buddhism and Hinduism came from reading Swami Vivekananda, D. T. Suzuki, and related figures who trace back to the World Parliament of Religions. These missionaries helped adapt Asian faiths to the US before Buddhism and Hinduism became countercultural. While Asian religions do not figure in *Catcher*, they play a progressively central role in Salinger's series of stories about the Glass family which, while lesser-known, make up the bulk of Salinger's corpus. This family of seven precocious children becomes defined by the suicide of the eldest, Seymour, told in the earliest Glass family story, "A Perfect Day for Bananafish" (1947). The subsequent Glass family stories, narrated mainly by the second-born, Buddy, struggle with the shadow of Seymour's suicide. Buddy attempts to memorialize Seymour as a spiritual titan of Buddhist and Hindu wisdom, even though there are no direct references to Asian religions in "Bananafish." Critics of Salinger have puzzled over how a character so supposedly enlightened as Seymour could destroy himself, and they have noted that the Seymour portrayed in "Bananafish" seems different from the Seymour in other Glass family stories (Bryan 226, Schwartz 96–97). While I will not dwell on the continuity problems with Seymour's character, which seem to be partially contingent on the timeline of Salinger's growing interest in Asian religions in the early 1950s, Seymour remains an important touchstone for my argument. While Seymour is prominent in most of the Glass family stories, I focus on *Franny and Zooey* because it shows how the youngest Glass child, Franny, uses Asian religions to find a positive way forward in life where Seymour did not. *Franny and Zooey* thus allows readers of Salinger to engage with Asian religions in a context where Seymour's suicide does not have the last word. Instead, *Franny and Zooey* envisions a particularly private but also life-affirming place for Asian religions in American life.

Franny and Zooey is a noteworthy site in Salinger's complex relationship to the Beat generation. The novel is engaged with Beat sentiment, even though it does not use the term *Beat*. The text's instigating incident is college-aged Franny's nervous breakdown, occasioned by her disenchantment with higher education at Yale and her lousy boyfriend, Lane. As she processes her distress, Franny gives a scathing critique of stuffiness, pretentiousness, and, as Holden Caulfield would say, phoniness. But whereas Franny's—and, by implication, Salinger's—diagnosis of US culture is similar to Kerouac's, the text's ultimate response is quite different. As an example of a more widespread pretentiousness, Franny complains that the poets in Yale's English department are "not *real* poets. They're just people that write poems that get published and anthologized all over the place" (18). Lane contemptuously responds, "Do you have to be a goddam bohemian type . . . to be a *real poet*? What do you want—some bastard with wavy hair?" (19, emphasis in original). Franny cannot give a precise answer but answers Lane's question "No" (21) and says a real poet should at least "do something beautiful" (19). Although Franny does not share Lane's harshness toward bohemians—read *Beats*—neither does she view them as the solution to societal pretentiousness.

Not much later, Franny's critique of Beat bohemianism becomes more specific. When Franny describes her malaise to her brother Zooey, she says, "Everything everybody does is so—I don't know—not wrong, or even mean, or even stupid necessarily. But just so tiny and meaningless and—sad-making. And the worst part is, if you go bohemian or something crazy like that, you're conforming just as much only in a different way" (26). This time, the target is not just ivory-tower literati but "everybody"—including Beat bohemians. Both Franny and Beats like Kerouac and Snyder share a criticism of mainstream society as inauthentic. But "go[ing] bohemian" would be, according to Franny, just another type of conformity, albeit an ironic conformity to a putatively anticonformist counterculture.

However, it is not just the general fact of conformity within groups that bothers Salinger but the specific content of Beat culture as well. A key case in point is sex. In contrast to the Beats, who celebrated sexual libertinism, Salinger is a sexual ascetic. In *The Dharma Bums,* Japhy Ryder self-servingly declares during an orgy that he has no patience for any religion "that puts down sex" (21). He misrepresents tantric teachings as authorizing sexual license, whereas those teachings more precisely stress overcoming ordinary sexual desire and exercising control (Fauré 50; Gyatso, *Practice* 192–97). By contrast, Salinger's renunciant view resonates with the Hindu scripture the *Bhagavad-Gita,* an excerpt from which appears in *Franny and Zooey* and which in later years Salinger claimed to read daily (Letter to S. Adiswarananda). The *Gita* praises celibacy and portrays sex as a spiritual fetter. The Swami Nikhilananda translation of the *Gita* that Salinger read says that a true student of truth acts by "restraining the self with firmness . . . dwelling in solitude . . . cultivating freedom from passion . . . [and] forsaking . . . pride and lust" (18.51–53). This idea appears in Salinger's fiction. In "Teddy" of *Nine Stories,* the title character says that he would have achieved liberation in a previous life, but took birth again because "I met a lady, and I sort of stopped meditating" (188). This remark concisely implies that a romantic and sexual attachment derailed Teddy's spiritual progress. Likewise, in *Franny and Zooey,* Lane's attachment to sex is portrayed as a vice. Lane implies that he and Franny had sex when he urges Franny to "*relax* about that Friday night" (5, emphasis in original), which he reassures her no one will find out about. Elsewhere, Lane uses a euphemism to complain that it has been too long since Franny had sex with him, calling it "no good. Too goddam long between drinks. To put it crassly" (43). Lane's pursuit of sex comes across as an expression of underlying selfishness and entitlement, a portrayal that puts Salinger at odds with pro-sex Beat Buddhism.

Franny and Zooey's acknowledgments of the Beats, while not extensive, nevertheless hint at the Beats' rich and ambivalent influence on the novel's response to stifling conformity. Although Salinger's fiction creates deliberate distance between his vision and that of the Beats, he still co-opts rhetorical elements of countercultural disruption, albeit for different ends. For example, in contrast to the outwardly eccentric Beats, *Franny and Zooey* reclaims a positive meaning for the word *fanatic* by recasting fanaticism as a radical inwardness. *Franny and Zooey* contains descriptions of religious pilgrimage as "terribly fanatical" (33, 100), with Zooey saying ironically that even Jesus Christ himself had a refreshingly "unhealthy fanaticism" (86). Inspired by this intense spirituality, Zooey once aspired to get a "nice, pilgrim-type rucksack. I was going to fill it with bread crumbs and start walking all over the country. Saying the prayer. Spreading the Word" (158). Given that *The Dharma Bums* postdates *Franny and Zooey*, it is noteworthy that both Salinger and Kerouac independently hit upon the rucksack as a symbol of noble, authentic religious itinerancy. For Salinger and the Beats, this sort of "fanaticism," even when expressed through Christian figures, is grounded in ideas from Asian religions.

But Salinger's sense of positive radicalism, however superficially similar to Beat rhetoric, is very different from that of midcentury American countercultures. For Salinger, good fanaticism is one of renunciation, not the chip-on-their-shoulder provocations of Beats and, later, hippies, who made a show of defying bourgeois norms of self-sufficiency. We see this view in the dialogues of *Franny and Zooey*. At one point, Zooey chastises Franny by telling her, "If you're going to go to war against the System, just do your shooting like a nice, intelligent girl—because the enemy's *there*, and not because you don't like his hairdo or his goddam necktie" (162–63). The exaggerated capital S coupled with the condescending description "nice, intelligent girl" is a dismissive characterization of the concerns of the contemporary counterculture. Furthermore, the fact that Franny eventually seems to take Zooey's advice, and gains happiness as a result, suggests that the novel vindicates Zooey's view. Zooey's exhortation to Franny to either "go to war against the System" full bore or stop complaining is somewhat disingenuous because Zooey knows Franny is not actually interested in activism, and he does not sincerely encourage her to go in that direction.

Instead, the authenticity Zooey advocates, and the novel largely validates, is private and politically passive, implicitly affirming the existing social order of nuclear families and stable work. Indeed, the happy resolution of *Franny and Zooey* is a consolidation of the frayed relationships within a nuclear family, and the novel takes place almost entirely within a single apartment. Whereas Japhy Ryder speaks of a "rucksack revolution" (73), Franny and Zooey discover that the profoundest realizations come through quiet, home-based introspection rather than activism or physical wandering. For them, as I will show, the pilgrim does not become a literal incitement to the itinerant lifestyle Beat Buddhists valorized, but rather stands as a symbol of the triumph of contemplative discipline over worldly distractions.

TRANSCENDING LANGUAGE AND RELIGION IN *FRANNY AND ZOOEY*

The novel's critiques of societal inauthenticity notwithstanding, *Franny and Zooey* nevertheless seeks to reconcile Asian religions with the American mainstream by presenting Buddhism and Hinduism as fully compatible with Christianity. The novel does this by drawing parallels between Christian and Hindu saints and texts and by weaving Hindu and Buddhist concepts into a loosely Christian plot. *Franny and Zooey* articulates a Perennialist stance more extensively than even the expansive vision of Kerouac, whose investments in Christian imagery made him somewhat unique among countercultural Beat Buddhists. *Franny and Zooey*'s interfaith synthesis, coupled with the novel's social quietism and focus on a middle-class nuclear family, is an effort to make Asian religions acceptable to the mainstream. But Salinger's subtle privileging of Hindu and Buddhist philosophy goes against orthodox Christian beliefs such as the linearity of time and the uniqueness of Christ. To soften the impact of these heterodoxies (from a Christian point of view), the novel's self-conscious verbal excess reveals a sophisticated project to convey Hindu- and Buddhist-inspired transcendence to its readers while building bridges to Christian and more generally normative American ways of being.

Franny and Zooey connects Western and Eastern religions through juxtaposition: The characters consistently group Western and Eastern terms together in their speech. Franny's main source of religious inspiration is the anonymous nineteenth-century memoir *The Way of a Pilgrim*, in which an itinerant Russian Christian wanders the countryside, practicing and teaching about the Jesus Prayer: "Lord Jesus Christ, Son of God, have mercy on me." As Franny explains, this prayer is a short sentence that one says continuously until its repetition becomes an automatic act of the heart, perpetually driving one toward greater virtue and direct experience of God. Franny compares the Jesus Prayer to similar practices in Nembutsu Buddhism, medieval Christian mysticism, and Hindu syllabic chanting (*Franny* 37–39). In a similar juxtaposition later on, Zooey's letter from his older brother, Buddy, lists the Hindu Upanishads, the Buddhist Diamond Sutra, and the Christian mystic Meister Eckhart as favorite sources of inspiration (59–60). Zooey also quotes D. T. Suzuki, saying that Zen realization is like being "with God before he said, Let there be light" (65). He further groups the Western term *saints* with Eastern words "arhats, bodhisattvas, [and] jivanmuktas" (65), which are various types of spiritual masters in Buddhism and Hinduism. These allusions, to list only a few, consistently juxtapose Eastern and Western religious traditions, suggesting that all faiths strive toward a common goal (Greene).

This meeting of East and West happens in the characters' writing as well as speech. After one particularly emotional exchange between the two title characters, Zooey absconds into his older brothers' former bedroom to look at a bulletin board filled with quotations compiled by Seymour. The narrator says, "No attempt whatever had been made to assign quotations or authors to categories or groups of any kind. So that to read the quotations from top to bottom, column by column, was rather like walking through an emergency station set up in a flood area" (*Franny* 175). Then the text shows us several of these quotations, and the reader can experience this seemingly chaotic fragmentation for him- or herself. The excerpts come from the *Bhagavad-Gita*, Marcus Aurelius, the eighteenth-century Jesuit priest Jean Pierre de Caussade, Leo Tolstoy, and a book of Zen koans, among other texts. In this diverse pastiche of authors, genres, and content, no unifying theme is apparent. Zooey does not give us much help either; all we know is that he "sat at Seymour's old desk, inert but not asleep, for a good twenty minutes" (180). He seems to be meditating, but we don't know about what. The text thus coyly invites the reader to contemplate the quotations along with Zooey. Doing so, the reader may find that the only thought large enough to generate a coherence behind these quotations is not an idea or a word, but an intuition of the whole of human striving beneath all its diverse expressions in fiction, poetry, philosophy, and religion. In this way, a diversity of words prods the reader toward their implicit unity's unnamable source.

But the fact of Seymour's suicide dampens this uplifting message. Zooey's contemplation of Seymour's bulletin board hearkens back to an earlier scene where Zooey reads a letter from Buddy that says, "You were the only one who was bitter about S.'s suicide and the only one who really forgave him for it" (68). Zooey's silent ruminations are both philosophical and personal; he reflects not only on the quotations themselves but also on the sad question of how his brother, who had invested so much in this wisdom, would choose to kill himself. These quotations are food for the reader's thought, but only Franny's eventual religious realization shows that she will succeed where Seymour had failed.

Having cast all religious paths as legitimate but limited purveyors of spiritual truth, the novel nevertheless does not treat all traditions as equal. In fact, the novel progressively subordinates its Christian elements to its Hindu and Buddhist influences. It does so by inserting Buddhist and Hindu ideas into a Christian plot. The story follows a recognizably Christian paradigm, but its spiritual payoff bears the language of Hindu and Buddhist nonduality rather than a Christian triumph of eternal life over death. On the level of plot, Franny is a Christ figure. Like Christ, she gives spiritual teachings to skeptical audiences, denounces the hypocrisy of her contemporaries, endures extreme suffering that brings redemptive benefits for others, and dramatically reemerges in a restored and improved state. Her skeptical audiences include her boyfriend Lane, her mother Bessie, and her brother Zooey. The contemporaries she criticizes are pretentious college professors and students, the pedantic Pharisees and Sadducees of her own time and place. She endures verbal harassment by the mostly well intentioned Zooey, who tells her, among other things, that "you're beginning to give off a little stink of piousness" (158). Zooey's unrelenting harangues drive Franny toward a crisis of suffering—a mental crucifixion—to the point where Franny is absolutely abject, sobbing, and in a "wretched, prostrate, face-down position" (172). Her suffering redeems Zooey as he repents of his harshness and utters a feeble apology (172). After this scene, a chastened Zooey also begins to open up to his grief over his brother Seymour's suicide of several years before. At the novel's end, Franny experiences a spiritual resurrection in which she feels "as if all of what little or much wisdom there is in the world were suddenly hers" (201). Thus, in *Franny and Zooey*, the Christian drama plays out in miniature, giving Salinger's American readers a familiar story arc to hold on to.

But this Christian plot does not deliver an orthodox Christian message. While the form of the story follows a Christian arc, the content of the characters' spiritual striving owes more to Buddhist and Hindu philosophy. This orientation is evident in the characters' word choices, especially Zooey's. He says that someone who teaches the Jesus Prayer in *The Way of a Pilgrim* is "a sort of Christian guru" (112). Here *Christian* is an adjective modifying the noun *guru*, a Sanskrit word for a spiritual teacher in the Hindu tradition. This phrase thus casts Hinduism as the general norm, and Christianity as the specific variant. In a later passage, Zooey calls Christ himself "a supreme *adept*" (171, emphasis in original). According to the *Oxford English Dictionary*, an *adept* is a trained expert, especially in something occult. By using this word, Zooey frames Jesus' greatness as the result of practice, not divine exaltation. This understanding makes sense in a Hindu framework, where the wisdom of highly realized masters is the fruit of their own diligence. And this understanding contradicts the traditional Christian notion of Jesus as the uniquely incarnate Son of God, as stated in the Nicene Creed. Zooey further undermines the doctrine of Christ's uniqueness by calling him "*a* supreme *adept*" rather than "*the* supreme adept" (emphasis added). The novel's mentions of Christ thus give American readers a familiar point of reference while describing him from the standpoint of Hindu ideas. This view of Christ is in accord with that of Sri Ramakrishna, whose followers regarded Christ as "an Incarnation of God" alongside "Krishna" and "Chaitanya" (Gupta c. 13). Moreover, Sri

Ramakrishna's biography, *The Gospel of Sri Ramakrishna,* pointedly uses the word *gospel* in its title in an effort to echo the New Testament (Gupta). Like Ramakrishna, Salinger's content is less Christian than such words suggest. Near the novel's end, right before Franny's epiphany, Zooey says, "The only thing that counts in the religious life is de*tach*ment" (198, italics in original), a Buddhist sentiment that would seem counterintuitive to many of Salinger's Western and Christian readers. Conditioned by deft lexical moves ranging from emphatic nouns to unobtrusive articles, the novel's Christian plot leads the reader to a resolution defined mainly by Asian mysticism.

Franny and Zooey's use of Christian placeholders for Hindu and Buddhist messages continues right up to the end of the story, when Zooey utters the novel's most famous line. After reminiscing about Seymour's encouraging him to keep up his work for the sake of an unspecified Fat Lady, Zooey declares to Franny, "*There isn't anyone out there who isn't Seymour's Fat Lady* [. . .] And don't you know—*listen*—to me, now—*don't you know who that Fat Lady really is?* . . . Ah, buddy. Ah, buddy. It's Christ himself. It's Christ himself, buddy" (201–2, italics in original). Although Zooey emphasizes "Christ himself," his formulation does not conform to Christian orthodoxy. Zooey says that "there isn't anyone out there who isn't Seymour's Fat Lady," but he also says that the Fat Lady is "Christ himself." If everyone is the Fat Lady, and the Fat Lady is Christ, it then follows that everyone is Christ, which goes against traditional Christianity's emphasis on Christ's uniqueness. Zooey's gloss on the Fat Lady makes much more sense in a Hindu framework in which the ultimate Divine is present in everyone. This maneuver is the last in a long line of nominally Christian tropes that the novel sets up to convey Hindu metaphysics.

Although the text gives implicit preeminence to Hindu and Buddhist philosophy, the novel does not rest on these doctrines as the truth itself. This hierarchy that subtly favors Asian traditions still occurs on the provisional level of language and concepts and as such is not ultimate. Rather, the novel ultimately attempts to convey the transcendence of all explanations, of whatever syntax or sect, by tapering its discourse down to pure silence. This trend accelerates as Zooey's former's ponderous speechifying substantially diminishes in the novel's last quarter. During one of his unsolicited lectures to Franny, the frustrated protagonist asks, "Are you finished?" (159). Zooey does not answer her question, saying, "You said you'd hear me out" (159), implying that he will not stop talking any time soon. A few pages later, when Franny entreats him to stop, Zooey answers, "I will, in a minute, in just a minute" (165). On the next page, when he still shows no signs of relenting, Franny again howls, "*Will you shut up, please?*" and Zooey replies, now reducing the timeframe by a factor of sixty: "In just a second, in just a second" (166, original emphasis). Later, in the novel's closing scene, Zooey signals his conclusion by saying, "One other thing. And that's all. I promise you" (198). And since it is the end of the book, he is true to his word, and the book closes with a moment of "primordial silence" (202).

This narrative trend is encapsulated in Zooey's famous words themselves: "*There isn't anyone out there who isn't Seymour's Fat Lady* [. . .] And don't you know—*listen*—to me, now—*don't you know who that Fat Lady really is?* . . . Ah, buddy. Ah, buddy. It's Christ himself. It's Christ himself, buddy" (201–2). After Zooey has spent most of the novel speaking in long, discursive paragraphs, now his language tapers into more rhythmic cadences, repeating the words and phrases "don't you know," "buddy," and "Christ himself." Thus his speech finally becomes less like tedious hectoring and more like the stabilizing mantras that he and Zooey discussed earlier. As the book ends on a note of "primordial silence" (201), the reader sees language diminish from unwieldy exposition, to rhythmic mantra, and finally to complete quiet. In the novel's last paragraph, Franny feels "as if all of what little or much wisdom there is in the world were suddenly hers. . . . For some minutes, before she fell into a deep, dreamless sleep, she just lay quiet, smiling at the ceiling" (201). This time, a reference to Seymour, here using the image of the Fat Lady, is more unequivocally positive because it serves as a vehicle of spiritual insight, even though Seymour did not fully realize that insight himself. This ending not only renews Franny but recuperates Seymour as well.

Furthermore, with this conclusion, the novel invites the reader to share in Franny's enlightenment. Her silence is the white space on the last page after the text ends, and in this space the effects of Zooey's mantralike speech reverberate for both her and the implied reader. The book's spiritual messages and mantralike repetitions automatically fill the silence of Franny's spiritual rapture. Thus, the novel attempts to perform the very mantra practice its characters discuss. By playing with language to show the limits of words, philosophies, and religions themselves, an array of speech melts into silence, and a plurality of traditions merges into transcendence. Through these techniques, Hinduism and Buddhism come across not as exotic contrasts to the American mainstream, as they do in much Beat literature, but as enriching complements to Christianity and vehicles for spiritual insight.

The payoff of Franny's enlightenment is not the exuberant, adventuresome freedom of Kerouac's Dharma bums or Snyder's poetry. *Franny and Zooey* is invested more in promoting Hindu notions of duty in ways that relate ambivalently to the American freedom of self-invention. As the *Bhagavad-Gita* states, a "man" is on the right track "when a man performs an obligatory action only because it ought to be done, and renounces all attachment" (18.9). Zooey makes the same point more informally by stressing the importance of "doing whatever the hell your duty is in life" (169). In Franny's case, that duty is being an actress. Zooey, channeling standard Asian views of reincarnation, pontificates that "somewhere along the line—in one damn incarnation or another, if you like—you not only had a hankering to be an actor or an actress but to be a *good* one. You're stuck with it now. You can't just *walk out* on the results of your own hankerings" (198, emphasis in original). But while the word *stuck* sounds like the opposite of freedom, Zooey's advice still points toward a path of individualistic self-determination. He says, "An artist's only concern is to shoot for some kind of perfection, and *on his own terms*, not anyone else's" (199, emphasis in original). That is, one develops spiritually not by turning away from such a calling but by learning to carry out one's karmic legacy without attachment, after which one is freed from the cycle of desire and pursuit.

This approach relates difficultly to Enlightenment individualism because it is both individualistic and nonindividualistic at the same time. Consider John Locke's theory of the blank slate, an idea that is an important aspect of Taylor's buffered self (Taylor 125, 127). One's mind is open to learning and character formation but has no predetermined direction and cannot have its self-determining agency undermined by outside factors like demons or spells. Salinger does retain a notion of individualism as a private mind that bears personal responsibility. But he challenges one aspect of the buffered self by redefining the individual, not as a blank slate, but as a long continuum influenced by the karmic inertia of previous lifetimes. Franny learns this lesson by accepting her duty to act. Her feeling of inner peace indicates that she has internalized Zooey's advice, alleviating the tension between her brother and herself, and will return to her acting pursuits as a more grounded and happier person. Her spiritual epiphany will give her the quiet strength, the reader is led to assume, to acknowledge the inauthenticity around her without succumbing to it or feeling personally victimized by it. The enlightened individualism Franny expresses makes her true to her highest spiritual self in largely private ways that do not involve changing society or rejecting mainstream American religions or identities.

That Franny's duty is acting is ironically symbolic. It is common to view acting as a frivolous activity that is, for most of its devotees, a fun but unproductive use of time and perhaps a waste of money. And the few who can make a living at it are living a dream and would not need encouragement to continue. Considering this stereotype, Franny's duty to act makes more sense as a stand-in for the broader concept of *action* in general. The Sanskrit word *karma* literally means *action,* and it also refers to the results of actions in Buddhism and Hinduism, often across many lifetimes (R. King, *Indian Philosophy*

77, 97, 161). Thus the novel's ideal reader will share Franny's call to act in whatever way most fulfills that person's karmic legacy, forged from a history of past longings that are, in a crucial sense, one's own.

While Salinger's vision engages in nuanced cross-cultural religious philosophy, it also continues enlightened individualism's tendency to ignore details of the specific cultures these religions come from. According to literary scholar Som P. Ranchan, with *Franny and Zooey,* Salinger "has brought [Vedanta] into a New York Apartment. . . . The vision of Ramakrishna is made real with such fun, mischief, metaphysical seriousness and profound, symbolic gravity" (106–7). I agree that Salinger is noteworthy for adapting the ideas expressed formally in the *Bhagavad-Gita* into a contemporary domestic setting with telephones, television, and snappy dialogue. But by saying that through Salinger "Vedanta thus ceases to be the sacred preserve of the monks" (106), Ranchan, like Salinger, overlooks the millennia of Indian Hindus for whom the Vedas and monks have long been just one aspect of a popular lived religion. Like most American literature about Asian religions, *Franny and Zooey* gives only a great-texts-and-great-sages view of these traditions and is not in touch with the lived experience of historically Buddhist and Hindu populations.

However, Salinger does give a bit more exposure to some "cultural" elements of Asian religions, such as mantra recitation and belief in reincarnation, than most other writers of enlightened individualism. It is a testament to Salinger's careful synthesis that these elements do not come across as alien to American life. The novel selectively transmits from Asian religions spiritual tools for living within the emerging US middle-class conformity against which the Beats and hippies openly rebelled. The novel's private focus, positive depictions of Christianity, and praise of dutiful work is an implicit tolerance of the social norms of US society.

This kind of inwardness, quietist though it is, does still lead to expressions of enlightened individualism. I offer a concluding example, this time from "Seymour—An Introduction" (1959). Buddy narrates a twilight marbles game between his eight-year-old self and a friend, during which ten-year-old Seymour suggests, "Could you try not aiming so much? . . . If you hit him when you aim, it'll just be luck" (236). Seymour's suggestion, starkly contrary to the typical spirit of the game, is so stunning that Buddy does not even finish the game and goes home in an awed daze. A few pages later, Buddy's narration makes the allusion to Zen explicit: "When he was coaching me . . . to quit aiming my marble . . . he was instinctively getting at something very close in spirit to the sort of instructions a master archer in Japan will give when he forbids a willful new student to aim his arrows at the target" (241). Buddy then says, quite disingenuously, "Mostly, however, I would prefer not to compare

Seymour's marble-shooting advice with Zen archery simply because I am neither a Zen archer nor a Zen Buddhist, much less a Zen adept" (242). Buddy's uptight concern for categorization and propriety is an example of what Alan Watts would call *square Zen*. More to the point, Buddy's anecdote is an Americanized homage to Eugen Herrigel's *Zen in the Art of Archery* (1948), the book that later inspired Pirsig's far more famous title *Zen and the Art of Motorcycle Maintenance*.

By transposing Zen archery onto a marbles game, Salinger adapts Buddhist principles to transform Americanized individualism into a more enlightened spiritual exercise. While marble games have been widespread throughout the world (Comeaux 324), it is not hard to see marbles in a US context as closely aligned with traditionally atomistic notions of American individualism: It involves competition, the high-stakes risk-taking of playing "for keeps" (327–28), and precocious entrepreneurial hustle, as suggested by the common metaphor "playing for all the marbles." Furthermore, Buddy's narration invokes American identity: "It was that time of day when New York City boys are much like Tiffin, Ohio boys" (235); the game of marbles unites American children regardless of location or urban/rural differences. By infusing marbles with a Zen sensibility of nonattachment and spontaneity, Salinger keeps the American scenery but redirects marbles' restless individualist impulse into a more Buddhist practice of deemphasizing the distance between subject and object. Even before Seymour tells Buddy not to aim, Buddy is already unattached to his own marbles, musing that he "was losing steadily . . . but painlessly" (235). In Salinger's world, to draw inward and be true to oneself without worrying about the surrounding American culture is the truly radical and countercultural act.

ROBERT PIRSIG AND THE LEGACY OF THE 1960s

Salinger's visions of Asian religions in American life were largely an outgrowth of and response to the Zen boom of the 1950s. Some eighteen years after Salinger wrote about the incipient trends of the times, Robert Pirsig reflected in hindsight on these trends, trends that deserve some attention before I dive fully into Pirsig's work. According to Pirsig, during the late 1950s, "there were rumblings from the beatniks and early hippies at this time about 'the system' and the square intellectualism that supported it, but hardly anyone guessed how deeply the whole edifice would be brought into doubt" (146). From Pirsig's perspective, one can see prescience in the depth of Franny's alienation from society and the countercultural responses that arose from such experiences. In the years following *Franny and Zooey,* a number of "bastard[s] with wavy hair" became famous for offering a hip alternative to the mainstream, such as Timothy Leary, Ram Dass, Allen Ginsberg, John Lennon, and others. Hippies made Asian religions even more visible than before in US culture, and they were eager audiences for Asian teachers like Maharishi Mahesh Yogi, A. C. Bhakdivedanta Swami Prabhupada, Eido Tai Shimano Roshi, and Chögyam Trungpa, all of whom relied on countercultural patronage and catered to that audience to varying degrees.

The strong link between hippie culture and Asian religions brought about a variety of literary responses during the 1960s, some of them uncomplementary. For instance, Kurt Vonnegut skewers Maharishi's Transcendental Meditation in his essay "Yes, We Have No Nirvanas." Criticizing the guru's approach as superficial and consumerist, Vonnegut declares that "Maharishi had come all the way from India to speak to the American people like a General Electric engineer," naively teaching that "every time you dive into your own mind, you are actually dealing effectively with the issues of the day" (177, 79). This context helps one to see *Slaughterhouse Five* as a satire of Asian metaphysics. Billy Pilgrim believes that he has been abducted by transcendent aliens who see "all time as you might see a stretch of the Rocky Mountains. All time is all time" (85–86). This notion is closely related to ideas in Buddhism and Hinduism, adapted in Transcendental Meditation, that time is an illusion (Loy, "Mahayana"; W. King 218–19). But Billy's belief in this idea is, in Vonnegut's portrayal, a form of escapism; he consoles himself with the idea that "according to the Tralfamadorian concept, of course, Nathan was alive somewhere and always would be" (199). Billy's mysticism, and, by extension, Maharishi's, is a way of avoiding "dealing effectively with the issues of the day."

Whereas Vonnegut looks askance at Asian religions but sympathizes with the counterculture, the converse is the case for Saul Bellow. His novel *Mr. Sammler's Planet,* according to literary scholar Sukbhir Singh, is influenced by Hindu ideas but also "aims at an open derision of the intellectual and behavioral extremes of the New Left or the counterculture followers in America" (436). Bellow has, in Singh's words, "deep contempt for the counterculture of the sixties" (440), and his novel "conveys the message of karma yoga as a cure for contemporary moral decay" of the "sixties" (441). Whereas many hippie figureheads such as Leary viewed Asian religions as complementary to countercultural lifestyles, Bellow saw them as opposed.

The questions of how to assess the confluence of Asian religions and American countercultures, and of how the mainstream and the counterculture relate more generally, remained salient after the post-1968 decline of the hippie movement. From around 1970 to the Watergate scandal and the end of the Vietnam War in 1975, the hippie movement gradually grew into the past tense; even though its spirit was still present, its kairos was on the wane, its energy sputtering through both internal burnout and conservative backlash (Dickstein 272–74, Morgan 169–70). Did this crossroads represent a decisive triumph of the mainstream over the counterculture? And would Asian religions in the US fall by the wayside without the fuel of an energetic and visible hippie movement?

This is the situation that Pirsig reflects on, and he brings to it a well-traveled perspective that resists granting primacy to any one viewpoint. Pirsig served militarily in Korea in the late 1940s and gained interest in Buddhism there. He subsequently learned about Hindu philosophy at Banaras University in India (Adams). He is, notably, the only writer in this study whose interest in Asian religions *began* while he was in Asia. Pirsig also straddles the two supposedly disparate disciplines of composition and philosophy: He taught composition at Montana State University and did graduate work in philosophy at the University of Chicago.

Both Pirsig and Salinger served in the military overseas: Salinger in the European theater of WWII and Pirsig in Korea before the Korean War (Slawenski, Adams). And both writers gained sudden fame from one runaway bestseller, after which they lived lives of seclusion. I do not presume to say which of these shared factors, if any, might have contributed to similarities in their outlooks on Asian religions and American society, but as I proceed, these similarities will, I hope, become clear.

Yet for all the authors' personal parallels, their respective texts take very different artistic approaches to depicting Asian religions in US life. Most of *Franny and Zooey* takes place in a single apartment; the text is almost all dialogue with minimal physical action, and the total narrative timeframe is just two days. By contrast, Pirsig's *Zen and the Art of Motorcycle Maintenance* uses a sweeping canvas. There is an abundance of scenery on a cross-country motorcycle trip; and the narrative spans a number of years, jumping between the narrative frame of the motorcycle trip and the narrator's look back at his years of pursuing philosophical questions of how to live authentically in a stultifying technocracy. Also, whereas Salinger's characters are thoroughly fictional and do not much resemble Salinger's own family, Pirsig's *Zen* is closely based on his own life, to the point where the narrator is a version of Pirsig himself, and the events depicted "must be regarded in [their] essence as fact" (Pirsig, author's note). (For this reason my discussion will use "Pirsig" and "the narrator" interchangeably.) Additionally, whereas *Franny and Zooey* involves numerous bridges to Christianity, Pirsig's *Zen*, although referring to God occasionally, barely mentions Christianity or Jesus at all. Salinger's and

Pirsig's disparate presentations nevertheless converge upon similar messages. Just as Salinger seeks to make Asian religions mainstream in contrast to Beat Buddhist provocation, Pirsig, writing more in hindsight to the counterculture, uses Asian ideas of nonduality to rise above the divisions between hippie and mainstream, or "square," culture. Both authors' visions work to advance more mainstream-friendly formations of enlightened individualism.

TAMING THE ROAD IN *ZEN AND THE ART OF MOTORCYCLE MAINTENANCE*

Like *Catcher in the Rye, Zen* was a surprise bestseller whose popularity rested on the text's ability to answer the yearnings of its historical moment. Literary scholar R. John Williams is right to stress the novel's role as a "postcountercultural text" (174; also see Dickstein 276–77). Pirsig considers how to reckon with the social crises of the 1960s from the somewhat less desperate standpoint of the 1970s, writing out of the sense that antagonistic social factions in the US, while still present, have fallen into an uneasy détente. Pirsig's historical exigency is that "in recent times we have seen a huge split between a classic culture and a romantic counterculture—two worlds growingly alienated and hateful toward each other" (Pirsig 68). The narrator acknowledges that, from a post-1960s perspective, "by now these battle lines should sound a little familiar" (68): The romantic counterculture views the mainstream, classical bourgeoisie as "Oppressive. Heavy. Endlessly Gray. The death force." Conversely, the classic mainstream views the romantic counterculture as "Frivolous, irrational, . . . interested primarily in pleasure-seeking . . . [a] real drag on society" (67). Pirsig writes that "clichés and stereotypes such as 'beatnik' or 'hippie' have been invented for the antitechnologists, the antisystem people, and will continue to be" (17). He views the contemporary divide between the fading counterculture and the ascendant mainstream as an embodiment of a larger "conflict of *visions of reality*" (53, emphasis in original). The novel thematizes these sides as "classic" and "romantic": "The classic mode . . . proceeds by reason and by laws" whereas "the romantic mode is primarily inspirational, imaginative, creative, intuitive" (67, 66). In his own time, the narrator tells us, "the names 'beat' and 'hip' grew out of" this conflict" (53). Unfortunately, the narrator laments, "There is no point at which these visions of reality are unified" (68). Or is there?

Although I am calling *Zen* a novel, it is a difficult text to classify. It is by turns a novel, philosophical treatise, essay, memoir, and autobiography. Pirsig's autobiographical narrator intersperses his philosophical ruminations throughout a frame narrative of a motorcycle trip with his eleven-year-old son, Chris. This present slips into flashbacks of the narrator's earlier life as a renegade intellectual whose metaphysical obsessions led to philosophical breakthroughs—but also to mental illness. *Zen*'s conceit is that the narrator uses the cross-country motorcycle trip to visit places he used to live and thereby reconstruct his memories of the important philosophical ideas he developed before undergoing disruptive electroshock therapy. In the narrative present of the road trip, the narrator also adopts the conceit of having an ongoing conversation with the reader to develop the philosophical ideas of his former self, whom he calls Phaedrus. Normally, when philosophy uses too much narrative, the argument is getting sidetracked; and when narrative becomes too philosophical, it loses momentum and succumbs to didacticism. The achievement of *Zen* is to interweave narrative movement and philosophical explication in a surprisingly effective synthesis. Although much of my analysis examines *Zen*'s philosophical points outside of their narrative contexts, the text's narrative structure is complex and important, and I will revisit this aspect of Pirsig's work near the end of this section.

One of the themes the narrator develops the most recurrently is the classic/romantic divide. As his philosophical forays build, the narrator sees the two sides of the classic/romantic dichotomy as having a large set of contrasting attributes, not all of which I will analyze but which can be summarized in the following table:

CLASSIC (66–68)	ROMANTIC (66–68)
Rational (67)	Emotional ("feelings rather than facts") (66)
Objective (223–24)	Subjective (223–24)
Square (163, 212–13)	Beat/Hip (17, 53)
Scientific/Technological (66)	Artistic (66)
Masculine (67)	Feminine (66–67)
Western (116–17)	Eastern (116–17)

While all the connections between these traits have significant social and ideological meanings, I want to focus on how Pirsig links classical understanding with the "West" and romantic thought to the "East." For Pirsig, the "East," or Asia, is mainly romantic, emotional, and mystical, while the West is primarily classical, rational, and concrete. These stereotypes are quite common in Pirsig's time and still are today. Pirsig's view of the classic West and romantic East was heavily influenced by F. S. C. Northrop (Pirsig 116–17, R. Williams 209), and this mindset is precisely what Edward Said would describe as *Orientalist* just a few years after *Zen*. Pirsig does not challenge these stereotypes with the polemical energy of Said, but he does attempt to show that these characterizations are oversimplifications that are not as solid as they appear.

Pirsig's attempts to transcend this divide involve critiques of classic and romantic expressions, while also having sympathy with both. The narrator's former self, Phaedrus, values the systematic pursuit of knowledge but shares the Beats' distaste for square intellectualism. He derides academia as a pompous "Church of Reason," critiquing its demands of conformity, lack of creativity, and inability to acknowledge scientific rationality's tendency to produce more questions than answers (386, 105–9). Weary of philosophy's pursuit of abstract truths that do not meaningfully connect with his lived experience, he begins to feel as though "it was reason itself that was ugly" (130). He then enters the philosophy program at the University of Chicago in an effort to introduce new and revolutionary ideas to unite classic and romantic modes. But his effort fails; his ideas are not accepted by the faculty. He grates against the rigidity of analytic philosophy that insists on rigorous definitions for everything and seems to have no room for his innovative ideas of Quality (more on this term soon) (389). Phaedrus's problems with the establishment, particularly in higher education, resonated with the Beats (and the critiques expressed in *Franny and Zooey*). According to a 2006 interview, in his teaching days, Pirsig was "reading Kerouac, and trying to live in truth" (Adams). Even though Pirsig did not identify with the Beats, he was directly influenced by Kerouac, and *Zen* is a road novel of cross-country travel and self-discovery.

But although Pirsig shared the Beats' distaste for square intellectualism, he was also unconvinced by countercultural critiques of "the system." Pirsig argues that the countercultural "flight from and hatred of technology is self-defeating" (18). Indeed, "to some extent the romantic condemnation of rationality stems from the very effectiveness of rationality in uplifting men from primitive conditions" (121). And yet Pirsig is still sympathetic to the counterculture and says their point of view is valuable; he is "not . . . out of sympathy with their feelings about technology" (18). Furthermore, lingering countercultural attitudes are "here to stay because it's a very serious and important way of looking at things that *looks* incompatible with reason and order and responsibility but actually is not" (53, emphasis in original). Indeed, the novel ends up being an extended refutation of its own early impression, "There is no point at which these [classic and romantic] visions of reality are unified" (68).

Pirsig offers what he hopes is "a solution for it all" by proposing what he calls the doctrine of "Quality" (147, 233–34). Pirsig defines *Quality* as an event of recognition that precedes the split between subject and object (233–34). Whereas the objective classic mode is opposed to the subjective romantic mode, a Quality perspective unites and transcends these divisions and is therefore a faculty that both Beat and square people could cultivate in common. This is not just an abstract idea but a way of living more holistically, one that the author sees exemplified in the activity of motorcycle maintenance, which relies both on classic knowledge and on romantic feel (more on this in due course).

Given the book's title, this Quality-based outlook has a curiously indirect relationship to Buddhist and Hindu philosophy. For a book with *Zen* in the title, there is surprisingly little discussion of Zen. In fact, the book deals much more with Greek philosophy and the subsequent history of Western thought than with Zen per se. The main intellectual figures *Zen* is concerned with include Plato, Aristotle, Newton, Kant, and the lesser-known Henri Poincaré; Pirsig gives no comparable attention to any specific thinkers from Asia. He explains his idea of Quality largely in terms of recuperating the ancient Greek Sophists (368). A more accurate title, then, would have been *Quality and the Art of Motorcycle Maintenance*. Most of the text's major ideas can be explained sufficiently with Western philosophy, which is the route most articles on the novel take. For example, Steve Odin calls the novel's ideas "an extension of mainstream twentieth-century American philosophy" (87). In spite of its title, which, as I previously mentioned, alludes to Herrigel's *Zen in the Art of Archery* (1948), the novel's debt to Zen is not immediately clear.

Furthermore, the novel even includes pointed objections to Buddhist and Hindu thought. Early on, the narrator recounts his studies at Banaras Hindu University, which taught the traditional doctrine of "*Tat tvam asi,* 'Thou art that,' which asserts that everything you think you are and everything you think you perceive are undivided. To realize fully this lack of division is to become enlightened" (136). This terminology is directly connected to the book's title; of the many disciplines for realizing this truth is "the Sanskrit *dhyana,* mispronounced in Chinese as 'Chan' and again mispronounced in Japanese as 'Zen'" (137). And yet Phaedrus finds this view "hopelessly inadequate" because it seems to him to dismiss the reality of human suffering (137).

What, then, does Pirsig gain by invoking Zen? For one thing, the word *Zen* performs work for Pirsig that relies more on Zen's vaguely exotic connotations than on its specifics. The prefatory author's note states:

> What follows is based on actual occurrences. Although much has been changed for rhetorical purposes, it must be regarded in its essence as fact. However, it should in no way be associated with that great body of factual information relating to orthodox Zen Buddhist practice. It's not very factual on motorcycles, either. (n.p.)

Pirsig is preemptively defending himself against the charge that he is superficially appropriating Eastern thought. His answer is not that he really does do Zen justice after all, but rather that he takes liberties across the board, so one should not single out his mentions of Zen for scrutiny. This line of reasoning still leaves the question, why use *Zen* in the title only to disclaim its legitimacy? The answer is that Pirsig invokes Zen not as a religion but as an exotic-sounding stand-in for any kind of holistic, sustained introspection. Moreover, Pirsig's mea culpa on motorcycles does not add up: In fact, the book is so factual about motorcycles that it was cited approvingly in a highly technical article about the history of best practices in mechanical work (Krebs). Pirsig is trying to have it both ways. He wants to invoke the air of mystical authority surrounding Zen without discussing the specifics of Zen traditions with rigor or detail. Herrigel's book that inspired Pirsig's title is much more attentive to Zen traditions and pedagogy than Pirsig is. But it was Pirsig's *Zen* that triggered the massive trend of using "Zen and the Art of . . ." as a template for book titles (Williams 197–98, 229–37). We can infer, then, how *Zen* was a pivotal contribution to the ongoing branding of Zen in the US, up to and including its casual use as an adjective for anything calming, as in, "I'm trying to be Zen about waiting in this line."

Although *Zen* does not depend heavily on the specifics of Zen itself, it does end up affirming some more general tendencies in Buddhist and Hindu philosophy, including even their shared focus on nondual metaphysics, which I outlined in the introduction. A noteworthy component of *Zen*'s spiritual vision comes not from Zen directly but from Daoism, which strongly overlapped with the Chan Buddhism in China that later became Zen in Japan (Hamar). When Phaedrus reads the *Tao Te Ching*, he substitutes the word *Quality* for *Tao* and finds "not a discrepancy. What he had been talking about all the time as Quality was here the Tao, the great central generating force of all religions, Oriental and Occidental, past and present, all knowledge, everything" (Pirsig 248). If Quality is the origin of "all religions," then every religious figure depends wholly on this Quality, including Buddhism. Therefore, it would be a matter of simple deduction that "Quality is the Buddha" (251). In keeping with Pirsig's initial disclaimer, the narrator hedges this equivalence by admitting he is not sure it is "true" (250). But the fact that Pirsig brings up this point at all shows that he cares about making connections across cultures, something he also wants to do with the social divides in the US.

As the narrator's explication of Quality continues, he increasingly frames his ideas in cross-cultural terms. The narrator says that "the old English roots for the Buddha and Quality, *God and good*, appear identical" (251, emphasis in original). This sentence equates "the Buddha" with "God," and "Quality" with "good." These bold equivalences are not philosophically precise; for example, the Buddha is not the creator of the universe. Thus, it is not entirely clear what Pirsig means when he says that "Plato is the essential Buddha-seeker" (361), but Pirsig is at least interested in seeing common ground between cultures and religions. He wonders, "Can the *dharma* of the Hindus and the 'virtue' of the ancient Greeks be identical?" (371). The narrator's answer to his own question is an emphatic yes: "*Quality! Virtue! Dharma! That* is what the Sophists were teaching" (371, emphasis in original). The narrator says that his ideas about Quality are original "in the history of Western thought" (231). But, as his later comparisons indicate, they are not original in "Eastern" thought. Pirsig's Quality doctrine is consonant with Buddhist and Hindu formulations of nonduality, if not with Zen in particular.

Pirsig's contribution, then, is not the idea that there is a higher reality that transcends subject-object division. Rather, he brings a distinctive notion of how this Buddhist and Hindu idea can apply to contemporary American life. The book's title comes into focus in one of the few passages where Pirsig does discuss Zen and motorcycles together:

> Zen Buddhists talk about "just sitting," a meditative practice in which the idea of a duality of self and object does not dominate one's consciousness. What I'm talking about here in motorcycle maintenance is "just fixing," in which the idea of a duality of self and object doesn't dominate one's consciousness. When one isn't dominated by feelings of separateness from what he's working on, then one can be said to "care" about what he's doing. That is what caring really is, a feeling of identification with what one's doing. When one has this feeling then he also sees the inverse side of caring, Quality itself. (290)

Motorcycle maintenance is the book's primary example of overcoming the classic/romantic divide through Quality. The motorcycle itself combines romantic, open-road freedom with the precision of classical engineering. And this act of taking care of a motorcycle requires both classical rationality and romantic sensitivity. Good motorcycle maintenance, according to Pirsig, involves both systematic problem solving and a certain intangible feel. When a mechanic is in the meditation-like zone of "just fixing," the experience of Quality incorporates classic and romantic modes as inseparable from one another.

Pirsig's acceptance of concepts from Asian religions is connected, crucially, to his rapprochement with the counterculture. He declares that at the moment of pure Quality perception, or not even perception, at the moment of pure Quality, there is no subject and there is no object. There is only a sense of Quality that produces a later awareness of subjects and objects. At the moment of pure Quality, subject and object are identical. This is the *tat tvam asi* truth of the Upanishads, but it's also reflected in modern street argot. "Getting with it," "digging it," "grooving on it" are all slang reflections on this identity. It is this identity that is the basis of craftsmanship in all the technical arts. And it is this identity that modern, dualistically conceived technology lacks. (284)

Here Pirsig has completely reversed course from his earlier critique of the Hindu affirmation *tat tvam asi*, "Thou art That," and its continuation in Zen (136–37). Moreover, his embrace of Buddhist and Hindu nonduality involves giving credence to Beats and hippies by taking on some of their better-known slang. Pirsig credits members of the counterculture with a unique ability to understand Quality by "digging it" (Beats) and/or "grooving on it" (hippies). Even if Pirsig disagrees with a countercultural rejection of technoculture, he thinks we have something to learn from Beats and hippies about making room for intuitive feeling and the casual, informal comfort that comes with being groovy.

Pirsig envisions a social payoff from his idea of Quality that strongly affirms what I have been calling enlightened individualism. The narrator asserts that

> this is how any further improvement of the world will be done: by individuals making Quality decisions and that's all. . . . I think it's about time to return to the rebuilding of *this* American resource—individual worth. There are political reactionaries who've been saying something close to this for years. I'm not one of them, but to the extent that they're talking about real individual worth and not just an excuse for giving money to the rich, they're right. We *do* need a return to individual integrity, self-reliance and old-fashioned gumption. We really do. (352, emphasis in original)

By describing "individual worth" as a fundamental "American resource," Pirsig places himself firmly in the tradition of American individualism that concerns the writers in this study. His promotion of "self-reliance and old-fashioned gumption" is particularly reminiscent of historian Frederick Jackson Turner's description of American frontier individualism. According to Pirsig, American individualism needs to be renewed through "Quality," which he rhetorically connects with Zen and which, as I have shown, acknowledges more-explicit philosophical antecedents to in Hindu and Buddhist thought. Concepts from Asian religions are again the key to renewing American individualism, which has been stifled by a myopic establishment. But the meaning of this individualism is changed, not simply "renewed," by "individuals making Quality decisions." The Quality Pirsig talks about, as exemplified in mindful motorcycle maintenance, cannot be identical to traditional rugged American individualism if it is based on overcoming the division between subjects and objects. Pirsig's enlightened individualism uses tropes of self-reliance to move toward a mode of experience that takes the individual outside of himself, thus bending the buffered self of Enlightenment individualism beyond its traditional parameters.

Zen further enacts this transcendence of subjects and objects on the level of form. Admittedly, I have engaged the novel's philosophical side more than its narrative side. But it is worth pointing out that by binding a classic discursive argument and a romantic narrative inextricably together, the novel's form enacts its bid to overcome the classic/romantic divide. Much of the interest of *Zen* comes from the synergy between its big ideas and personal moments. As R. John Williams puts it, for all its grand visions, it is at its core a story about family, a journey, and a search to overcome the dark places in oneself (184). For example, right after the narrator recalls Phaedrus's decisive insight into the nature of Quality, there is a cut to a hiking scene in which the narrator and Chris reach a high plateau, break out into the open, and see a wide blue sky (234). It's also important that the narrator and Chris have a troubled relationship and quarrel throughout the trip. In the novel's final scene, the narrator realizes the flaws in his parenting and recognizes how these shortcomings amount to philosophical hypocrisy: "Advice has been given again and again to eliminate subject-object duality, when the biggest duality of all, the duality between me and him, remains unfaced" (395). But as the narrator realizes how much he loves and emotionally depends on his son, both of their attitudes improve and the narrator concludes, "We've won it" (406). In *Zen*, the ideas give depth to the narrative, and the narrative gives life to the ideas.

In this respect, a noteworthy parallel theme with Salinger emerges: the importance of healing fractured nuclear family relationships. *Franny and Zooey* (like *Catcher in the Rye*) is concerned with reaffirming the bond between brother and sister. Franny and Zooey butt heads but eventually affirm their love for one another; this dynamic also occurs against the background of their mother, Bessie, whose badgering annoys Zooey but is ultimately motivated by caring. Likewise, in *Zen*, for all its geographic and temporal sprawl, the crucial moment is the recuperation of the narrator's relationship with his son, Chris. This domestic perspective makes a pointed contrast to the adventuresome, childfree world of Beat Buddhism. Beat Buddhist characters go on enriching spiritual quests that often involve, as with Ray Smith and Sissy Hankshaw, getting *away* from one's restrictive immediate family. By contrast, Salinger's and Pirsig's narratives suggest that ideas from Asian religions do not have to be threatening to the mainstream. Rather than celebrating a departure from family life, Salinger and Pirsig show Buddhist and Hindu principles of nonduality bringing normative nuclear families closer together, even as these writers still retain links to Beat critiques of mainstream conformity.

Another important point of contact between Salinger and Pirsig is their elision of Asian cultures, a broad trend within enlightened individualism that Salinger and Pirsig take even further than the Beats they write against, for whom touches of Asian culture are hip signs of rebellion. Salinger's and Pirsig's interest in Asian religions is limited to abstract philosophy and does not extend to contemporary Buddhist and Hindu populations around the world or immigrants in the US who practice these religions. Pirsig takes this abstraction even further than Salinger: Whereas *Franny and Zooey* gives considerable exposure to specific texts and figures from Asian religions, Pirsig does not, and his allusions to Zen, as I have discussed, remain vague and indirect.

It is also noteworthy that Pirsig's inattention to cultural specifics applies even to his own contemporary moment. The small scale of *Franny and Zooey*'s action makes its lack of reference to political events understandable. But with Pirsig's repeated emphasis on social trends of the 1960s, it is surprising how infrequently the book mentions history and politics. Pirsig invokes the themes of the 1960s but not the details. He does not mention the Vietnam War, Woodstock, the Kent State shootings, the Civil Rights Act, or any of the famous flash points of the time. As a result, *Zen* makes it seem as though the divide between hip and square originates from idealized competing "visions of reality" without accounting for how specific and often traumatic historical events pushed social activism and the backlashes against it. While *Zen* does make insightful observations about the recurrence of classic/romantic divides across time, it is politically aloof with respect to its contemporary moment. One thus finds a fuller sense of the context of *Zen*, as well as *Franny and Zooey*, in their dialogues with Beat Buddhism, a conflicted give-and-take that rejects sociopolitical rebellion but retains and repurposes countercultural rhetorics of authenticity. This slippage between substance and style, and the surrounding reflections on the fate of countercultural adaptations of Asian religions, continue to be staged in future generations of writers, including the postmodernists to whom I now turn.

CHAPTER 3

Secret Rituals and American Autonomy

Thomas Pynchon's Vineland
and Don DeLillo's Underworld

ANTI-BEAT WRITERS such as Pirsig deliberately embrace the mainstream while acknowledging the legitimacy of countercultural concerns—and still co-opting countercultural rhetoric. Pirsig thinks that the countercultures were wrong to reject technocracy. But some writers who are more sympathetic to countercultural and radical impulses offer a different interpretation. For them, the countercultures' mistake was not their critique of the mainstream, but their sweeping, unrealistic belief that a utopian revolution could cure society's ills. In this view, the countercultures' belief in their own inevitable victory is one more example of the faults of placing ultimate trust in a single cause, whether a social movement, national government, or religion.

This type of response is most evident in postmodern fiction. Although the impulses of postmodern fiction began before the height of countercultures, for example, in experimental texts such as William Gaddis's *The Recognitions* and John Barth's *The End of the Road* (1955, 1958), the meaning of the countercultures in the midst of a re-ascendant bourgeois order became a noteworthy theme in postmodern fiction after 1980. Japhy Ryder's rucksack revolution and Timothy Leary's psychedelic revolution had failed to transform society to the extent that their champions had hoped and claimed. The utopian impulses behind these movements are thus unsurprising objects of critique in the postmodern context of a more general skepticism toward grand narratives (Lyotard, McHale). The refusal of closure typical of postmodernism leads to a suspicion toward the transcendence such narratives offer. This suspicion can drive people, ironically, to the dark comfort of reactionary paranoia (Coale), which offers its own grand narrative of sinister conspiracies (Hofstadter 29–31, Sedgwick 124–25).

These considerations at first make postmodernism seem an odd fit for the argument of this study. How can writers make texts of enlightened individualism if they believe in neither enlightenment nor individualism? My answer is that, paradoxically, this very refusal of transcendence is what enables some postmodern writers to synthesize Asian religions with liberal American individualism. I study how this distinctive synthesis takes shape in Thomas Pynchon's *Vineland* (1991) and Don DeLillo's *Underworld* (1997). These works repurpose postmodern skepticism to envision a distinctive way of using stripped-down, Asian-based spirituality to transform American individualism. Instead of celebrating Asian religions' philosophies of transcendence, these novels innovatively adapt Buddhist and Hindu secret rituals as context-specific tools to pierce through American culture's more isolationist and paranoid tendencies.

Of course Pynchon and DeLillo do not represent all postmodernists; I wish to show that the writers of *Vineland* and *Underworld* are positively indebted to American individualism to a greater degree than other postmodern writers who incorporate Asian religions into their fiction, such as Kurt Vonnegut, William Gaddis, and John Hawkes (Singh; Kohn, "Buddhist Duality," "Merging"). But it would not be an overstatement to call Pynchon and Delillo *the* exemplars of postmodern fiction, as evidenced in criticism by scholars such as Samuel Chase Coale, John McClure, and Theophilus Savvas. The preeminence of Pynchon and DeLillo thus indicates, in ways too striking to ignore, that enlightened individualism has unexpectedly made its way into postmodernism.

Vineland and *Underworld* use resources from Asian religions to highlight—and challenge—two surprisingly similar dynamics of paranoia: countercultural paranoia toward governmental secrecy and mainstream paranoia toward Asian religions in the US. Both of these postures of mistrust are based on real scandals, and many observers justifiably blamed sinister secrecy for enabling a great deal of misconduct. But, as both novels help diagnose, legitimate objects of critique such as the Vietnam War often inspired paranoid habits of thought that led to famous overreaches like beliefs in extraterrestrials in Roswell, New Mexico, or the belief that the moon landing was fake. Similarly, a healthy critique of the Asian religious secrecy that fostered patterns of sexual misconduct also played into excessive stigmatization against these religions in general.

Vineland's and *Underworld*'s response to the problem of secrecy is surprising: These novels do not simply decry secrecy; instead, they seek to envision a more positive secrecy, adapted from Asian religions, that can counteract more-sinister secret abuses by both the government and Asian religious organizations. By disrupting paranoia through the productive secrecy of adapted Asian religions, Pynchon and DeLillo turn secrecy's suspiciousness into a strength to be skillfully adapted. This repurposed secrecy offers ways of forming new American communities through the bonds of shared esoteric wisdom. This vision partially recuperates both Asian religions and American individualism, transforming both: Asian religions lose their hazy transcendence, and American individualism relinquishes its faith in heroic isolationism. Through this newfound humility, Asian esotericism and American individualism mutually redeem one another.

To understand the climate of paranoia that *Vineland* and *Underworld* respond to, it is important to note that in the 1960s and 1970s, many damning exposures shattered governmental credibility, including atrocities in Vietnam, the Watergate break-in, illegal domestic spying, and numerous other misdeeds (Bernstein and Woodward, Ellsberg). Concerning various massacres in Vietnam, soldiers' defense that they were just "following official orders" cast further suspicion on secretive authority (Turse 89). And well beyond the 1960s and 1970s, the government has frequently invoked secrecy to protect citizens' security, and most people now think of sinister governmental secrecy as the norm (Knight, *Conspiracy* 28–32), an originally countercultural view that has since become mainstream.

Secrecy has also played an ambivalent role in Asian religions in the US. In many sects tied to both Buddhism and Hinduism, students may practice certain meditations only after receiving a formal initiation from a qualified master, and they may not reveal the practice to those who have not received the initiation. This type of secrecy is standard protocol for the Self-Realization Fellowship, Transcendental Meditation, Siddha Yoga, and all four schools of Tibetan Buddhism (Williamson 162–63, Coleman 104). In his discussion of Tibetan Buddhism, James Coleman subtly captures the resulting mistrust: "Aside from [its] complexity, the casual student is soon confronted by another unique barrier—secrecy" (104). The word *unique* marks secrecy as an exception to the American ideal of transparency. Americans are supposed to dislike secrecy: What does the secret-keeper have to hide, and how might these secrets infringe upon personal liberties? Indeed, in the 1980s, a number of scandals arose surrounding sexual misconduct by Buddhist and Hindu teachers (Coleman 139, Goldberg 210–18, Seager 185–87, Williamson 115–18). These scandals cast broader suspicion on Asian religions in the US. Critics faulted institutional secrecy as a cover for abuses of power (Seager 186, Williamson 266). The "guru-based Asian religions" were also easy targets for labeling as cults; their emphasis on guru devotion provoked criticisms of fanaticism and brainwashing (McCloud 98). In a political context that increasingly values "transparency" (West and Sanders 1), inherently secretive institutions today struggle to gain mainstream legitimacy. The backlashes against Asian religions also fit into a US tradition of mistrusting religions and organizations seen as ritualistic, cultish, and secretive, such as Catholicism, Freemasonry, and the Mormon church.

While I do not mean to conflate the scope of governmental transgressions and religious misbehavior, my point is that American people have mistrusted both their government and Asian religions for comparable reasons related to secrecy. Even though the Asian religious counterculture may seem to be against the mainstream, the problem of secrecy links the two. Allen Ginsberg reflects on this very connection in his 1990 poem "Elephant in the Meditation Hall." The poem refers to many of the Hindu and Buddhist teachers in the US beset by "scandal" (985), including Richard Baker Roshi, Rajneesh, and Ginsberg's own teacher, Chögyam Trungpa (985). It then turns to much larger scandals in the government, including the Iran contra scandal and various US operations that destabilized other countries. Ginsberg concludes, "Scandals in Buddhafields? big mistakes in Hemispheres, on moons, Black Holes everywhere!" (986). We need a sense of proportion, Ginsberg's speaker seems to say, but we should remember that power corrupts across many sectors. Ginsberg responds to events that have contributed to negative reactions toward secrecy that grow out of liberal norms of transparency. However, Pynchon and DeLillo model ways to resist paranoia and react with more empowerment to these problems. Buddhism's and Hinduism's foreign origins, combined with their traditions of secrecy, have long made them targets for American mistrust. Pynchon and DeLillo emphasize this secrecy but seek to turn it into an asset to human flourishing in the US.

Each novel pursues this itinerary in different ways. In *Vineland*, Pynchon imagines a secret heterodox ninja art whose practitioners use it to courageously resist sinister governmental secrecy and its associated oppression. *Vineland*'s nuanced portrayal of gloriously impure American adaptations of Japanese culture further counteracts 1980s stereotypes and paranoia against Japan. Whereas Asian arts empower *Vineland*'s characters, in *Underworld*, obscure Asian mantras inspire fear. But DeLillo undermines American suspicion toward Asian religion by suggesting its hidden kinship with Catholicism, a faith that had been stigmatized for much of American history but that that had nevertheless moved firmly into the mainstream by the 1950s (Herberg).

Underworld pairs Western and Eastern chants in a series of uncanny moments, inviting the reader to overcome boundaries its main characters refuse to challenge. The act of reading *Underworld* thus becomes an esoteric initiation in its own right, one in which the reader can arrive at hidden knowledge of the power of Asian mantras to recuperate American yearnings for freedom.

While *Vineland* and *Underworld* both embrace Asian religions' potential to recuperate American ideas of freedom, these adaptations depend on denying the promise of transcendence such religions typically offer. This refusal relates complexly to the role of transcendence in Taylor's immanent frame. As John McClure argues, Pynchon's and DeLillo's fiction portray important examples of *partial faiths* that reach toward transcendence without fully claiming it. Indeed, both *Vineland* and *Underworld* portray characters who are cross-pressured between the lure of transcendence and the immediacy of the mundane. But each novel ends in a different place. *Vineland*'s principal characters find closure in a surprisingly stable spiritual vision, even if that vision is stripped of total transcendence. By contrast, DeLillo's characters remain caught in the cross-pressures of the immanent frame without a clear resolution.

Pynchon's and DeLillo's syntheses are also a reflection on countercultural worldviews. The same Beats and hippies who led critiques of governmental secrecy were also, by virtue of being a primary constituency of Asian religions in the US, exploited—and arguably duped—by religious secrecy in the guru scandals of the 1980s. How can one reconcile this contradiction, and how might Asian religions in the US recover? Pynchon and DeLillo portray practices and communities that model recuperative possibilities. Readers of *Vineland* and *Underworld* can find ways to preserve certain empowering aspects of Asian religious secrecy while giving up on the corruption to which a devotion to ultimate transcendence is susceptible.

THE TROUBLE WITH TRANSCENDENCE IN *VINELAND*

Scholars have long understood that Pynchon has strong sympathies with radical and countercultural voices (Molloy, O'Bryan 2). Previous scholarship is thus correct in saying that Pynchon's invocations of marginalized religions, such as those from Asia, are consonant with his affection for marginalized countercultural communities (McClure). But while Pynchon scholars agree that religiously themed journeys, however comic, are prominent in his novels, the degree of spiritual attainment Pynchon's characters achieve is a matter of dispute (Eddins; Kohn, "Seven Buddhist Themes"; Molloy), and discussions of *Vineland* reflect these larger patterns in Pynchon scholarship (Cowart, McClure, Porush). But a closer examination of *Vineland* shows that Asian religious disciplines promote identities that retain some debts to American ideals of autonomy and individual rights; even the countercultures Pynchon portrays find value in these things. In fact, it is *Vineland*'s exploration of Asian religions that makes this recuperation of American liberal ideas possible for its countercultural characters.

In keeping with longstanding themes of Pynchon's works, *Vineland* contains many critiques of consumerism and state violence. Many of these references seem to imply a negative judgment of the US in general. For example, the third-person narration describes the midcentury blacklist on Hollywood actors suspected of Communist ties as "one of American misoneism's most notable hours" (289), implying that US fear of what is new has had many other expressions. Elsewhere, federal agent Brock Vond thinks of members of a nascent protest movement as "logs" that, once "disengage[d]" from their idealism, can "get sawed into lumber, to be built into more America" (216). Vond's train of thought is a compact expression of the vices of authoritarianism, conformism, and deforestation, one that evokes an America that stands for perpetrating violence and crushing dissent. Such troubling descriptions also come from aging, paranoid hippies on the other end of this power relationship. Members of the bohemian Traverse and Becker families label "the tragic interweaving" of governmental leadership and conspiracies as the "last unfaceable American secret" (372), implying a series of such sinister secrets that has become a feature of American life. In these descriptions, "America," specifically the US, uses sinister secrecy to prop up cruel bombast and oppression.

And yet many of the complaints and longings *Vineland* expresses are also framed as a yearning for more-extensive fulfillments of specifically US systems and ideals, a point that previous critics of *Vineland* have missed. When aging hippie Zoyd Wheeler finds himself framed for marijuana possession, Zoyd pleads, "What about 'innocent until proven guilty?'" His lawyer replies, "That was another planet, think they used to call it America, before the gutting of the Fourth Amendment" (360). Here the problem is not America itself, but rather a lack of American legal protections of individual rights. Similarly, Zoyd's ex-wife Frenesi Gates and her partner Flash lament "the State law-enforcement apparatus, which was calling itself 'America,' although somebody must have known better" (354). In this description, American authoritarianism is a corruption, not an authentic expression, of the best US spirit. And later, when seeking to recover a kidnapped Frenesi, a crew of rescuers "peered at the maps, each with that enigmatic blank in the middle, like the outline of a state in a geography test, belonging to something called 'the US,' but not the one they knew" (250). The unknown is literally a gap in a map. But the language evokes a sense that the country itself has transformed into something sinister that used to be better. The novel asks, What has happened to the country?

These nuances arise out of the novel's conversancy with historical specifics. The novel's critiques of the US are not abstract, but are rather aimed at Nixon and Reagan in particular. One radical character diagnoses the poor state of the US as the fault of "the whole Reagan program . . . [that] dismantle[s] the New Deal, reverse[s] the effects of World War II, restore[s] fascism at home and around the world, flee[s] into the past, can't you feel it, all the dangerous childish stupidity" (265). Just as the critiques are concrete, so are the points of praise. In this account, specific leaders are undoing the positive parts of America's legacy, such as the New Deal and the defeat of the Nazis in WWII. In a departure from most of Pynchon's work, *Vineland* appeals with surprising sincerity to several American achievements and ideals; these are redeemable aspects of America that need renewal.

Vineland portrays Asian religions as resources for renewing these American ideals, a portrayal that puts the novel in the orbit of enlightened individualism. Although *Vineland* references Tibetan Buddhism and Hinduism, the tradition it deals with the most is a modernized form of Buddhist-inspired ninjutsu that is at once a riff on the Western commercialization of martial arts and a salutary source of courage, resistance, and insight. This discipline enables its followers to respond to sinister governmental secrecy by taking refuge in positive secretive communities of their own.

In order to accentuate the positive role of an adapted, transcendence-less secrecy, *Vineland* conversely critiques a misguided secrecy borne out of loyalty to protecting promises of total transcendence. While never losing its sympathy with radical politics, *Vineland* repeatedly critiques countercultural engagements with Asian religions, which were often naive in their absolute faith. Many of the novel's characters have sincere enthusiasm for Buddhism and Hinduism, but their superficial appropriations of them come across as escapism. Pynchon's talent for inventing humorous names highlights this satire. For instance, the leader of the rebellious community The People's Republic of Rock and Roll, playfully abbreviated as PR3, is named "Weed Atman." This name embodies radicals' convergent interest in marijuana and Asian religions, as *atman* is the Sanskrit word for the soul in Hinduism (Cowart 99–100). Furthermore, Weed observes that people believe in him with reckless devotion, which he mentally paraphrases: "Yes, my guru! Anything—chicks, dope, jump off the cliff, you name it!" (Pynchon 229). The worship surrounding Weed suggests that 1960s radicals often mistook fervor for insight; it also parodies the radical guru devotion that swept many followers of Hindu-inspired meditation movements during the 1960s (Williamson 222). One might infer that if followers like these were not so blinded by their faith in transcendence as to overlook apparent transgressions, they would have been quicker to fight the sexual misconduct in some Asian religious groups which became exposed more frequently in the 1980s.

In a subtle but crucial example of misguided faith in Asian-inspired transcendence, Frenesi's own thoughts about transcendence join spiritual naïveté with political utopianism. Frenesi, who spends much of the 1960s filming the radical movements she participates in, reflects on her visions within these movements by framing the appeal of radical politics in terms of Asian mysticism:

> Frenesi dreamed of a mysterious people's oneness, drawing together toward the best chances of light, achieved once or twice that she'd seen in the street, in short, timeless bursts, all paths, human and projectile, true, the people in a single presence, the police likewise simple as a moving blade—and individuals who in meetings might only bore or be pains in the ass here suddenly being seen to transcend, almost beyond will to move smoothly between baton and victim to take the blow instead, to lie down on the tracks as the iron rolled in or look into the gun muzzle and maintain the power of speech—there was no telling, in those days, who might unexpectedly change this way, or when. Some were in it, in fact, secretly for the possibilities of finding just such moments. (Pynchon 117–18)

Frenesi frames political protest in the language of spontaneous Zen enlightenment, in which immense spiritual realizations occur at unpredictable moments with no apparent buildup (Cheng 595–600). One goes "almost beyond will" toward a change that occurs "unexpectedly." The protesters mystically overcome their flaws and disagreements, merging into "a single presence." These descriptions of transcending shortcomings, and even selfhood itself, parallel the Zen principles stated in Herrigel's *Zen in the Art of Archery*. Just as the protesters merge into "a single presence," as D. T. Suzuki writes in his introduction to this volume, the Zen archer "becomes one with the perfecting of his technical skill" (10). And just as Frenesi's transcendent activist faces police brutality without fear, the Japanese swordsman is totally "released from the thought of death" (Herrigel 108).

However, Frenesi's transcendence has fault lines. Whereas Zen teaches the overcoming of all divisions whatsoever (Suzuki, *Essays* 73–74), for Frenesi, the division between "the people" and the authorities who wield "the gun" remains. Also, Frenesi's grammar makes *transcend* a conspicuously empty signifier. As a transitive verb, one is supposed to say what is being transcended; intransitive uses of the word are rare or obsolete (*OED, transcend*). But Frenesi uses the word intransitively, asserting that the protesters simply "transcend" without stating over what. Throughout this passage, words such as *oneness, true, single presence,* and *transcend* all convey Frenesi's religious fervor. But the vagueness of her diction is a facet of her revolutionary optimism that subsequent events destroy.

In the 1960s, Frenesi is a major player in the PR3 community, but sinister government plots involving infiltration and betrayal bring it down. In the aftermath of PR3's bust, the narrator reflects, "In those days it was possible to believe in acid, or the immanence of revolution, or the disciplines, passive and active, of the East" (Pynchon 251). The transcendence these spiritual paths offer matches the "liberation" and "joyous certainty" of 1960s radical movements (210). But both kinds of unlimited hope, the novel suggests, are unrealistic. The distance conveyed in the phrase "in those days" implies that such belief is no longer possible in 1984, the year of the novel's present, or 1990, the year of its publication. For Frenesi, and presumably many others, the Watergate scandal "ended the gilded age" of the 1960s, when sweeping political change seemed possible (72). During the Reagan 1980s, characters further resign themselves as "the Repression went on" (72). Looking back from the 1980s, as the ascent of the new Right brings steep cuts in social spending, the countercultural aspirations of the 1960s seem more distant than ever. *Vineland* thus critiques both government actions against counterculturual movements and these movements' own misplaced faith in spiritual devotion to transcendence as a solution to political problems.

Many other characters along with Frenesi express a craving for "transcendence" as a solution to American problems (112, 180, 223). However, the word *transcendence* is consistently vague and unstable, suggesting that transcendence is an incoherent concept whose pursuit is misguided. All these apparent abuses of transcendence, the novel suggests, are not merely correctible sloppiness but markers of a contradiction in the very idea of transcendence. What this means is that *Vineland*'s critique encompasses not only American countercultural adaptations of Asian religions but also Asian religions' own focus on transcendence. *Vineland* comes across as being especially skeptical about transcendence as emphasized by monastic elites and Western adapters who focus on textual scholarship and philosophical doctrine (Cheah 22–26, McMahan 5). Buddhism and Hinduism consistently teach mediation as a path to supreme happiness irrespective of material conditions (Iyer 19, Seager 13), but for Pynchon this goal is a mystifying distraction from meaningful engagements with the gritty world. In Pynchon's portrayal, a salutary adaptation of Asian religions in the US must abandon a pure commitment to ultimate transcendence in favor of more attention to provisional techniques such as adapted secrecy, to which I now turn.

NINJUTSU: FIGHTING SECRECY WITH SECRECY

While *Vineland* questions devotion to transcendence as misguided and inadequate, the novel validates many countercultural concerns. The countercultural communities in *Vineland* are paranoid, but their paranoia is not false fear: The government really is working against them. To recapitulate just a few interrelated examples: Federal agent Brock Vond, the novel's main villain, manipulates Frenesi into a betrayal that kills Weed Atman and brings down PR3. After Frenesi goes into hiding, the government recurrently checks on Zoyd to make sure he stays out of touch with her. Years later, a renegade narcotics agent, not content to leave well enough alone, plants a ceiling-high column of marijuana in Zoyd's home. These acts of subterfuge train most of the novel's radical characters to become "paranoid" (117, 207, 262). *Vineland*'s plot speaks to tactics the government actually used against suspected radicals during the 1950s and 1960s, including secret surveillance, infiltration, blackmail, evidence tampering, and raids (Donner, Schultz). Accordingly, in *Vineland*, no one knows when a raid will come or which friend might have been pressured into betraying a radical cause.

This fear of governmental secrets comes across vividly during a 1980s family reunion between the Beckers and the Traverses, two families with substantial ties to union politics, anarchist movements, and other progressive or radical groups. Those in attendance variously discuss

> Hitler, Roosevelt, Kennedy, Nixon, Hoover, Mafia, CIA, Regan, Kissinger, that collection of names and their tragic interweaving that stood not constellated above in any nightwide remoteness of light, but below, diminished to the last unfaceable American secret, to be pressed, each time deeper, again and again beneath the meanest of random soles, one blackly fermenting leaf on the forest floor that nobody wanted to turn over, because of all that lived, virulent, waiting, just beneath. (Pynchon 372)

The implied speakers engage in the paranoid tendency to attribute diverse events to a single sinister cause (Apter 366). Through a "tragic interweaving," the plurality of "that collection of names" boils down to the singularity of "the last unfaceable American secret." This passage also displays the paranoid reflex of seeing signs of conspiracy everywhere (Sedgwick 130–31), even "beneath the meanest of random soles." Those conversing are unwilling to expose the secret, staying within the broad implication that political leaders are covertly working against their citizens. Scholars such as Frank J. Donner, Bud and Ruth Schultz, and others have documented many governmental antiradical operations during the 1960s, making the vagueness of the Becker-Traverse conversation unnecessary. But that is the point: The picnickers do not mystify the "secret" for lack of data. They do so because the secret itself is so "virulent" that facing it would be unbearable. Here, secrecy and paranoia are inseparable: Secrecy allows conspiratorial forces to evade accountability; the secrets thus become so dark that those who resist cannot fully handle them and are left with no choice but paranoia.

Vineland's response to this paranoia is striking. The novel finds no subversive joy in exposing dark government secrets. The novel suggests that rather than reveling in muckraking, victims of governmental oppression should fight secrecy with secrecy, as shown by the ninjutsu of Buddhist heretic Inoshiro Sensei and his main student, DL Chastain, who is Frenesi's longtime friend, onetime lover, and collaborator. This esoteric discipline, I will show, repurposes secrecy in ways that actually promote, not undermine, American values of freedom and autonomy. By creating a refuge of benevolent secrecy, the novel disrupts paranoia's universal suspicion of secrecy and opens up a greater receptivity to esoteric disciplines than American individualism has traditionally brooked. *Vineland* shows how certain protocols of secrecy, which developed in Japan from the fifteenth century onward (Morinaga 2), can adapt to the needs of contemporary Californian countercultures and thus ultimately advance a version of enlightened individualism.

To understand how secrecy works in *Vineland*, it will help to first outline secrecy's broader functions in the Japanese context that inspired Pynchon. As Japan scholar Maki Isaka Morinaga explains, secrecy serves several purposes in systems of esoteric transmission. First, sharing an art with only a small, select group of followers is a form of quality control. If just anyone could discuss and spread the teachings, then "uncontrolled dispersion can deteriorate secret teachings in their quality" (37). Secrecy is also a way of reinforcing the seriousness of what is taught and thus promoting organizational loyalty and cohesion. A secret is so serious that outsiders should not even know the first thing about what it is. Teachers of secret arts thus "transmit not only knowledge, but also power and authority" (2). Furthermore, secrecy bestows what Morinaga calls a "value upgrade" on the knowledge it entails (37). That is, information conveyed through secret transmission is more valuable than the same information presented freely, because secrecy lends that knowledge an ethos of exclusivity and preciousness—sometimes even if, Morinaga surprisingly maintains, that knowledge is also available through public channels (37–42). These understandings of secret transmission are widespread across Japanese arts, including dance, swordsmanship, unarmed combat, theater, and even flower arranging (Morinaga). All in all, when used in the skillful ways Morinaga describes, secrecy is an intensifying constraint that directly promotes discipline, carefulness, discretion, and seriousness. This formation contrasts with the sinister secrecy of the American government as portrayed in *Vineland*.

The secrecy of *Vineland*'s ninjutsu lends itself well to Morinaga's understanding of secrecy in Japanese arts. Along these lines, DL is "sworn to keep silent" about her training (124). Some of the moves she learns "are never spoken of," even by those who practice them (127). Many of these esoteric techniques "would only make sense ten years or more from now—requiring that much rigorous practice every day for her even to begin to understand—and until she did understand, she was forbidden to use any of them out in the world" (127). In these passages secrecy is understood not just as a prohibition against disclosure but as a state of mind, a training method, a way of reinforcing how much responsibility, care, discipline, discretion, and quiet patience this art requires.

The features of secrecy such as the ones we see in *Vineland*'s ninjutsu can, according to Morinaga, operate regardless of the specific content of the secret art (2–3). But for *Vineland*'s ninjutsu in particular, its mode of secrecy also goes hand in hand with its inherently secretive content, for it relies on stealth, misdirection, disguise, evasion, and subterfuge. This focus on secret subterfuge rather than ethereal transcendence turns out to be just what the counterculture needs, in *Vineland*'s portrayal. Because this adapted ninjutsu comes from Japan and retains some Buddhist spiritual content, as I will soon discuss, it caters to preexisting countercultural affinities for Asian spiritual traditions. But *Vineland*'s ninjutsu steers this interest in adapting Asian paths away from transcendence and toward a gritty resistance from more sinister secrecy. The novel portrays this kind of cross-cultural adaptation as more worthwhile than Frenesi's wide-eyed devotion; ninjutsu is not naive and airy like many countercultural versions of Buddhism and Hinduism, but practical and appropriately worldly. The immanent resistance this ninjutsu offers enables *Vineland*'s countercultural characters to fight against governmental abuses of power, a struggle that, as I noted in the previous section, reaffirms some traditional notions of American freedom and autonomy.

Vineland adapts ninjutsu for American countercultures by presenting it as a refuge for the derelict. Toward this end, Inoshiro justifies his own deviations from traditional ninjutsu as acts of solidarity with "drunks, and sneaks," whom he identifies with and wishes to empower with "our equalizer, our edge" (127). This is a marked contrast from the historical role of ninjas as mercenaries hired by feudal lords to carry out covert missions against their enemies (Tomiki). By making ninjutsu work for society's rejects rather than its rulers, Inoshiro promotes an impulse of subversive resistance that finds a home in American countercultures, such as the ones DL identifies with.

A key example of this application is when DL participates in a mission to rescue Frenesi from being kidnapped by Brock Vond and his nefarious governmental squadron. DL's ninja skills are instrumental in rescuing Frenesi and helping the rescue party evade detection when those who bust PR3 give chase through a mountain. DL also uses her skills to fool or disable guards at opportune moments (252–57). Here DL's actions illustrate how an adapted Japanese tradition can answer the needs of American countercultures by resisting a sinister government, thus fighting secrecy with secrecy. Whereas secrecy typically goes against liberal norms of transparency, here it functions as a refuge that appeals to certain notions of liberal rights. The secrecy of *Vineland*'s ninjutsu represents a kind of resistance and autonomy, a Japanese-inspired art through which the oppressed do not have to give away everything. The "power and authority" (Morinaga 2) that this ninjutsu confers through its secrecy is a ballast to counteract its practitioners' systemic disempowerment.

In addition to enabling specific acts of resistance, *Vineland*'s ninjutsu is noteworthy for the complex ways it relates to Buddhist content. Ninjutsu's debts to Zen Buddhism retain some spiritual lessons, but ninjutsu remains distant enough from Zen to avoid a focus on transcendence. The Buddhist goal of overcoming duality contrasts starkly with the ninja's focus on "gaining an advantage" over an adversary (Seager 13; Hayes, back cover). And the nonviolent tendencies in Buddhist philosophy exist in an unresolved tension with their refracted instantiation in violent ninjutsu, a tension that *Vineland* never fully resolves. Still, Inoshiro's ninjutsu uses the Buddhist concept of karma to teach that one has important missions in life, and one's actions have consequences (132, 163, 382). And, like other Japanese arts, ninjutsu inherited Zen's focus on acting with carefully cultivated mindfulness, patience, and discipline (Herrigel, Morinaga), so, accordingly, *Vineland*'s ninjutsu teaches the importance of deep concentration and meditation (Pynchon 155, 140). Through these means, DL trains to the point where "she didn't think so much" (128). Her circumvention of thought is similar to Herrigel's account of the Zen of Japanese archery, an active meditation that overcomes the separation between tool and user without transcendent abstractions. But while these ninjutsu lessons are rooted in Zen, they are distant enough from Zen's transcendent orientation to be accessible to the novel's unprivileged characters who cannot access Zen serenity "someplace scenic up in the mountains" (123). Thus ninjutsu's secrecy imbues ideas like mindfulness and karma not with the ethereal transcendence of Zen but with the intensity of a covert discipline. This shift in emphasis reinscribes Buddhist ideas into a secretive art that helps countercultural communities who need freedom, not transcendence.

A key implication behind this secrecy is that if one uses these ninja techniques without due patience, then one has violated the spirit of the overall secrecy. Accordingly, when DL acts against ninjutsu's protocols of secret discretion, the novel portrays this recklessness as negative. DL's biggest mistake, as John McClure points out (54), is when she accidentally puts a delayed death touch on Japanese businessman Takeshi Fumimota, thinking he was Brock Vond. When reflecting on this action, and her larger career as a ninjette, DL "could appreciate how broadly she'd violated the teachings of her sensei. She had not become the egoless agent of somebody else's will, but was acting instead out of her own selfish passions. If the motive itself was tainted, then the acts, no matter how successful or beautifully executed, were false, untrue to her calling, to herself, and someday there would be payback" (Pynchon 253). Elsewhere, when spite overtakes her, DL imagines Inoshiro yelling at her, "Didn't you learn anything?" (259). Inoshiro's American affiliates similarly remonstrate DL for paying "no . . . fucking . . . attention" (155). DL's interest in revenge rather than a larger mission causes her to use her techniques outside the bounds of her teaching. Even though she does not break her vow of secrecy in the narrow sense of disclosing the techniques to others, she violates the pervading spirit of secrecy by going against the care and restraint urged by her teacher.

By portraying this secretive ninjutsu in a positive light, *Vineland* achieves a noteworthy payoff of its cross-cultural adaptation, that is, its demystifying of contemporary American fears toward Japan. The 1980s, when Pynchon was writing *Vineland* and when the novel's present is set, saw a boom in American popular appropriations of Japanese culture, as seen in productions such as the film *The Karate Kid* (1984); the bestselling ninja novels of Eric Van Lustbader (1980, 1984); and the comic books, cartoons, and films about the *Teenage Mutant Ninja Turtles* (1984–present). Yet at the same time, American fears about Japanese economic competition were rapidly escalating (S. Johnson, Lohr, Lutz). Even Zen was implicated, and many Americans came to believe that Japan's business success arose from Zen principles of mindfulness, a notion that R. John Williams says has some basis in fact (although this Zen influence, as Williams shows, was also mediated through American consultant W. Edwards Deming) (189–92).

But in Inoshiro's ninjutsu, Pynchon presents a Japanese import Americans should not be afraid of. It uses secrecy in a positive, not suspicious, way. Inoshiro is not an ethereal Eastern wise man, but a somewhat disreputable strip-mall hustler whose surreptitious activities have an endearing underdog quality. The dubious shortcuts in Inoshiro's pedagogy substitute "the original purity of ninja intent" with "the cheaper brutality of an assassin" (Pynchon 126–27). He also makes lewd advances on DL and has mysterious dealings with the Japanese mafia (122, 127; 125–26). In spite of these points of shadiness, *Vineland* actually casts its version of ninjutsu in a more benign light than it does historical ninjutsu by being a refuge for the downtrodden rather than a covert tool of power.

And yet the seriousness embedded in this ninjutsu's secrecy coexists in a postmodern manner with irreverent tropes of selling out to the marketplace. The consumerist element of this cross-cultural adaptation further undermines the stereotype of the exotic and inscrutable Japanese warrior. The bastardized techniques Inoshiro teaches DL have parodic names such as "the Enraged Sparrow, the Hidden Foot, the Nosepicking of Death, and the truly unspeakable *Gojira no Chimpira*" (127), the last of which roughly translates to "Godzilla's Dick" (Fargo 75–76). DL's ninjutsu establishment in the US further satirizes contemporary commercializations of martial arts. Led by an all-female community of "ninjettes" (Pynchon 163), the Sisterhood of Kunoichi Attentives offers seminars including "Kiddie Ninja Weekends" and "help for rejected disciples of Zen" (107). These humorous riffs make the supposedly vicious art of ninjutsu seem funny and nonthreatening. This strange combination of serious messages and kitschy consumerism suggests that no one is pure, and even spiritually tinged Japanese arts can still adapt flexibly to American life. In *Vineland*'s adapted ninjutsu, secrecy need not mean utter seriousness all the time.

Furthermore, DL puts this secret ninjutsu to use by working with another Japanese character who undercuts stereotypes. As punishment for accidentally attacking Takeshi Fumimota, the order DL operates under sentences her to restitution by working *with* Takeshi. DL then helps Takeshi with his business in "karmic adjustment," using her secret techniques to travel stealthily around the world and do jobs to ease the passage of beings stuck in limbo into their next lives. Although Takeshi is an opportunistic businessman, his affability goes against stereotypes of the ruthless workaholic Japanese corporate soldier. By calling Takeshi's freelance business "karmic adjustment," he links karma with the language of insurance (172). The novel thus irreverently connects Japan's supposedly mystical past with its contemporary economic rise. Takeshi is a likable character who jokes in the face of danger (164–65), urges DL to "lighten up!" (176), and shows gratitude to those who help him (66–67). Ultimately, the novel portrays Takeshi's monetizing of other beings' spiritual problems as a myopic capitulation to consumer capitalism. But this lighter portrayal also undermines US fears of Japanese business. The characterizations of Takeshi and Inoshiro suggest that instead of fearing Japan, Americans should discerningly adapt Japanese practices in ways that can be useful to countercultural goals.

VINELAND'S LANDSCAPES AND CROSS-CULTURAL ADAPTATION

This secret ninjutsu has particular benefits for Californian countercultures, as the preceding examples show. But by presenting this instance of an adapted Japanese art, the novel also hints at broader possibilities of cross-cultural adaptation for those who skillfully reshape Asian traditions for American needs. We see this theme reflected in the novel's landscapes, through which *Vineland* creatively portrays America as heir to Japanese spiritual wisdom. In *Vineland* America has better Zen scenery than Japan. Inoshiro Sensei contrasts a lofty realm of supposedly pure Zen from the hard reality of his tutelage. The martial arts he teaches are "for all the rest of us down here with the insects, the ones who don't quite get to make warrior" (127). Presumably, those who do "make warrior" have more exalted options. They are the ones whom DL imagines in clichéd tales of Japanese apprenticeships "someplace scenic up in the mountains" (123). In contrast to this elevated vision, her own tutelage takes place "down here in the ensnarling city" (123). However, the book does portray a "scenic" locale suitable for spiritual development. It is not in Japan but in the redwood groves of Vineland County. The narrator describes one morning in which "the fog here had burned off early, leaving a light blue haze that began to fade the more distant trees" (35). This serene image recalls the motifs of Chinese and Japanese landscape painting, which often employ an ethereal "haze" effect (Slawson 119). Later, DL's up/down dichotomy reappears at the Sisterhood of the Kuniochi Attentives. The narrator says, "Out the window, screened by eucalyptus trees, could be seen once-white walls overgrown with ivy, a distant bright of freeway tucked into the unfolding spill of land toward 'down there'—while up here the wind blew among the smooth gold and green hills, it seemed endlessly" (Pynchon 155). The scenic beauty DL cannot inhabit in Japan is present in California. Through these images, *Vineland* positions America as a fertile field for Japanese wisdom, provided that that wisdom is based on the fecund aspects of secrecy rather than sterile and vacuous promise of airy transcendence. In this respect, *Vineland* has something in common with Gary Snyder's nature poetry and, perhaps in a less extreme version, Kerouac's geographical transposition.

It is fitting, then, that DL's culminating realization occurs in the US, not Japan (380). Looking back on her career as a ninjette, DL reflects, "Had it only been, as she'd begun to fear, that many years of what the Buddha calls 'passion, enmity, folly'? Suppose that she'd been meant, all the time, to be paying attention to something else entirely?" (380). In this traditionally Buddhist list of the "three poisons," folly—an ignorance of the interdependence of all phenomena—is the most fundamental, leading alternately to "passion" for what one craves and "enmity" toward what one hates (H. Smith 112, 387). DL's self-described passion for "enlightenment through ass-kicking" is a symptom of what the "three poisons" doctrine diagnoses (Pynchon 198). Because she sees the world in a subject-object, us-versus-them framework, she counterproductively craves enlightenment as though it is an object to be grasped. She had thrived on her hatred for Brock, but she finally realizes that the life of an adventuring martial artist, driven by "passion" and "enmity," is less rewarding than establishing friendships, especially her developing love for Takeshi, the "something else" she should have cultivated. As McClure points out, this "something else" is Takeshi, not a spiritual path (55). Thus, DL's realization is more circumscribed than in its traditional Buddhist context. *Vineland* dramatizes the view that only certain aspects of Japanese wisdom can flourish in America, and it comments on Asian religions' development in the US. Inoshiro Sensei's down-to-earth ninjutsu fits American—and specifically countercultural—needs. The novel suggests that Americans should leave Zen and its pretentions to transcendence behind. *Vineland* thus envisions a new kind of spirituality within the immanent frame beyond what Taylor's framework elucidates. Taylor says that for the immanent frame to remain open, there must be transcendence (544). But *Vineland*'s unique adaptations of ninjutsu remain in an open immanence without complete transcendence.

In addition to leaving traditional Asian transcendence behind, *Vineland*'s ninjutsu enables a shift in US individualism. Whereas traditional US liberalism uses freedom from oppression as a platform for enterprising self-determination, *Vineland*'s characters use the freedom-promoting resistance of ninjutsu's secrecy to foster community among the downtrodden. The revolutionary impulse and craving for freedom are still present, but they frame the individual as embedded more in communities of family and caring than in prevailing conceptions of US individualism. DL's self-discovery involves being less driven by selfish agendas and more open to human connections. DL has her greatest realizations at the same place where Prairie Traverse reunites with her father, Zoyd makes peace with his ex, and a joyfully raucous family barbecue takes place under majestic redwood trees with an affectionately rendered "profusion of aunts, uncles, cousins, and cousins' kids and so on" (368). Here again, the landscape is important. Mentions of a "soda cooler beneath an oak tree," "long redwood tables," and "the fog of Vineland" indicate that the attendees belong to the landscape (368–69). Significantly, these descriptions extend motifs of picturesque fog and endless hills where Buddhist realization takes place (35, 155). *Vineland* thus promotes a kind of enlightened individualism that sees the self partially transcended in a secretive community within distinctly American amalgamations of landscapes and spiritual paths.

UNDERWORLD'S SECRET INITIATION

Pynchon's interest in Asian religions is an outgrowth of his observations of, and considerable sympathy with, countercultural communities in California for whom adaptations of Asian religions were a major resource. But for his foremost postmodern colleague, Don DeLillo, the significance of Asian religions is less of a given. It was not inevitable that a New York–based writer with an advertising background would have become as familiar with Asian religions as DeLillo has. Moreover, whereas Pynchon's fiction foregrounds characters on the margins of society, DeLillo's characters tend to be mainstream inhabitants of corporate America with nuclear families and decidedly un-countercultural pursuits.

Perhaps because of this difference, critics have mostly overlooked DeLillo's references to Asian religions: To date, only one essay has appeared on this topic. In this remarkable piece, Robert Kohn shows that Tibetan Buddhism pervades DeLillo's novels ("Tibetan Buddhism" 157). He further argues that DeLillo's longstanding interest in Tibetan Buddhism led him toward deeper explorations of Catholicism, the religion of DeLillo's upbringing, in his later fiction (157). But DeLillo's allusions to Asian religions are not limited to Tibetan Buddhism. In a 1982 interview, when critic Tom LeClair asked DeLillo about Zen in his novels, DeLillo replied that it "has more to do with people playing at Eastern religion than anything else. I know very little about Zen. I'm interested in religion as a discipline and a spectacle, as something that drives people to extreme behavior" (LeClair 10). In other words, for DeLillo, "Eastern religion" matters less for its distinctive characteristics and more as a timely example of religion's appeal as a refuge from the mundane. DeLillo made a related point during a special appearance at the Library of Congress in 2013, which I attended. I asked him what interested him about Asian religions in his novels, and he replied that "these rituals, the depth of these religions, the age of these religions, impressed me greatly." Asian religions were "different from everything I knew," a fascinating phenomenon "at the edge of our culture." In this view, Asian religions are significant in DeLillo's writing not for their specific content but rather as signs of mysterious otherness.

While *Underworld* departs, as I will show, from this exoticizing dynamic, DeLillo's gloss on his allusions to Asian religions holds true for most of his earlier novels. In *Americana* (1971), DeLillo's first novel, the narrator feels uncomfortable toward his undergraduate Zen professor, whom he describes as "indifferent to westernization" (174). In *Running Dog* (1978), the main character hires a man to perform Tibetan rituals on his behalf against a backdrop of political intrigue and murder. In *The Names* (1982), a deadly cult has a cell in India, where the narrator remarks that "masses of people suggested worship and delirium" (276). In *White Noise* (1985), the main character recalls that one of his ex-wives lives at an ashram where "the usual rumors abound of sexual freedom, sexual slavery, drugs, nudity, mind control, torture, prolonged and hideous death" (25). In *Mao II* (1991), DeLillo explores the brainwashing techniques of the Korean-based Unification Church (Kauffman 372–73n1), which, while based on Christianity and not Hinduism or Buddhism, gained a sense of exoticism from its Asian headquarters. These instances exaggerate American discomfort with Asian religions and obscure their specific content.

But *Underworld* is different. Several critics have rightly argued that *Underworld* marks a turning point by celebrating religious experience even as it continues to critique fanaticism (McClure 94, Hungerford 74, Schneck 215–16). More specifically, I find that *Underworld* is not merely "playing at Eastern religion" but engages with specific Asian ideas and practices, especially Tibetan Buddhism, more than anywhere else in DeLillo's corpus. This engagement means that even as *Underworld* showcases the apparent strangeness of Asian religions, the novel also gives readers the tools to see beyond this sense of distance. Specifically, by portraying the proximity between Buddhist, Hindu, and Catholic religious forms, *Underworld* suggests how Asian religions can transform an atomistic version of American individualism into a more enlightened freedom that shifts the American frontier spirit into a courageous openness to others.

This recuperative knowledge is hidden—that is, made secret—by the novel's form and social context. In *Underworld,* what makes wisdom from Asian religions secret is not, as in *Vineland,* initiation requirements from within specific Asian arts themselves. Rather, what hides Buddhist and Hindu insights beneath the surface of *Underworld*'s narrative is the mainstream American paranoia toward Asian religions that *Underworld* portrays. This paranoia represses Asian religious wisdom and thus makes *Underworld*'s mainstream characters unable or unwilling to recognize it when it appears. In *Underworld*'s Cold War context, which spans the 1950s to 1990s, the USSR is Americans' fundamental object of paranoia. But this context casts a paranoid light on a variety of other phenomena as well. *Underworld* dramatizes a cultural trend aptly diagnosed by anthropologist George E. Marcus: "The cold-war era itself was defined throughout by a massive project of paranoid social thought and action that reached into every dimension of mainstream culture, politics, and policy" (2). Accordingly, the novel's characters represent the majority of Cold War Americans for whom the sight of crowds of "Buddhists beating drums" is a disreputable, cultish image (171). *Underworld* portrays American paranoia as so pervasive that characters' behaviors and aversions can be implicitly attributed to paranoia even if they do not make overtly paranoid comments.

Thus the patterns in which mantras appear and reappear in *Underworld* showcase the paranoid mentality that "everything is connected" in a sinister way (DeLillo 825). This technique superficially casts Tibetan Buddhism as uncanny and implicitly untrustworthy. Like Freud's notion of the "uncanny" (*unheimlich*), Tibetan mantras come across as that which "was intended to remain secret, hidden away, and has come into the open" (Freud 132). Furthermore, in *Underworld,* Tibetan Buddhism is Catholicism's "double" (*doppelgänger*), an eerie twin that embodies this secret (141–42). It is different enough from Catholicism to appear separate, but similar enough to create discomfort. Thus *Underworld*'s characters are dimly aware of these religions' similarities but refuse to acknowledge them. Their resistance is shortsighted, as phrases from Asian religions unexpectedly recur in characters' minds. The sudden reappearance of mantras further fits Freud's definition of the uncanny as an involuntary resurfacing of a repressed idea (151).

Underworld, then, functions as an esoteric text in its own right, with manifold hidden connections that elude its characters and can be known only to well-informed or "initiated" readers who patiently excavate its secrets. As conspiracy scholar Peter Knight states of *Underworld,* "that everything is connected remains, for the reader as well as much as for the novel's characters, a subliminal suspicion and an act of discovery, rather than a tritely proven observation" ("Everything" 830). This is especially true when it comes to the hidden wisdom the novel offers that originates from Asian religions. By imitating Asian religious secrecy in its very form, *Underworld* invites the reader to resist characters' discomfort with Buddhism and Hinduism. The implication for the alert reader is that if Catholicism can change from being a stigmatized sect to being an accepted part of the American mainstream, so could

Buddhism and Hinduism. If brought fully to the surface, these ritual parallels, as I will point out, could have helped ease characters' paranoia by illuminating common strivings across cultures—and defamiliarizing the characters' own familiar spiritual comforts. Furthermore, *Underworld* suggests that ideas of nonduality conveyed through certain Asian mantras, even when the novel questions this transcendence, can fulfill American cravings for freedom better than characters' isolating individualism. As I will eventually show, the novel's conclusion, a mysterious afterlife in cyberspace, shows how Buddhist interdependence can transform individual desire into a more embedded freedom to experience connections with others. Ultimately, *Underworld* urges its readers to attain a level of insight that its characters mostly fail to achieve. Not only is this insight hidden from the novel's characters; it is also presumably beyond a majority of *Underworld*'s readers, who would not have the knowledge of Asian religions needed to see the connections I will discuss. This knowledge gap further heightens the exclusivity of *Underworld*'s hidden Asian-inspired wisdom. Thus what *Vineland* does on the level of plot *Underworld* accomplishes on the level of form. While *Vineland* narrates secret initiation, *Underworld is* a secret initiation. I will now attempt to reveal this secret.

UNCANNY MANTRAS

At first glance, *Underworld* does not seem to emphasize themes of US individualism. But there are important moments where *Underworld* expresses characters' longings in the form of the frontier landscape of the American West, particularly for the main character, Nick Shay, and his brother Matt. For example, in Arizona, Matt reflects:

> The landscape made him happy. It was a challenge to his lifelong citiness but more than that, a realization of some half-dreamed vision, the otherness of the West, the strange great thing that was all mixed in with nation and spaciousness, with bravery and history and who you are and what you believe and what movies you saw growing up. (449)

Matt's sense of wonder at a mythos of "nation and spaciousness" speaks to the freedom to have plenty of room to roam as a distinctively American frontier aspiration. And his mention of "bravery and history" invokes the American pioneer spirit of forging ahead in an inhospitable frontier. The Arizona landscape inspires similar reflections from Nick, whose career takes him to Arizona "out from the East" in a microcosm of the historical US frontier (86). Nick likes how the West is sheer "geography, all space and light and shadow and unspeakable hanging heat" (86). Traveling to the Sonoran Desert on "impulse," he marvels at how the landscape is "all distance. It was hardpan and sky and a wafer trace of a mountain, low and crouched out there, mountain or cloud, cat-shaped, catamount—how human it is to see a thing as something else" (64). The vast desert is a theater of possibility that embodies the freedom to envision reality as one wishes.

Nick's and Matt's fascination with the desert signals longstanding tropes of American frontier individualism. At the 1893 World's Columbian Exposition, the same event that hosted the World Parliament of Religions, Frederick Jackson Turner famously argued that American individualism depends on the Western frontier. He said that "the conditions of frontier life," shown in *Underworld* as the expansiveness and heat that impress themselves on Nick, give rise to "that dominant individualism, working for good and evil, and withal that buoyancy and exuberance that comes with freedom" (37). But Turner also acknowledged the pitfalls of this mindset, warning that "Individualism in America has allowed . . . all the manifest evils that follow from the lack of a highly developed civic spirit" (32). These pitfalls are on display in *Underworld*. In an explicit microcosm of the nation he inhabits, Nick asserts, "I've always been a country of one" (DeLillo 275). This atomistic individualism leads to isolation, distance from his family, and dishonesty. For example, Nick cheats on his wife with a woman at a swingers' convention as a fleeting respite from the problem, as he puts it, that "there's too much loneliness in America" (298).

Nick and Matt unsuccessfully pursue their longings in ways that set the stage for the novel's uncanny link between Catholicism and Tibetan Buddhism. At the age of seventeen, Nick accidentally shoots and kills a bar waiter. After spending some time in the criminal justice system, Nick spends a corrective term at a Jesuit school, where a priest teaches him the power of words (DeLillo 295–97, 540–41). "These names are vital to your progress," says Father Paulus (542). He starts with mundane objects, such as the parts of a shoe, but moves on to more overt religious content by giving Nick *The Cloud of Unknowing*, a medieval Christian meditation manual of unknown authorship. Taken with the book's emphasis on short, intense prayer, Nick becomes "preoccupied with this search for the one word, one syllable. It was romantic. The mystery of God was romantic. With this one word I would eliminate distraction and edge closer to God's unknowable self" (DeLillo 296). Nick's ascetic drive to "eliminate distraction" paves the way for an obsessive and unsuccessful spiritual practice.

Nick settles not on a single syllable but on the phrase *todo y nada*, "all and nothing," a paradoxical description of God adapted from the writings of sixteenth-century Catholic mystic St. John of the Cross. After years of practice in which Nick "repeated it, repeated it, repeated it" (297), he becomes a family man and affluent professional. But the intensity of his prayer leads him to focus on power rather than goodness, and he remains unable to sustain fulfilling relationships. Nick assiduously teaches his children the power of obscure words (102, 105, 119), but otherwise spends little time with them. Also tellingly, the reader first learns of Nick's prayer when he explains it to the aforementioned swinger with whom he cheats on his wife (294–301). Although Nick's chanting does not redeem him, it suggestively sets up the novel's ongoing engagement with religious incantation, which offers hidden possibilities for positive religious practice in spite of religion's apparent failure for most of the novel's characters.

Nick's work with Christian prayer has an uncanny parallel when Matt goes to Vietnam as a military videographer. The narrator recounts that "they sent him to Vietnam, to Phu Bai, and the first thing he saw when he entered the compound was a flourish of spray-paint graffiti on the wall of a supply shed. *Om mani padme hum.* Matt knew this was some kind of mantra, a thing hippies chanted in Central Park, but could it also be the motto of the 131st Aviation Company?" (462, original italics). The mantra is eerie for three reasons: Matt does not expect to see it; he does not know who painted it; and he does not know what the words mean. He puts the mantra out of his mind, but later it spontaneously resurfaces. One of the first things Matt films seems frivolous: "He tossed a frisbee to a gook dog and watched the animal leap and twist" (462). But when editing this footage, Matt unexpectedly reengages with the mantra:

> When he found a dot on the film he translated it into letters, numbers, coordinates, grids and entire systems of knowledge.
> Om mani padme hum.
> In fact the dog didn't leap at all but only watched the frisbee sail past, more or less disdainfully. A dot was a visual mantra, an object that had no properties except location.
> The jewel in the heart of the lotus. (463–64)

Since Matt does not understand the mantra, he cannot know its English translation, "the jewel in the heart of the lotus." The narrative thus introduces knowledge Matt does not have into his free, indirect train of thought, furthering the novel's evocation of paranoid connections.

The scene parallels Nick's contemplative prayer practice, but with unsettling differences. Whereas Nick deliberately seeks out a short prayer, Matt encounters the *Mani* mantra unexpectedly. Nick's practice occurs in America, whereas Matt is in faraway Vietnam. Nick deals with a familiar Western Catholic tradition, whereas Matt has a brush with the exotic traditions of Tibet. Although both mantras require translation, the Sanskrit of *om mani padme hum* is even more foreign than the Spanish of *todo y nada*. Just as Nick and Matt are brothers, these two scenes are siblings, but Matt's mantra is Nick's prayer's uncanny twin.

In addition to these connections, *todo y nada* and *om mani padme hum* have comparable meanings. Both use paradox to describe infinite reality in ways that parallel other comparisons between Christian and non-Christian mysticism (Llewelyn; Honda; Aitken; Loy, "Zen Cloud"; D'Souza). In his commentary on the phrase *todo y nada,* Thomas Merton explains that God includes everything and is therefore "all." But God also surpasses all things, and therefore is no *thing* in particular (53–54). "All and nothing" describes God's being; God is everything and nothing at the same time. The Tibetan mantra *om mani padme hum* involves a similar paradox. *Mani* means *jewel* and *padme* means *lotus*, while *om* and *hum* are invocational sounds with no semantic content (Studholme 110, 116). The 14th Dalai Lama explains that the jewel symbolizes compassion, while the lotus symbolizes emptiness (Gyatso, *Practice* 136). The jewel of compassion requires the clarity of subject and object, while the lotus of emptiness transcends all distinctions. In sum, ultimate reality is both multifaceted and empty (Gyatso, *Practice* 136; Mingyur 102–3). The "jewel" of compassion is an all-inclusive love that parallels the "all" of St. John's God. Likewise, the "lotus" of emptiness echoes the "nothing" of the unconditioned God.

While the mantras' meanings resemble one another, they remain distinct. St. John's Catholic mysticism seeks a total "blackout of desire" (Merton 54), whereas the Tibetan practice exploits specific images and feelings as a means toward supposedly higher realizations (Seager 131, Coleman 107–8). In the words of Catholic theologian Lawrence Cunningham, St. John's spiritual vision "is not the Void of Eastern thought nor the Great Doubt of the Buddha" (2006). Furthermore, Buddhist emptiness is not simply nothingness, but rather a condition of possibility (Mingyur 59–60). These two prayers are similar enough to be compared—indeed, the novel invites the reader to do so—but different enough to defy comparison. In this fraught kinship, the Catholic prayer occurs within the familiar context of a Jesuit school, whereas the Tibetan prayer is associated with the foreignness—and the wartime trauma—of Vietnam. In the Vietnam War, Buddhism was the religion of the exotic Vietnamese, both ally and enemy. But *Underworld* challenges Buddhism's foreignness by intertwining it with Western religion. For Nick, if only he were aware of this possibility—which seems to have mysteriously appeared in the mind of Matt—the nonduality of the Buddhist mantra could usefully offset the intensity of the St. John of the Cross mantra by easing Nick's obsession with his and God's "self." Thus the informed reader has access to potentially productive secret wisdom from Asian religions that the characters, in their paranoid-tinged surface experiences, do not.

Underworld's mantras reference Hinduism as well as Buddhism. The novel explores Hinduism through an unlikely source: Lenny Bruce, who thinks about mantras in the middle of his performances. He wears a "Nehru jacket" (DeLillo 546, see also Rosen), a high-collared buttoned shirt made famous in the West by Jawaharlal Nehru and also favored by the Beatles. The historical Bruce was partial to this fashion (Friend), but the novel further emphasizes its connection to Hinduism. The garment is Bruce's "Hindu statesman number" and a "Hindu tunic" (DeLillo 584, 585). It could have been an "Indian tunic," or not mentioned at all. But the adjective *Hindu* is important because it shows that one can *have* a "Hindu statesman number." The spiritual dignity of the word *Hindu* can set up higher-impact ridicule than the less religious label *Indian*. With Bruce's irreverence, nothing is sacred.

But Bruce, in DeLillo's imagination, develops misgivings about this irony during his own performances. Throughout his routines, Bruce mockingly yells, "*We're all gonna die!*" (547, 584), a line "he'd come to love" as a "high-pitched cry of grief and pain that had an element of sweet defiance" (547). Bruce's "cry" is a dark response to the Cuban Missile Crisis, and his decision to put it at the center of his routine is a bold exercise in black humor. However, the historical Bruce never used this phrase (Rosen 106), so one must account for why DeLillo has Bruce say this. The answer lies in what Bruce thinks but does not say:

> He should have been standing here chanting *We're not gonna die We're not gonna die We're not gonna die*, leading them in a chant, a mantra that was joyful and mock joyful at the same time because this is New York, New York and we want it both ways.
>
> When he thought they were gonna die, he'd chanted the die line repeatedly.
>
> But that was over now. He'd forgotten all that. There were other, deeper, vaguer matters. Everything, nothing, him. (DeLillo 629, original italics)

Bruce's sudden shift from a frivolous "Hindu statesman number" to a desperate "mantra" establishes Asian mantras as a return of what has been repressed. Furthermore, Bruce's mantralike chanting is ironically reminiscent of Ginsberg's call to "make mantra of American language now," this time in a darker, more paranoid register. Still, by wishing to lead people in "a chant, a mantra," Bruce wants to stop doing a "Hindu statesman number" and become, if not an actual Hindu priest, at least a sincere figure of spiritual solace. Rather than turning the news of the day into macabre jokes, Bruce now wants to address "other, deeper, vaguer matters," which he identifies as "everything, nothing, him," an allusion to *todo y nada*. The song lyric "New York, New York" also becomes a mantra, embodying the consummately American hopes and fears of the city. Bruce spontaneously turns one of his bawdy segments into a reflection on the horrors of sex slavery, during which time there is "an unguarded plea in Lenny's eyes" (629). But the audience predictably cools to his sobering change of course. Bruce's hopes are not realized, and because he resignedly returns to the "old jokes" (633), his audience will continue to see his association with Hinduism as ironic, even though the reader sees his underlying wish for sincerity.

By linking mantras and seriousness, but ultimately giving up on both, Bruce joins Matt Shay in only flirting with Asian religions. The novel is not implying that these characters' problems would be over if they took up these traditions in earnest, but it suggests that they miss chances to engage with traditions that have the power to help them understand and cope with their positions as US Americans. These Asian chants have more in common with Western incantations than the characters realize. Rather than determining a direction for themselves, the characters of *Underworld* remain fraught by something like the cross-pressures Charles Taylor describes, caught between competing pulls of immanence and transcendence. They have spiritual urgings that nudge them beyond their mundane immediate surroundings, but they continue to be pulled both ways, toward transcendence and toward immanence, without a clear resolution. Again, characters' unwillingness to engage more deeply with motifs from Asian religions renders the wisdom hidden. It is up to the reader to divine the secrets of how Asian ideas of nonduality could more fully answer the American longings Bruce alludes to.

INTERFAITH INTERNET

The only character who decisively overcomes the dualistic thinking that afflicts many of *Underworld*'s characters is Sister Edgar. Ironically, the novel's preeminent Catholic does the best job of internalizing Asian mantras, as her afterlife in the World Wide Web uniquely synthesizes Eastern and Western motifs. Thus Sister Edgar uncovers the secrets the novel's other characters miss, even without her directly and intellectually knowing about Asian mantras. Initially, Sister Edgar seems to be an extreme version of a stereotypical Catholic schoolteacher, a joyless disciplinarian who uses scare tactics and humiliation to subdue her students. She practices charity and yet disdains those she serves, keeping them at arm's length. In a routine excursion sometime during the 1980s, Sister Edgar thinks that "latex was necessary here. Protection against the spurt of blood or pus and the viral entities hidden within, submicroscopic parasites in their soviet socialist protein coats" (DeLillo 241). Edgar's thoughts show how Cold War paranoia pervades her everyday interactions.

Years later a young girl named Esmeralda is raped and murdered in Sister Edgar's parish, and the despairing nun joins a crowd looking at a billboard where the girl's face is rumored to appear miraculously. In the crowd, Sister Edgar opens up to others in a way she has not before. She lets the unwashed people she had previously shunned embrace her, and she feels "an angelus of clearest joy" (822). Her ecstasy is a turning point in her spiritual life (McClure 95–96), but after this transformative experience, "there is nothing left to do but die" (DeLillo 824), and the by-now elderly Sister Edgar passes away peacefully. Here is one of the novel's rare religious moments with unambiguously positive effects. Moreover, Sister Edgar's death evokes the Buddhist motif of departing from the world once one overcomes a harmful cycle of dualistic perception. Thus Sister Edgar's death prefigures the more definitive Buddhist awakening she undergoes posthumously.

After she dies, Sister Edgar passes into an afterlife "in cyberspace, not heaven" (825). Religion scholar Thomas A. Carlson has argued that this realm has predominately Christian associations (226–27). But while Christian tropes are present, an even more revealing framework is the *bardo* of Tibetan Buddhism. From a Christian perspective, Sister Edgar's experience would be a bitter disappointment compared to perfect happiness in heaven. But Buddhists expect a problematic, limited afterlife. In fact, Edgar's existence in cyberspace borrows from the *Bardo Thodol* (*The Tibetan Book of the Dead*). This text has come up repeatedly in DeLillo's novels (Kohn, "Tibetan Buddhism" 158), and it is a document that, as Buddhist studies scholar David McMahan puts it, has "become somewhat exaggeratedly representative of Tibetan Buddhism in the West" (*Making* 53). According to the *Bardo Thodol,* beings in the bardo realm between death and rebirth possess "not a body of gross matter" but an ethereal form (Evans-Wentz 158). Similarly, in cyberspace, Sister Edgar has "shed all that steam-ironed fabric" of her earthly clothes and is described as a "fluctuating impulse," not matter (DeLillo 824, 826). Also, in the bardo, one can pass through solid objects and traverse immense distances instantly (Evans-Wentz 158–59). Along the same lines, Sister Edgar is "open—exposed to any connection you can make in the world wide web" (DeLillo 824).

Such parallels might also apply to a Christian afterlife, but although bardo beings can move freely, they are not truly free. They are "driven by the ever-moving wind of karma[;] thine intellect, having no object upon which to rest, will be like a feather tossed about by the wind" (Evans-Wentz 161). Therefore, the bardo is "terrific and hard to endure" and one is liable to feel "sorrow," "terror," or "awe" (161). Similarly, Sister Edgar "feels the grip of systems" (DeLillo 825). The fact that she is "exposed to any connection you can make in the world wide web" is not liberating, but unsettling. Just as the bardo is fearful, Edgar is "so uneasy. . . . She senses the paranoia of the web, the net. There's the perennial threat of *virus* of course" (825, my emphasis). Since Sister Edgar was a germaphobe in life, DeLillo's pun extends her anxiety even into death.

Despite devoting her life to God, Sister Edgar is unprepared for this afterlife. But the narrator of the *Bardo Thodol* insists that there is nothing to fear, for the bardo's frightful contents are illusory productions of one's own mind (Evans-Wentz 103–4). By recognizing that these appearances are not real, one can experience the clear light of undifferentiated reality (89). Thus, even in the bardo one can attain enlightenment, or at least be spontaneously born in a celestial realm guaranteeing rapid progress toward enlightenment (110–12). Lacking this esoteric knowledge, Sister Edgar has trouble seeing things for what they are. For instance, when she sees a website on the atomic bomb, a religious feeling arises from this sublime vision: "The jewels roll out of her eyes and she sees God. No, wait, sorry. It is a Soviet bomb she sees" (826). Because of DeLillo's consistent use of free indirect discourse, the reader recognizes the mistake as Sister Edgar's, not the narrator's. Here, what attracts the gaze is actually a cause of suffering, a potentially liberating idea emphasized in Buddhism that Edgar does not realize at first.

Sister Edgar's misrecognition ties back to the Tibetan mantra *om mani padme hum*, as evidenced in the striking description of her awed crying. The narration says "the *jewels* roll out of her eyes" rather than the more obvious "the *tears* roll out of her eyes" (my italics). The word "jewels" hearkens back to the translation of *om mani padme hum*, "the jewel in the lotus." The *Bardo Thodol* teaches that reciting *om mani padme hum* can deliver one from the bardo into nirvana (Evans-Wentz 149–50n1). If Sister Edgar's cyberspace afterlife is a version of the bardo, this mantra is the secret password that can rescue her from it. But she enacts only half of it herself. The closest approximation of a lotus that could complement Sister Edgar's teary jewels is the bomb blast she sees. It is a "spray plume" and a "superheated sphere" with "solar golds and reds" (DeLillo 825). Its round form and bright colors vaguely recall lotuses of Buddhist art, but as an ironic blossom of destruction.

And yet after this highly refracted iteration of the Mani mantra, Sister Edgar does gain liberating insight. In contemplating this bomb blast, "Sister begins to sense the byshadows that stretch from the awe of a central event.

How the intersecting systems help pull us apart, leaving us vague, drained, docile, soft in our inner discourse, willing to be shaped, to be overwhelmed—easy retreats, half beliefs" (826). Her ability to "sense the byshadows" and understand "intersecting systems" arrives in a realization of previously elusive wisdom that occurs beneath the level of conscious thought. Next, Sister Edgar gains peace by merging with, of all people, J. Edgar Hoover. Hoover appears elsewhere in the novel with no causal connection to Sister Edgar. But he has shared her name, germaphobia, celibacy, and Cold War paranoia. In this culminating moment, Hoover is

> hyperlinked at last to Sister Edgar—a single fluctuating impulse now, a piece of coded information.
> Everything is connected in the end.
> Sister and Brother. A fantasy in cyberspace and a way of seeing the other side and a settling of differences that have less to do with gender than with difference itself, all argument, all conflict programmed out. (826)

Sister Edgar transcends "difference itself" in a realization of Hindu and Buddhist teachings that ultimate reality is undifferentiated (Coleman 37–38, Rambachan 43). "Everything is connected" now becomes a cosmopolitan, rather than a paranoid, statement. Still, Sister Edgar's release is "a fantasy," and the reader is left wondering to what extent such overcoming of "all conflict" is truly possible; this transcendence, in keeping with postmodern contingency, is tenuous at best.

Having narrated this release, the novel ends with bittersweet hope. At this point, "a word appears in the lunar milk of the data stream[,] . . . a single, seraphic word" (826). A long description of the word's many associations, including "the thick lived tenor of things" and "its whisper of reconciliation," builds up to the unveiling of the word itself, the novel's last: *peace* (827). By lyricizing the many meanings that inhabit this one powerful word, the novel ends with another chant. *Peace* is a short prayer like those recommended by *The Cloud of Unknowing*. The word further offers a pointed contrast from the Cold War and the Vietnam War that take up much of the narrative.

The novel ties the word *peace* to multiple religions. One can "summon the word in Sanskrit, Greek, Latin, and Arabic, in a thousand languages and dialects living and dead, and locate literary citations, and follow the word through the tunneled underworld of its ancestral roots." These four languages are all associated with major religions, including Hinduism (Sanskrit), Christianity (Greek and Latin), and Islam (Arabic). The next paragraph is one sentence that says, "Fasten, fit closely, bind together." This is one of the most recognized meanings of the word *religion*: "that which *ties* believers to God" (*OED*, my emphasis). It shares a common root with "*ligament*" (*OED*). In an echo of the novel's title, the metaphor of "the tunneled underworld" emphasizes the theme that "everything is connected in the end," even if entities appear separate (DeLillo 826).

The novel's concluding emphasis on religion and connectedness further reveals why Asian religions are uncanny in *Underworld*. The novel's ongoing juxtaposition of Eastern and Western chant invites the reader to see similarities between these practices. But by touching on Asian traditions just long enough to dismiss them, the novel's characters repress these links. Their avoidance does not succeed in banishing Asian religions; instead, it establishes them as Catholic Christianity's uncanny double. Through characters' repression, Tibetan Buddhism "was intended to remain secret, hidden away, and has come into the open" (Freud 132). The novel's end suggests that recognizing, not repressing, connections between religions can alleviate paranoia and bring "peace." This payoff contrasts somewhat from the use of secrecy in *Vineland*. Whereas in *Vineland*, secret wisdom must stay secret to keep its potency, in *Underworld*, Asian wisdom's exclusivity is not the endgame. In *Underworld* the socially conditioned secrecy of Asian wisdom does serve to underscore its value. That which is rare is all the more precious, so there is a sense of accomplishment among the few readers who can uncover this secret. But *Underworld*, unlike *Vineland*, gives voice to the dream of revealing this secret wisdom to everyone.

However, *Underworld* does not simply normalize Buddhism or Hinduism. The novel connects Christian and Buddhist chant, not in unquestioned beneficence, but in their strangeness, highlighting how difficult it is to integrate such practices into one's life. Even ending with the mantra *peace* does not simply vindicate chant. The narrator, in a direct address to the reader, says that "you try to imagine the word on the screen becoming a thing in the world . . . but it's only a sequence of pulses on a dullish screen and all it can do is make you pensive" (827). In other words, contemplating the word *peace* is not enough to establish peace "in the world," just as chanting Catholic or Tibetan mantras is not enough to heal characters' spiritual struggles.

The novel's ending, ambivalent though it is, still presents a hopeful vision based on a more enlightened version of US individualism. It hearkens back to the opening line, "He speaks in your voice, American, and there's a shine in his eye that's halfway hopeful" (11). At the outset, an "American" attitude is one whose "shine" suggests the twinkling "hope" of individual gain. The last page reiterates the second-person address by intoning, "They speak in *your* voice" (827, my emphasis). But the adjective *American* is absent this time, and there is instead a variety of images gesturing more broadly toward "the world," not just the US (827). This glimmer of cosmopolitanism is not abstract; it also focuses on the small objects of textured life such as "the slabbed butter melting on the crumbled bun" (827). Instead of the vast, austere expanse of an American frontier that awes Nick and Matt, this closing imagery's provocative attentiveness to small things brings a focus on connectivity and goodwill. The implied reader imagines that a frontier of peace is "extending itself ever outward[,] . . . a word that spreads a longing through the raw sprawl of the city and out across the dreaming bourns and orchards to the solitary hills. / Peace" (827). This epilogue uses ideas of Asian nonduality to contrast the rugged American individualism that limits Nick and Matt from achieving Sister Edgar's nascent enlightened individualism. By using the second person and describing what "you try to imagine" (827), the novel implores the reader to go beyond the limited insight of its characters, not to reach an ultimate transcendence, but to carry out a more open engagement with the aspects of Asian religions that can productively transform American individualism from a stance of atomism to interconnectedness. This is *Underworld*'s esoteric initiation.

Neither *Underworld* nor *Vineland* is centrally devoted to Enlightenment ideals of individual rights, and Pynchon and DeLillo cannot be called Hindu or Buddhist advocates. But even though Pynchon and DeLillo treat both Asian and North American enlightenments with distance, their fiction offers provocative visions of how effectively Asian religions can translate to American contexts. Moreover, their postmodern skepticism is precisely what allows Asian religions to advance their diagnoses of American paranoia. By delving into the anxieties of those touched by Asian religions, *Vineland* and *Underworld* suggest that paranoid thinking blocks a more informed skepticism of pathways to transcendence. Instead of wholesale acceptance or rejection of Asian religions, Americans should adapt Buddhism's and Hinduism's esoteric aspects that can most empower human vitality and freedom in the face of oppressive forces. By using secret Asian religious tools to reform American aspirations of freedom and happiness, these postmodern visions remain perched on the edge of enlightened individualism.

CHAPTER 4

Asian Religions and African Dreams

Alice Walker and Charles Johnson

THE WRITERS in the first three chapters have highly contrasting responses to Asian religions. But one common factor that lies in the background of their enlightened individualism is a white identity that, as religion scholar Joseph Cheah reminds us, tends not to draw attention to itself as racially marked (3–4). This choice of writers reflects a larger cultural reality: American converts to Asian religions, especially Buddhism, have been overwhelmingly white (Pintak; Selzer, "Black American Buddhism" 44). This fact has often led scholars to write the history of Buddhism's spread in America as a white history. For example, in a landmark study, Rick Fields calls a cohort of nineteenth-century American Theosophists, who drew heavily from Asian religions, "The White Buddhists" (83); Stephen Prothero similarly declares the influential Henry Steel Olcott to be "The White Buddhist."

But this is not the whole story. Particularly in the post–civil rights era, there has been increasing minority interest in Buddhism, and not only among immigrants from Asia. An especially significant development along these lines is Buddhist and Hindu adaptations in an African American context. This understudied phenomenon has significant implications for the larger picture of cross-cultural adaptation in multiethnic US literatures. In the US, nonwhite writers interested in Asian religions have an even more complex task than their white counterparts: They must write about a foreign tradition while occupying a minority position themselves, both within the culture at large and within communities of imported faiths.

A number of African American writers and artists have contributed to Asian religions in the US. In a Buddhist clergy where non-Asian teachers are overwhelmingly white, ordained black practitioners have written about their experiences, such as Jan Willis, Ralph Steele, and Joseph Jarman (Pintak). Articles on Buddhism among African Americans have appeared in the Buddhist periodicals *Shambhala Sun* (renamed *Lion's Roar* in 2015) and *Tricycle* (Pintak, Heuman). Periodicals have noted Buddhist and Hindu influences on black musicians such as John Coltrane, Wayne Shorter, and Herbie Hancock (Goldberg 264–66, K. Smith, Truman). These voices attest to an emerging literary scene invested in nurturing Asian religions not just for Americans, but for African Americans specifically.

In particular, the fiction of Alice Walker and Charles Johnson has played an innovative role in emerging discourses of Asian religions for African Americans, what Linda Selzer calls "Black Dharma" ("Black American Buddhism" 43). Both Walker and Johnson have been inspired by Buddhism and Hinduism: Walker has drawn eclectically from African, Amerindian, and Asian spiritual traditions, choosing not to identify with any one religion (Walker, *We Are the Ones* 98). Johnson has been a Buddhist since 1981 (Rushdy 401), but Hinduism also plays a notable role in his writings, as both religions place a similar—and, for Johnson, crucial—emphasis on the ultimate nondifferentiation between oneself and others. Furthermore, both writers believe that Asian religions have specific value for American minorities, especially African Americans. Although Walker and Johnson do not see themselves as carrying on Beat Buddhism in particular, they do share with the Beats and other countercultures a sense that Asian religions can be powerful resources for Americans with marginalized identities. Walker's and Johnson's enlightened individualism connects Asian teachings of nonduality to American traditions of social activism, and specifically racial politics. Their fiction dramatizes the idea that Asian teachings of nonduality are both a potent argument against racism and a resource for dealing with racial trauma.

Walker and Johnson have written in the midst of significant obstacles to Asian religions' reception among African Americans. These barriers speak to critical debates about blackness and cultural authenticity. Authenticity, understood as fidelity to one's ethnic roots, has been a central concept in African American literature and culture, and critics continue to debate its value vigorously (Chinitz, Eversley, Favor, E. Johnson). Ideas of black authenticity have alienated African Americans from Asian religions. Whereas for white Westerners, Asian religions' exoticism is usually a part of their appeal (Storhoff and Whalen-Bridge 4), for African Americans, Buddhism's and Hinduism's remote origins make them suspect. A black radio host once asked Charles Johnson, "People in the community are wondering how did a brother get *over there* with Buddhism?" (Whalen-Bridge, "Shoulder" 301, my emphasis). Many African Americans feel that it would endanger black heritage to follow foreign religions (Selzer, "Black American Buddhism" 45). Also, African Americans who are interested in Asian religions often feel uncomfortable going to Buddhist centers because most convert Buddhist organizations are predominately white (Pintak).

Walker and Johnson intervene in this cultural tension by reinterpreting Asian religions as expressions of authentic blackness. Both writers relate ambivalently to the idea that religious seekers should prioritize, as the Chink in Robbins's *Cowgirls* puts it, "their own history" (230). On the one hand, Walker's and Johnson's fiction relies on Buddhist and Hindu doctrines of nonduality to loosen the demands of authenticity. On the other, it also acknowledges authenticity's investment in roots by imagining an ancestral connection between Asian religions and African American culture.

Walker's and Johnson's efforts to bridge Asian thought and African Americans identities target multiple audiences. For African American readers, these texts strive to make Asian-inspired spirituality more accessible and more applicable to dealing with racial trauma. Buddhism's teachings on emptiness and nonduality are especially valuable, Walker and Johnson believe, for both critiquing racism and transcending reactionary hatred against whites. For non–African American readers, Walker and Johnson seek to portray black practitioners of Eastern religions as a natural and valuable part of America's religious landscape.

This project comes to life in Walker's and Johnson's fiction. My discussion of Alice Walker focuses on *The Color Purple* (1982) and *Now Is the Time to Open Your Heart* (2004). Then I turn to Johnson's *Middle Passage* (1990) and *Dreamer* (1998). As their work evolves, Walker and Johnson bring Asian religions from the underground to the surface. *The Color Purple* and *Middle Passage* imagine Hindu religious principles coming from African sources, hiding the influence of Asian religion as such. Later, *Now Is the Time* and *Dreamer* explicitly involve Buddhism, but they focus on African American spiritual seekers who transplant Asian wisdom into a contemporary American minority context. These works show each author's balancing act between promoting African American cultural pride and inviting spiritual influences from other cultures.

Although critics have discussed Buddhism's influence on Johnson and, to a lesser extent, on Walker, they have not explored the specific novelistic strategies by which both writers nativize Asian religions. My investigation of these two writers raises important questions for contemporary literary criticism, African American studies, and cultural and religious studies more broadly. What are the ethical obligations of spiritual innovators such as Walker and Johnson with respect to a religion's more traditional representatives? Is it possible, or even desirable, for Asian teachings to play a significant role in African American culture and politics? Can a notion as seemingly abstract as nonduality support effective political change? More broadly, to whom, if anyone, does a religion belong, and by what criteria? What are the relationships between ancestry and religion in an increasingly globalized age? I cannot fully answer these questions in this book, but the following discussion will provide a basis for pursuing them.

WALKER'S ASIAN ALTERNATIVE

For Alice Walker, political freedom and spiritual liberation are inseparable. In her 1995 essay "The Only Reason You Want to Go to Heaven Is That You Have Been Driven Out of Your Mind," Walker argues that African Americans should "decolonize their spirits" from Christianity and recover the pagan spirituality of their ancestors. Christianity, Walker says, is a religion that black people were "forced to have" instead of their gentler, Earth-based "traditional worship." She praises those who "speak in defense of the ancient Goddess / God of all pagans and heathens, Mother Earth," lamenting that "we are empty, lonely, without our pagan-heathen ancestors." If African Americans can recuperate a spirituality from their own roots, Walker asserts, they can achieve both spiritual transcendence and cultural pride.

Walker's self-declared project of spiritual recovery has led previous critics to focus on influences in her writing from African and South American religions (Lauret, Marvin, Simcikova). But this picture becomes complicated once we explore Walker's well-documented indebtedness to Asian religions, an influence critics have noted but without exploring issues of cultural difference. How can an apparently foreign spirituality be compatible with pride in one's ethnic roots? We can trace an evolving response to this tension by exploring latent Hinduism in *The Color Purple* and explicit Buddhism in *Now Is the Time,* two novels that narrate journeys of spiritual growth. I argue that *The Color Purple* and *Now Is the Time* mediate Asian traditions through African and Amerindian spiritual practices. In other words, characters in these novels learn Buddhist or Hindu metaphysics from African or Amerindian traditions. Through this process, Walker seeks to legitimize Asian religions for non-Asian minorities.

At the time of its publication, no one, including Walker, said much about *The Color Purple*'s Indian influences. But in later years Walker has detailed how she learned Transcendental Meditation (hereafter TM), a contemplative practice derived from Hinduism, in the late 1970s, and has maintained an active interest in Eastern spirituality ever since (White 298; Walker, *We Are the Ones* 90–105). TM's founder, Maharishi Mahesh Yogi, promoted the practice as nonreligious. It does not teach culturally specific Hindu deity worship but instead focuses on transcending thought and experiencing union with unconditioned consciousness ("The Technique"). Nevertheless, Maharishi's utopian vision that mass meditation can bring about world peace has a Hindu basis that also found its way into countercultural, mantra-based activism. As I mentioned in the first chapter, these ideas were exemplified in the 1967 attempt to levitate the Pentagon and end the Vietnam War through chanting (Hungerford 32, Roszak 124–25), as well as Allen Ginsberg's and Gary Snyder's roles in the 1967 San Francisco Human Be-In, in which thousands of mantra chanters sought to promote global harmony (Trigilio 2–3). This type of Asian-inspired optimism (or, less charitably, naïveté) gave TM considerable appeal among hippies, and Maharishi became a popular figure among the counterculture, a status advanced by his conspicuous association with progressive celebrities such as the Beatles (Iwamura 63).

At first Walker came to TM to help herself cope with the pain of her divorce in 1976 (White 466). But this personal impetus quickly led to a wish for others to enjoy the same benefits she experienced with TM, a motivation that had a significant impact on Walker's writing. In fact, Walker could hardly be more explicit about TM's influence, stating in a 2006 essay collection that "meditation . . . has helped me write my books. . . . *The Color Purple* owes much of its humor and playfulness to the equanimity of my mind as I committed myself to a routine, daily practice" (*We Are the Ones* 158). She adds that *The Color Purple* "was actually my Buddha novel without Buddhism" (99). Given these acknowledgments, it is surprising that critics have not explored how Asian religions relate to concerns of ethnic reclamation in Walker's novels. But if we investigate *The Color Purple*, we can see a delicate negotiation taking shape.

THE COLOR PURPLE'S IMPERSONAL GOD

In *The Color Purple*, sisters Celie and Nettie change their spiritual orientation from the patriarchal Christianity of their upbringing toward a noninstitutionalized spirituality that shares central features with classical Hindu metaphysics. Chief among these are the beliefs that all phenomena are manifestations of God and that God is impersonal, unconditioned being-itself (Iyer 93–94, Rambachan 83–85). However, the novel disguises India's influence on its spiritual themes by implanting Asian wisdom in characters with no knowledge of Hinduism. Instead, both Celie and Nettie meet a wise person of African descent who helps them realize that the Christianity of their youth is oppressing them and that a more humane alternative is available.

For Celie, that mentor is Shug, a blues singer who brings an immense reservoir of spiritual resources to personal problems. When Celie is overcome with grief at her father's death and anger at her husband's hiding Nettie's letter to her, she denounces God as "trifling, forgitful and lowdown" (Walker, *Purple* 192). Shug responds to Celie that God is not the problem, but rather Celie's idea of God as "big and tall and graybearded and white" (194). In an often-cited passage, Shug offers a more palatable definition of God:

God ain't a he or a she, but a It.
   But what do it look like? I ast.
   Don't look like nothing, she say. It ain't a picture show. It ain't something you can look at apart from everything else, including yourself. I believe God is everything, say Shug. Everything that is or ever was or ever will be. And when you can feel that, and be happy to feel that, you've found It. (195)

This pivotal definition echoes several key teachings of Hindu monism as expressed in TM. Here God is not separate from the world, but "God is everything," absolutely immanent. God is unconstrained by time, equally present as "everything that is or ever was or ever will be." Furthermore, Shug believes that this ultimate reality is impersonal rather than personal, as indicated by her preference for the gender-neutral pronoun *It*, with a capital *I*, over the white male God of Christianity.

These tenets strongly resemble Hindu conceptions of ultimate reality. In particular, Shug's concise catechism resonates with passages from Maharishi Mahesh Yogi's *Science of Being and Art of Living*, a seminal text of the TM movement that Walker likely read. Maharishi declares, "Everything in creation is the manifestation of the unmanifested absolute impersonal Being, the omnipresent God" (Mahesh 268). Not only do Shug and Maharishi agree that ultimate reality is impersonal, but Shug's use of the neutral pronoun *It* with a capital *I* to refer to God also parallels the language of TM. Maharishi, arguing that God and the world are inseparable, writes, "The world is the creation of the impersonal, absolute God. It is sustained by It and eventually dissolves into It" (269). Even if Walker is not deliberately quoting Maharishi in *The*

Color Purple, these parallels nevertheless point toward TM's influence on the novel.

Shug's speech conveys its spiritual importance through its form as well as its content. Shug's description of God is a vernacular creed: It bears repetitive, verse-like declarations of what God "ain't" versus what God "is." Her statements are evenly balanced between three negations—God looks like "nothing," "ain't a picture show," and cannot be viewed "apart from everything else"—and three affirmations—God "is everything," "everything . . . that ever will be," and can be known by "when you can feel that, and be happy to feel that." Shug's subtle formalism makes her speech doctrinal without being stiff; she makes a religious invocation without disrupting her or Celie's verbal idiom.

Shug's ideas help inspire Celie toward the payoffs of American individualism. Soon after Shug's stirring sermon, Celie stands up to her abusive husband and takes greater control of her life. As Celie discovers this courage within her, her words of defiance "seem to come to me from the trees" (206), indicating that Celie has internalized Shug's spirituality. Shug explains in her sermon to Celie that on her road to believing that "God is everything. . . . My first step . . . was the trees" (195). Celie's resistance to an abusive husband she was coerced into marrying is an assertion of her individual autonomy, and she soon takes advantage of this greater freedom by starting a successful business making pants (210–16). Celie expresses her spiritual growth in large part through monetizing her individual skill through business enterprise, a quintessentially American paradigm. And it is Shug's Hindu-based spiritual ideas—expressed with a touch of pagan veneration of nature—that enable Celie's journey.

Celie's spiritual development finds a parallel in Nettie, who independently develops similar spiritual beliefs while on an Anglican mission in Africa. But Nettie does not simply learn this view from African religions. Instead, she gradually intuits a middle way between Anglicanism and the religion of the fictional Olinka tribe to whom she ministers. Early in the mission, Nettie's encounter with a roofleaf ceremony plants the seed of spiritual unity in her mind. An Olinka man says to her:

> We know a roofleaf is not Jesus Christ, but in its own humble way, is it not God?
>
> So there we sat, Celie, face to face with the Olinka God. And Celie, I was so tired and sleepy and full of chicken and groundnut stew, my ears ringing with song, that all that Joseph said made perfect sense to me. I wonder what you will make of all this? (154)

This moment introduces Nettie to the idea that divinity is not confined to a personal Godhead but can pervade the world "in its own humble way." At this point, Nettie's investment in Anglican doctrine prompts her to dismiss this dawning awareness as merely the result of fatigue and overeating. But this passage's appeal to a variety of senses also enacts the beginnings of a spirituality of all-pervasive immanent divinity. These concrete sense experiences are what make Nettie receptive to the idea that the roofleaf is God as well as Jesus Christ. The sight of being "face to face with the Olinka God"; the taste of "chicken and groundnut stew"; and the hearing of "song" all suggest that God is manifest in festive, sensual, worldly life. And Nettie's question to Celie foreshadows Celie's exploration of Asian spirituality—even though the novel does not call it that—as well.

But while Nettie's experience with African religion is liberating, she does not fully embrace it. Moreover, the ways in which Nettie distinguishes her spirituality from both Anglican and Olinka views hint at TM's influence on the novel. In a 1973 interview, Walker says she understands African religion as centering on a belief in "all creation as living, as being *inhabited* by spirit" (Walker, "Interview" 41, my emphasis), a view that the Olinka religion expresses. By contrast, the Hindu metaphysics of TM declare that all creation *is* spirit (Mahesh Yogi 33–36, Rambachan 43–46). This principle of absolute unity is much closer to what Nettie, paralleling Shug, eventually asserts.

Summarizing what she has learned, Nettie reflects in one of her last letters to Celie before coming home, "God is different to us now, after all these years in Africa. More spirit than ever before, and more internal. Most people think he has to look like something or someone—a roofleaf or Christ—but we don't. And not being tied to what God looks like, frees us" (Walker, *Purple* 257). Nettie's liberation from Anglican and Olinka metaphysics is complete. The Anglican God, who is by implication more "external" than "internal," feels remote. On the other hand, the Olinka worship of the roofleaf plant is so immanent that it encompasses a limited range of phenomena. When Nettie explains that "the roofleaf became the thing they [the Olinka] worship" (154), the definite article *the* indicates that the roofleaf is the *only* thing they worship. Both systems, in Nettie's view, limit God. But although the Olinka religion does not fully satisfy Nettie, her contact with African people is a crucial catalyst in awakening her de facto Asian spirituality. In effect, the Hindu metaphysical framework Nettie comes to believe in emerges from Africa.

Nettie's remarks parallel Shug's and, eventually, Celie's belief in ultimate reality as impersonal, all-pervasive spirit rather than a personal deity. At the novel's end, Celie also identifies God with everything, saying, "Dear God. Dear stars, dear trees, dear sky, dear peoples. Dear Everything. Dear God" (285). But although both Celie and Nettie develop spiritualities indebted to Hindu metaphysics, their mentors are African or African American, not Indian. Why is this? Arguably, Walker does not acknowledge Hindu sources in *The Color Purple* because she wants African Americans to claim this religion as their own. Critics have noted that one of the major aspirations of *The Color Purple* is to speak about Africa without being constrained by European systems of thought (Gruesser 153). Although the novel largely deals with escaping the yoke of Christianity, any foreign religion could, by extension, undermine this project of ethnic reclamation. Acknowledging Indian sources might dilute, in the eyes of her readers, Walker's vision of a vital spirituality by and for those of African descent. Thus *The Color Purple* portrays the tension between Walker's interest in Hindu metaphysics and her commitment to celebrating a black spiritual heritage. Here, Walker's nascent enlightened individualism is still framed in terms of ethnic ancestry rather than the more liberal sense of freedom of association based on found affinities.

FROM HINDU TRANSCENDENCE TO BUDDHIST COMPASSION

As Walker's career progressed, her ideas about spiritual ancestry began to shift, culminating in a more direct acknowledgment of Asian religions in *Now Is the Time to Open Your Heart*. The ideas about ancestry Walker developed after *The Color Purple* are complex enough to warrant further discussion, which will better contextualize my reading of *Now Is the Time*. This novel biographically parallels *The Color Purple* because Walker wrote both novels under the influence of a specific meditation practice from Asia—TM for *The Color Purple* and tonglen for *Now Is the Time*. Also, both practices started as responses to a personal crisis but broadened into a social vision. In 1993 Walker's mother died (White 466). To help deal with her grief, Walker listened to recordings of Pema Chödrön, a Tibetan Buddhist nun, teaching tonglen meditation (Walker, *We Are the Ones* 98). Whereas TM aims to transcend all thought in the absolute unity of Being, tonglen uses detailed visualizations of suffering beings to arouse visceral feelings of compassion in the meditator (H. H. Sakya Trizin 82–84). The practice is intended to develop one's compassion. One imagines breathing in the suffering of others and breathing out one's own happiness to them (Walker, *We Are the Ones* 98; Chödrön 109).

This counterintuitive approach actually worked for Walker who, after practicing the meditation daily for a year, felt both relief from her own grief and increased compassion for others (Walker 98). During this time, Walker's devotion to Tibetan meditation coexisted with an ongoing concern for preserving African traditions. As I mentioned earlier in this chapter, Walker's 1995 essay "The Only Reason You Want to Go to Heaven Is That You Have Been Driven Out of Your Mind" is an important declaration of Walker's promotion of African and Native American "pagan" religions (Walker, "Only Reason"). In this text, Walker describes indigenous animistic religions as a more authentic ancestral resource for African Americans than the Christianity that slaveholders forced on them. Walker's advocacy of paganism involves an affirmation of the body against the "excarnation" of religion, which Charles Taylor defines as the shift from bodily participation in religion to a near-exclusive focus on the mind (554). Walker's use of the word *pagan* is thematically similar to Taylor's use of it to mean a world-affirming stance opposed to the instrumentalizing reforms of both ascetic religion and rationalist naturalism (612–13). For Walker, paganism is a way of experiencing "the magical intimacy we felt with Creation" which "the God of the Old Testament is always trying to wipe out." By linking paganism with African and Amerindian religions, Walker wants to recuperate a religion of world-affirming embodiment. Walker's goal is to promote both spiritual transcendence and an ethnically authentic affirmation of the world. (This materiality, however, does not include rituals distinctive to Buddhism or Hinduism, whose influence on Walker consists mainly of meditation techniques and philosophy.)

Christianity, Walker contends, is a poor candidate to do the cultural work she prizes, not only because it was imposed but also because it is foreign. Walker finds it bizarre that so many African Americans should follow "the longhaired rabbi from a small Jewish sect in a far-off desert." The term *far-off* underscores Walker's reservations about alien spiritual influences and reinforces her appeal to authenticity as the rediscovery of ethnic roots. And yet by the time Walker wrote "The Only Reason," she had already been practicing tonglen meditation rigorously. If one risks neglecting one's heritage by practicing a religion from a "far-off desert," what would be better about devotions from the far-off Himalayan Mountains?

The tension behind this question would prove productive for Walker. In the late 1990s Walker met Pema Chödrön, and the two engaged in a public dialogue that was marketed on video and CD under the title "Alice Walker and Pema Chödrön in Conversation" (1999). During their dialogue, Walker says, "The heart literally responds to this practice [of tonglen]. . . . If you keep going and doing the practice, the heart actually relaxes. That is quite amazing to feel" (Chödrön and Walker). According to Walker, tonglen meditation opens one's heart. With this description, the source for Walker's book title becomes clear.

Although *Now Is the Time to Open Your Heart* does not discuss tonglen in particular, its engagement with Buddhism and concern for developing compassion is a direct result of Walker's specific meditation practice.

In her dialogue with Chödrön, one can also see Walker's developing ideas about the role ancestry plays as a spiritual concept. Explaining to Chödrön how tonglen helped her, Walker says, "I'm always supported by spirits and ancestors and people in my tribe, whoever they've been and however long ago they lived. So it was like having another tribe of people, of ancestors, come to the rescue with this wisdom that came through you and your way of teaching." This thought continues Walker's investment in ancestry. She calls Tibetans, the people who invented tonglen, "another tribe" but then calls them, ambiguously, "ancestors." Of course the Tibetans of antiquity are ancestors, most obviously of present-day Tibetans. But Walker implicitly claims Tibetans as her own ancestors as well, showing how important it is for Walker to describe spiritual solace in terms of something that comes from one's forebearers. Through her efforts to promote Buddhism to African Americans and, as we will see, to Amerindians, Walker develops a more nuanced idea of spiritual ancestry that allows for direct acknowledgment of these traditions' Asian origins.

Walker continued to elaborate her case for claiming Buddhists as African Americans' spiritual ancestors at a Buddhist retreat in 2002. This retreat, held at Spirit Rock Meditation Center in Woodacre, California, was the first Buddhist retreat specifically for African Americans. In her presentation—the only one of Walker's many public talks that has been called a "dharma talk" (Walker, *We Are the Ones* 88)—Walker opens with a historical account of George Slaughter, a mixed-race child who was lynched for riding on a horse with an unacceptably fine saddle. Walker calls George "our murdered ancestor" because he is black, but she also invokes Buddhism to express a broadened concept of ancestry that transcends ethnic identity:

> I cherish the study and practice of Buddhism because it is good medicine for healing us so that we may engage the work of healing our ancestors. Ancestors like George. Ancestors like George's father.
> Both George and his father are our ancestors.
> *What heals ancestors is understanding them.* And understanding as well that it is not in heaven or in hell that the ancestors are healed. *They can only be healed inside us.* Buddhist practice, sent by ancestors we didn't even know we had, has arrived, as all things do, just in time. (109, emphasis in original)

This passage lists three ancestors, each less literally plausible than the previous one. George may not be related to anyone in the room where Walker speaks, but he is memorable as a figurative ancestor because he is a black youth killed by racist violence. But George's father is more difficult to regard as an ancestor because he is white and part of the mob that killed his son. To forgive such a villain and embrace him as one's ancestor requires a profound Buddhist sense of nonduality. Accordingly, Walker exhorts her listeners to feel compassion toward George's father, saying that he was "*unfree*" because of racism (107, italics in original). Finally, Walker takes the word *ancestor* even further: If Buddhism is "sent by ancestors we didn't even know we had," then this means that, spiritually speaking, Buddhists are African Americans' ancestors. In this usage, an ancestor is not necessarily someone in one's own family tree, ethnic group, or even country. An ancestor is someone from the past from whom one can learn valuable lessons. Of course this is not a new idea; Catholic parishioners routinely address their priests as *Father*. But Walker's application of this idea is striking for its implicit rejection of biological descent as a necessary criterion for ancestry.

For Walker, Buddhism's relevance for African Americans stems not only from histories of racial hatred, but also from spiritual tendencies within black Southern culture. In 2009 Walker wrote a letter of encouragement to the graduating class of Naropa University, a Buddhist school in Boulder, Colorado, founded by Allen Ginsberg's guru Chögyam Trungpa in 1974 (Hayward 91–93). In this letter she praises the school's mission of promoting Buddhist values but also brings up African American regional experience. Referring to Tibetan Buddhism, she writes,

> I see how beautifully it connects with, joins, African American Southern soul. If and when black people in the South begin to investigate Buddhism, a large part of their suffering will decrease and a large part of their peace of mind, which they have valued so highly, and with such persistence, will be enlarged. They will not fail to recognize the gift. (*Cushion* 53–54)

Walker's deep concern for African American Buddhism is apparent in how her letter changes course in order to make this point. This quotation does not fit neatly within the letter's larger organization. Moreover, Naropa University is not in the South, nor does it have a significant population of black students—just 1 percent as of the period 2012–13 ("Facts at a Glance"), close to the time Walker wrote her letter. But here, Walker is more interested in imagining what could be than what is already the case. Her qualifier "if and when" combines a sense of contingency and inevitability, yearning for a cultural development that she acknowledges has yet to "begin."

However, the "peace of mind" Southern blacks "have valued so highly" is ambiguous in the above passage. At a public appearance in 2013, which I attended, I asked Walker what specific characteristics of Tibetan Buddhism she sees as harmonizing with "African American Southern soul." Walker answered that historically, Southern blacks found peace of mind through communing with nature in a slow-paced, outdoor-centered culture. Thus, Walker said, Southern blacks "were meditating without calling it that." Walker proposed that Buddhist meditation would give a more "structured" way of expanding this peace of mind. Through Buddhist meditation, she said, "the black soul" meets "the Tibetan soul." By supporting events such as the Spirit Rock retreat, speaking alongside H. H. the Dalai Lama (Walker, "Creative Journey"), and promoting meditation at her public appearances, Walker is working to make Buddhism a greater presence in African American culture. She does so in ways that encourage more-transnational versions of American identity, forging alignments between Asian spiritual disciplines and Enlightenment-indebted American projects of civil rights and minority uplift.

BUDDHISM AND ETHNIC AMERICAN IDENTITIES IN *NOW IS THE TIME TO OPEN YOUR HEART*

Walker's expanded notion of spiritual kinship finds narrative expression in *Now Is the Time*. But whereas *The Color Purple* does not advertise its Hindu influences, *Now Is the Time* explicitly engages with Buddhism. In this novel, the protagonist, Kate Talkingtree, seeks to recover an ancestral spirituality through Amerindian cultures, a quest reflected in her self-made surname, which used to be "Nelson." Kate, like Walker, is part Amerindian, so her turn to the spiritual wisdom of the Amazon reflects a desire to recover the spirituality of her ancestral culture (see Walker, *Now Is the Time* 66, 90, 183; White, *Alice Walker* 389–90). But rather than receive Asian wisdom in Amerindian disguise, after her ancestral spirits help her see Buddhism in a new light, Kate returns to the Buddhism she had previously abandoned.

At the novel's beginning, Kate grows disaffected with Buddhism because of a politically out-of-touch teacher (4–6). He criticizes "hot revolutions, with guns and violence" and praises the "cool revolution" of the Buddha's teaching (4). Kate, bristling at this facile dismissal of disaffected masses with limited options, leaves the retreat and "[dismantles] her altar" at home (11). Corroborating Linda Selzer's diagnosis of African American suspicions toward Asian religions (Selzer, "Black American Buddhism" 45), the Buddhism Kate experiences is too white and affluent to understand the struggles of the poor and oppressed around the world. Like the anti-Beat inwardness of Salinger and Pirsig, this version of Asian religions uses meditation as an aloof withdrawal from the world rather than an active engagement with its problems. These impressions lead Kate to conclude that "she had reached an impasse on the Buddhist road" (4). Her disillusionment prompts her to notice that "she seemed to be the only person of color there" (5), confirming that this Buddhist retreat does not nourish Kate's sense of ethnic roots.

In this opening scene, Kate's growing reservations toward Buddhism converge with her critiques of Christianity. When the Buddhist teacher scolds political revolutionaries, it offends Kate in the same way that Christianity's doctrine of original sin does. Kate is supposed to be meditating, but she "kept looking out the window instead, just as she had looked out of the window of the Church of God and [sic] Christ, as a child, when she had been unable to believe human beings, simply by being born, had sinned" (5). In both cases, a foreign faith doles out undeserved criticism of people whose experiences the religious tradition does not understand. These thoughts strongly echo Walker's critique of Christianity in "The Only Reason." In her essay as well as this novel, the antidote to an alienated and alienating religion is to take refuge in a nature-focused tradition from an ancestral culture.

In search of a spirituality that better speaks to these concerns, Kate goes to the Amazon on a retreat consisting of teachings, nature walks, and trances induced by the psychedelic plant yagé. Her experiences there contrast with her experiences of Buddhism in America. Whereas the indoor meditation hall separates Kate from a surrounding grove of redwood trees (3, 6), the Amazon retreat is primarily outdoors in the middle of the rainforest (53–54). Whereas the people at Kate's Buddhist retreat are overwhelmingly white, her colleagues in the Amazon are white, black, Amerindian, and Hispanic. Whereas the center of gravity in the Buddhist retreat is an emphatically male teacher, in the Amazon the main object of reverence is a personified spirit called Grandmother, a primordial divine feminine. And whereas the Buddhist retreat focuses on listening to lectures from the teacher, in the Amazon the participants talk to and befriend one another.

The retreat leads Kate to identify more strongly with her various ethnic lineages. But significantly, Kate comes to sees herself as someone who can integrate different cultures precisely because she is American. While she is in the throes of yagé-induced nausea, she reflects:

> I am an American, Kate thought. Indigenous to the Americas. Nowhere else could I, this so-called black person—African, European, Indio—exist. Only here. In Africa there would have been no Europeans, no Native Americans. In Europe, no Africans and no Indians. Only here; *only here,* she said, as the waves of vomiting continued past the three hours and into the evening. I will bear this as long as it takes. This old medicine surely must care for, belong to, me. (53, emphasis in original)

Walker scholar Maria Lauret reads this passage as a nod to the mythos of the US as a uniquely diverse nation of immigrants, even as the novel recognizes many of the problems in American history (203). And yet, in the context of this passage, Kate uses the term *American* in a broader sense than the common usage. Here *American* does not mean "of the United States" but rather "Indigenous to the *Americas*" (emphasis added), a term that encompasses all of North and South America. Kate identifies, then, with the entire New World.

This passage justifies the practice of a particular religious discipline—in this case, the Amerindian use of yagé to connect with the Grandmother spirit—by appealing to an ancestral connection to the tradition's custodians. Because Kate is "Indigenous to the Americas," the Amerindian spiritual path she chooses naturally "belong[s] to [her]." By implication, Kate's sense of spiritual belonging gives her a culturally rooted satisfaction that Buddhism does not, since Kate is not Asian. While Kate's sense of heritage covers a vast territory, her affirmation of her multicultural identity is just as significant for its tacit disavowal of Buddhism as a major presence in her spiritual life. By celebrating her multiethnic identity but leaving an alien Buddhism behind, Kate defines herself as multicultural without being cosmopolitan. Ethnic kinship, not philosophical affinity alone, becomes a criterion for spiritual pursuits.

But while the novel emphasizes contrasts between Buddhism and Amerindian traditions, there are hints of commonality as well. Similar to introspective Buddhist meditation, the Amazon retreat, according to its teacher, will place its participants in "connection with our interior world" (Walker 143). In addition, even though Kate has stepped away from Buddhist practice, she still thinks of her Amazon retreat as the pursuit of "enlightenment" (51), the dominant English translation for the Sanskrit *bodhi*, the release from suffering that is Buddhism's ultimate goal (McMahan 18). Kate's experiences with psychedelics also remind her of Ram Dass (88, 209), also known as Richard Alpert, a countercultural teacher who helped popularize countercultural versions of Asian religions in the 1960s. (Ram Dass, using the name Richard Alpert, famously coauthored with Timothy Leary and Ralph Mentzer the seminal work *The Psychedelic Experience: A Manual Based on the Tibetan Book of the Dead* [1964].) It is also worth mentioning that although Walker does not directly cite Allen Ginsberg, Ginsberg combined his interest in Buddhism with South American psychedelics decades before Walker did, as recorded in *The Yage Letters* (1975), which Ginsberg coauthored with William Burroughs. In any case, the fleeting connections Kate draws during her retreat foreshadow a more complete synthesis between Asian and Amerindian faiths that occurs after the retreat ends.

After Kate returns to the US, a vivid dream catalyzes her experiences into a conscious integration of Buddhism and Amerindian religion. The connections that remain hidden in *The Color Purple* thus become explicit here. In this dream, Kate hears a sermon from the ancestral Grandmother spirit she learned about during the Amazon retreat. Whereas Grandmother seemed at first to be an alternative to sterile Buddhism, here, no less an authority than Grandmother herself declares the value of Buddhism. Grandmother admonishes Kate not to throw out the Buddha with the bathwater. She instructs, "*You don't understand about Buddha.... He would not mock those who take up arms against their own enslavement. Sometimes there is no way, except through violence, to freedom*" (196–97, italics in original). This is a direct rebuttal of Kate's previous Buddhist teacher, who condescendingly denounces all revolutionary violence. But Grandmother does not say, "White people don't understand about Buddha." She puts the onus on Kate; it is *she* who does not understand. This chastisement paves the way for Kate's reconciliation with Buddhism. The problem, the novel suggests, is that Kate tried to learn Buddhism from someone who does not understand the suffering of oppressed people around the world. Only by rediscovering Buddhism through the spirits of her own ancestors can Kate recover a positive Buddhist spiritual practice.

To accomplish this goal, Grandmother uses nature imagery to unite Buddhist and Amerindian traditions:

> *When Buddha sat under the bodhi tree, he was sitting under Me. He was sitting under Me, she repeated, as tree. And he was sitting on Me as grass.*
>
> *When you drink yagé, you complain about how bad it tastes. It tastes bad because you have killed it in order to have it. This is not necessary. For the Buddha, it was not necessary. Sitting under Me and on Me, he received the medicina.... This is possible, receiving the* medicina *this way, if you open your heart.* (197, italics in original)

Here, Grandmother proclaims the kinship of Buddhism and *medicina* as vehicles to spiritual insight. She even suggests Buddhism's advantages over the Amerindian path, saying that Buddhist meditation provides the same benefits of medicina without the plant-killing or the unpleasant taste. Grandmother thus characterizes the Amerindian yagé path as spiritual shock therapy, a remedial course on the way back to Buddhism. But in order for this return to Buddhism to work, Kate must avoid the pitfalls of what she experienced before. Grandmother warns that, for most people, spiritual retreat is not an option, because "the moment they try to open their hearts, . . . the powers that be rush to implant a religion, generally foreign to their natures, into them" (197). This reference to Walker's critique of Christianity, and her larger project of ancestral spiritual recovery, challenges Kate to rediscover a Buddhist practice that is not "foreign to [her] [nature]." Even though Buddhism is geographically distant from Kate's ethnic roots, the imagery in the above passage puts Grandmother and the Buddha in same place, suggesting that Kate should think of the Buddha as coming from the same ancestral culture as Grandmother.

Like Shug's description of God in *The Color Purple*, Grandmother's teaching contains liturgical elements. Grandmother offers a series of points and counterpoints, balancing spiritual affirmations with warnings against violence: "*How precious it is to have a human life to live! How sad to waste it in something so grim and blurry [as violence]. A thought can be like a gun; it can slay the enemy. Music can be like a sword; it can pierce the heart of the enemy*" (197, italics in original). These repetitive, poetic analogies read like a prayer for training the mind to avoid violent thoughts, as these can poison even normally benign activities. Also, after explaining that the physical medicina is not necessary for spiritual insight, Grandmother asserts, "That is why people take the time to learn how to do that; open the heart. That is why they go on retreat. That is why they learn to meditate" (197). This anaphora gives a repetitive, rhythmic call to regular, diligent spiritual practice. At the novel's end, Kate's return to Buddhism and to her estranged boyfriend demonstrate that she has, in fact, "opened her heart" to spiritual and romantic commitment. The fact that Kate has this dream without the aid of yagé indicates that she can now "*[receive] the* medicina" without chemical aids. In addition, Grandmother's remarks about the struggles of "*the very poor*" suggest that opening one's heart is not only for personal healing but is also necessary for social change on a larger scale. This is a powerful enactment of enlightened individualism that includes both a sense of a personal right to pursue happiness—Kate's healing is largely individual—and the social and community bonds through which one pursues broader justice for oppressed groups, all within a framework of Asian religions and nonduality.

Kate's nature-infused return to Buddhism gives new meaning to the description of the Buddhist teacher in the novel's first scene. The Buddhist teacher has "a shining bald head.... Every once in a while he reached up and stroked the silver earring in his left ear.... Because of the earring and because he seemed spotless in his flowing robes, she mentally dubbed him Mr. Clean" (4). This description casts the teacher as immaculate—"shining," "silver," and "spotless"—and lofty, emphasizing his "head" and his upward reach to his earring. He is haughty, distant from the earth, bereft of vivid color, and out of touch with the worldly experience of impoverished masses. He represents the fantasy of a disembodied mind that arrogantly judges the world from a sterile remove.

By contrast, Kate's yagé-induced visions approach Buddhism from the earth, emphasizing the ground which the Buddha touches and sits on, as well as his position under the bodhi tree. This Earth-centered imagery teaches Kate to re-approach Buddhism from the lowly ground, not from the lofty position of the complacent teacher's "shining bald head" (4). Also, near the novel's end, Kate dreams that a snake, a creature demonized in Christianity but venerated as close to the earth in Amerindian lore, tells her that the Buddha is *"in alignment"* with Amerindian teachings on "[making] friends" with one's fears (211, italics in original). The snake "[smiles] benignly, like Mr. Clean from the Buddhist retreat she'd left an eternity ago" (211). This reference to the teacher who alienates Kate from Buddhism shows how far Kate has come. Whereas she reacts with distaste to the teacher before, she can now appreciate his good qualities, seeing him in the snake without resentment. This change in perspective allows Kate to rebuild her altar, return to the lover she left to go on her retreat, and have an informal wedding-like reception feast with friends who fly in from around the world. The novel ends with Kate placing an anaconda clock on her altar in the Buddha's lap, symbolizing the harmony of Amerindian and Buddhist spirituality, a synthesis that spans cultures and continents.

The deliberateness of the novel's transnationalism is further reflected in its acknowledgments. These encapsulate the differences in identifying influences between *Now Is the Time to Open Your Heart* and *The Color Purple*. Walker dedicates *The Color Purple* "To the Spirit, / Without whose assistance / Neither this book / Nor I / Would have been / Written." The label "Spirit" is general enough to encompass the novel's African, Native American, and Asian influences without specifically highlighting any one of them. By contrast, Walker begins *Now Is the Time* by thanking *"all devas, angels, and bodhisattvas who accompany, watch over, and protect explorers, pioneers, and artists"* (italics in original). Instead of using one all-encompassing spiritual term, here Walker deploys multiple specific terms for venerated beings in Judaism and Christianity ("angels") and Buddhism ("devas" and "bodhisattvas"; see McMahan 66 and Seager 24, respectively). Here, Walker's religious terminology emphasizes cultural differences rather than overlooking them. This perspective arises from Walker's evolving dedication to specific religious disciplines. At a Spirit Rock retreat in 2002, Walker emphasizes how important it is for people to have a spiritual "practice." She exhorts that "whatever it [the practice] is, now is the time to look for it, to locate it, *definitely*, and to put it to use" (Walker, *We Are the Ones* 110, emphasis in original). In this context, to "locate" a practice is not only to select one but to know where it comes from.

By bringing Buddhist and Amerindian paths together in *Now Is the Time*, Walker narrates a more nuanced, ethnographically detailed negotiation between traditions than she offers in *The Color Purple*. Nevertheless, both novels emphasize the primacy of finding spirituality that is related to one's own ethnic roots, even as Walker's sense of what that means broadens over time. Celie's, Nettie's, and Kate's spiritual journeys succeed because Asian religion is mediated through contact with an ancestral culture. Many scholars have criticized such appeals to ethnic authenticity on the grounds that they promote an essentialist and oversimplified view of a singular origin (Favor, Hall, Levin). But critics also acknowledge that many ethnic and diasporic communities derive strength, identity, and dignity from an affective connection to an ancient tradition, effectively reclaiming dignity that long histories of oppression have sought to take away (B. Bell, Hall, Spivak).

Walking a fine line in this debate, Walker wants to teach her readers to go beyond one's own culture *through* one's own culture. Finding spiritual solace in one's ancestors—however loosely defined—opens up ways of relating to sacred paths from elsewhere. Thus Walker envisions how one can reach across cultures for transcendence while still catering to the demands of culturally authenticity. For example, while Kate sees herself as an "American," this train of thought ultimately leads to a sense of transcendence that goes beyond the Americas to an ultimate spiritual reality that encompasses all things. This process underlies Walker's 2006 exhortation to "understand oneself as an earthling, not an American, Canadian, African, or Indian" (Walker, "Conversation with David Swick" 306). The benefit of Walker's approach is that it loosens the demands of authenticity to overcome skepticism toward cross-cultural spiritualities. But it also risks substituting one essentialist myth of origins for another, more appropriative version, without critically analyzing the concept of ancestry.

We can thus see a change in how Walker deals with channeling Asian wisdom to African Americans. An allegory of literal ancestry in her earlier work gives way to overt recognition of Asian traditions in her later work. The reader can see an evolving sense that literal ancestry is less important, although one's ethnic group remains an indispensable reference point when engaging with

Asian religions. Whether discussing African origins or African American solidarity, Walker emphasizes ethnic identity to convey her view of Asian religions' relevance for African Americans. Her literary project thus constitutes a groundbreaking effort to make Asian nonduality a tool for improving America as a multiethnic society, and *Now Is the Time* is therefore a significant formation of what I have called *enlightened individualism*.

JOHNSON'S ASIAN RECONCILIATION

Whereas few critics have discussed Walker's Asian influences, Charles Johnson has already inspired voluminous scholarship on his debts to Asian thought (Byrd; Little, *Imagination*; Nash, *Fiction*; Selzer, *Context*; Storhoff). But by discussing Johnson alongside Walker, a juxtaposition that no critic has made, I will make the relationship between these two writers' commitment to both Asian religion and African American culture clearer. Existing analyses tend to say that Walker's writing emphasizes race (Lister vii; Selzer, "Race and Domesticity" 2; Tapia 29), whereas Johnson is eager to transcend race and all forms of dualism (Little, *Imagination* 136; Nash, *Fiction* 132; Conner 58–59). But both authors are engaged in projects more similar than these divergent accounts suggest. Just as Walker finds it important for ancestral cultures to mediate initially foreign religions to contemporary ethnic contexts, Johnson's novels strive to give Asian religions an African or African American pedigree.

For all these crucial similarities, though, Walker and Johnson relate quite differently to Christianity. Whereas Walker offers Asian religions as a liberating alternative to Christianity, Johnson presents them as complements to Christianity. Walker critiques what she views as the imposed, white male God of Christianity, which she sees as an illegitimate object of veneration for African Americans. By contrast, Johnson focuses on the positive role of the black church in the Civil Rights movement, predicting that Christianity "will continue to be the dominant spiritual orientation of black Americans" ("Sangha" 48). Johnson approves of African American Christianity's "compelling and time-tested moral vision" even though he doesn't fully agree with its "dualistic" view of "good and evil" (48–49). The example of Christianity suggests that Johnson tends to see more good in certain mainstream facets of US American identity than Walker does. This observation can begin to explain why Johnson is friendlier to Christianity than Walker and why Johnson does not seem to share Walker's deep interest in present-day Africa. Accordingly, Johnson is much more explicit than Walker in connecting Asian religions to political traditions of American liberalism, especially, as I will show, in Johnson's treatment of Martin Luther King in *Dreamer* (1998).

To understand Johnson's unique connections between Asian nonduality and American activism, it helps to consider how Johnson's intellectual development shows a curious commitment both to specific forms of social progress *and* to resisting any single school of thought. Johnson is not as connected to countercultural spiritualities as Walker; he has not directly mentioned Beat or hippie adaptations of Asian religions. But Johnson did come of age engaging with countercultures during their late-1960s peak, especially various forms of Black Nationalism. Although there is much more to say about this subject, for my purposes here I will simply mention that while the Black Power movement of the 1960s and early 1970s did not share the Beats' or hippies' interest in Buddhism and Hinduism, it was still countercultural in its rejection of mainstream conformity and valorization of the marginalized (Roszak 44–45). Johnson was sympathetic to the cultural pride of the related Black Arts movement, as reflected in his admiration for Amiri Baraka (Little, "Comic Book" 581–82). But Johnson's early work as a political cartoonist shows an irreverent desire to undermine any fixed or extreme position, including that of the Black Power movement (588). Seen in this light, Johnson's blossoming interest in Asian religions in the 1970s (596) comes across as a way of transcending countercultures and mainstream cultures alike, thus furthering his project of undercutting all orthodoxies, rather than carrying on a specifically countercultural legacy. But as I will show, unlike Salinger or Pirsig, Johnson's interest in transcending cultural divides has led him toward, not away from, social and political engagement.

Making his shift toward Asian paths even stronger, Johnson considered himself fully a Buddhist in 1981 after finishing his second novel, *Oxherding Tale* (McWilliams xxx). By calling himself a Buddhist, Johnson has shown himself to be more willing than Walker to declare a religious affiliation, but Johnson has also resisted identifying with a specific school in Buddhism. Although he was officially registered with a Rinzai Zen temple in Japan as of 2003, Johnson has declared a "shamelessly nonsectarian" orientation (*Turning the Wheel* xviii), having had many Buddhist teachers from different schools without identifying strongly with any of them (Whalen-Bridge, "Shoulder" 308). The common thread behind Johnson's Buddhist path is his focus on Buddhism's psychological analyses of the human mind, analyses that intersect with his philosophical training as a phenomenologist (Nash, "Conversation" 214). He treats Buddhism not as a set of beliefs but as a philosophical and spiritual method for undermining fixed ideologies.

For most of his career, Johnson's writing has not called attention to his Buddhist practice. Asian religions—Hinduism as well as Buddhism—are a driving force in his novels, but they are expressed primarily in the novels' form rather than their exposition. And although Johnson discusses Buddhist philosophy a great deal in interviews, he has only briefly alluded to the fact that he is a Buddhist. More recently, that changed. After his 1998 novel *Dreamer*, Johnson said that he had entered a new phase in his career in which he wants to devote himself publicly to Buddhism, especially through his essays (Whalen-Bridge, "Shoulder" 300). Five years after the publication of *Dreamer*, Johnson's essay collection *Turning the Wheel: Essays on Buddhism and Writing* made this emerging project even more explicit. In a key essay from this collection, "A Sangha by Another Name," Johnson boldly argues that Buddhism's emphasis on nonduality is the best antidote to racism, concluding that "through the Dharma, the black American quest for 'freedom' realizes its profoundest, truest, and most revolutionary meaning" (57). This is an especially direct declaration of enlightened individualism that we see expressed and developed in various ways in much of Johnson's work. By examining *Middle Passage* and *Dreamer*, we see how Johnson makes this case in narrative form. First, I show how *Middle Passage* imagines a Hindu-like religion originating from an African tribe, much like Walker's *The Color Purple*. Then I turn to *Dreamer*, whose primary conveyor of Asian wisdom to America is, surprisingly, the Reverend Dr. Martin Luther King Jr.

MIDDLE PASSAGE'S NONDUAL ANCESTORS

Middle Passage is the tale of the spiritual education of Rutherford Calhoun, a freedman living in the antebellum US. From the novel's beginning, Johnson tailors Rutherford's vices to a Buddhist corrective. According to the second of Buddhism's four noble truths, suffering arises from attachment to self, phenomena, and experiences (Rahula 29–30). Rutherford is a textbook case: "I hungered—literally *hungered*—for life in all its shades and hues: I was hooked on sensation, you might say, a lecher for perception and the nerve-knocking thrill, like a shot of opium, of new experiences" (Johnson, *Middle Passage* 3, emphasis in original). Rutherford is selfish, and his thieving and womanizing prevent him from developing trust-based relationships with others; indeed, he stows away on a slave ship to avoid marriage. But by interacting with the Allmuseri tribespeople whom the crew enslaves, Rutherford arrives at a boundary-shattering epiphany that destroys his grief-sustaining belief in the division between subject and object.

Through the Allmuseri, Johnson gives Rutherford access to Asian wisdom from an African source. That is, Johnson gives the Allmuseri a religion whose central tenets developed and coalesced in Asia, not Africa. Rutherford summarizes for the reader what he has learned by talking to and observing the Allmuseri. As in both Buddhism and Hinduism, the Allmuseri have a nondual metaphysic: "The failure to experience the unity of Being everywhere was the Allmuseri vision of Hell. And that was where we lived: purgatory. That was where we were taking them—into the madness of multiplicity—and the thought of it drove them wild" (65). In this view, slavery is a manifestation of the false belief in differentiation between self and other. Also, the Allmuseri take karma and rebirth seriously: "No word was uttered or deed executed that did not echo throughout the universe. Seeds, they were, that would flower into other deeds—good and evil—in no time at all. For a people with their values, murder violated (even mutilated) the murderer so badly that it might well take them a billion billion rebirths to again climb the chain and achieve human form" (140). Along the same lines, the Allmuseri share with Buddhists and Hindus the belief that external reality is the creation of one's own mind, making "each man utterly responsible for his own happiness and sorrow" (164). The conjunction of monism, karma, rebirth, and the primacy of mind over matter clearly mark the Allmuseri religion as philosophically Asian.

Critics have previously observed that the Allmuseri embody a kind of recognizably Asian wisdom, but these critics have not sufficiently explored the cultural implications of this grafting (Little 142, Storhoff 174–75). Johnson's move advances his project, shared with Alice Walker, of making black Buddhists seem less strange by imbuing Buddhism, or something like it, with an African ancestral pedigree. But although both Johnson and Walker invent fictional tribes for *Middle Passage* and *The Color Purple,* respectively, Johnson's creative license is greater. Unlike Johnson, Walker has spent time in Africa (White 110–11). Not coincidentally, then, Walker's Olinka do not have any obviously non-African characteristics. Although Nettie arrives at a philosophically "Eastern" perspective from her contact with the Olinka, the Olinka themselves do not profess any distinctively Asian doctrines. By contrast, Johnson freely grafts Asian religion onto his African creation. This bold displacement simultaneously appeals to African nativism and highlights Buddhism's relevance to everyone, regardless of genetic ancestry. Johnson's Allmuseri are more than a tribe of people: They are embodiments of spiritual transcendence.

The Allmuseri, paradoxically, are both particular and universal. They bear cultural particulars of places and names. But their being symbolizes the idyllic origins of all of humanity, as Rutherford's description suggests: "Their palms were blank, bearing no lines. No fingerprints. . . . They might have been the *Ur*-tribe of humanity itself. I'd never seen anyone like them. Or felt such antiquity in the presence of others; a clan of *Sphaeriker.* Indeed, what I felt was the presence of countless others *in* them, a crowd spun from everything this vast continent contained" (Johnson, *Middle Passage* 61, original italics). If fingerprints mark individuality, then the lack of fingerprints symbolizes a lack of differentiation, indicating that the Allmuseri are wise parents of humanity who are more in touch with primordial reality than other, less mature peoples. Rutherford's remark that the Allmuseri "might have been the Ur-tribe of humanity itself" resonates with the current prevailing theory that the human species originated in Africa, thus making Africans everyone's ancestors. Walker raises a similar point in a dharma talk, reminding her audience that because humans came out of Africa, one may think of African heritage not only for African Americans but for everyone (Walker, *We Are the Ones* 119). Johnson takes this idea further, eventually revealing the Allmuseri to be a blend of tribes from around the world. We learn that the Allmuseri are a seafaring people who took influences from India, Central America, and even Europe (Johnson, *Middle Passage* 76–77, 65). In short, the Allmuseri are everyone's ancestors, but also everyone's contemporaries.

Despite this evidence of shared ancestry, Rutherford initially has difficulty relating to the Allmuseri. He has enough of a conscience to admire the Allmuseri's noble qualities but not enough to believe that these qualities are his to inherit. He laments, "I wanted their ageless culture to be my own. . . . But who was I fooling?" (78). But as his knowledge of the Allmuseri increases, Rutherford realizes that "the Allmuseri seemed less a biological tribe than a clan held together by values" (109). He reflects that his brother, a Christian pastor devoted to charity, "might well have been one of their priests" (109). This shift from "biological" considerations to "values" sets up Rutherford's ability to learn from the Allmuseri.

Rutherford's move away from genetic determinism also helps him realize that the Allmuseri are not "ageless" (78) but change as others do. As Rutherford watches the Allmuseri grow increasingly despondent from their enslavement, Rutherford realizes that they are not a "timeless product" but "were process and Heraclitean change, like any men" (124). Furthermore, the "emptiness" Rutherford sees in tribesman Ngonyama's eyes is not simply the emptiness of loss but emptiness in the Buddhist sense of lacking of a fixed essence: Change is possible. If Rutherford and his shipmates "had changed them" (124), then by implication the Allmuseri might conversely change him. Rutherford initially thinks of the Allmuseri as living saints who "fell *sick*, it was said, if they wronged anyone" (78, emphasis in original). This naive view is discredited when the Allmuseri mutiny and kill most of the crew, even as they accept the karmic gravity of their actions, wondering whether their chance at freedom is worth the spiritual cost of their violence (140–41). Rutherford's growing awareness of change and emptiness is a crucial part of his maturation.

Overcoming ethnic essentialism makes Rutherford more capable of adopting the Allmuseri's good qualities.

Rutherford's increasing receptivity to others begins without his realizing it. When an Allmuseri carves meat so skillfully that he "leaves no knife tracks" (76), one observer insists this feat must be a "trick" of "mirrors" (76). This offhanded remark actually presages Rutherford's ability to see his reflection, both literally and figuratively, in the Allmuseri. Here, Rutherford compares the Allmuseri's meat carving to his own skill as a lock-picker (76). Soon afterward, Rutherford gives some of his food to an Allmuseri girl after "her eyes burned a hole in my forehead" (78). For the first time, Rutherford feels penetrated by someone else's gaze, hinting at the erosion of Rutherford's solid sense of self. Also, whereas Rutherford previously could not see himself as an Allmuseri (78), he later sees his reflection in an Allmuseri's eyes and realizes that they both are "remade by virtue of [their] contact with the crew" (124). Later, Rutherford encounters an Allmuseri God kept in a cage in the cargo hull, and he intuits that the God's name is Rutherford (171). This series of face-to-face moments progresses from mundane—the Allmuseri's carving skill is like Rutherford's thieving skill—to transformative: The God as Rutherford signals an underlying divinity that transcends the apparent separation between beings.

As everyone onboard faces increasing threats from storms, navigational errors, disease, and insurrection, Rutherford reassures them of their safe return, in what he calls a "useful fiction" (162). Gary Storhoff reads this phrase allegorically, stating that the novel reimagines American history overall as "useful fiction" that can inspire positive change (150–51). In fact, the novel's primary "useful fiction" is the Allmuseri themselves. Through this fictional tribe, Johnson joins Asian religions to the origins both of Africans and of humanity in general. By locating Asian religions in Africa, Johnson's "useful fiction" is that Asian philosophy's origins are black. This move seeks to make black practitioners of Asian religions seem less strange, both inside and outside of African American communities. But by also emphasizing the Allmuseri's status as "the Ur-tribe of all humanity" (Johnson, *Middle Passage* 65), Johnson positions the tenets of Asian religions as universal wisdom relevant to everyone.

This wisdom—centered on a belief in ultimate reality as undifferentiated—matures in Rutherford's mind through his performance of acts of kindness. As he comforts the ship's occupants, his heretofore occasional glimpses into nonduality coalesce into the following epiphany:

> In myself I found nothing I could rightly call Rutherford Calhoun, only pieces and fragments of all the people who had touched me, all the places I

had seen, all the homes I had broken into. The "I" that I was, was a mosaic of many countries, a patchwork of others and objects stretching backward to perhaps the beginning of time. What I felt, seeing this, was indebtedness. What I felt, plainly, was a transmission to those on deck of all I had pilfered, as though I was but a conduit or window through which my pillage and booty of "experience" passed. . . . Even I was the more peaceful as I went wearily back to help Cringle at the helm. (162–63)

Here Rutherford has a realization of Buddhist nonself and Hindu nonduality. Without Rutherford's realizing it, this epiphany fulfills his wish for the Allmuseri "culture to be my own" (78). Just as the Allmuseri bear "the presence of countless others *in* them" (61, original emphasis), Rutherford sees himself anew as "a patchwork of others." This feeling of "indebtedness" allows him to feel ancient legacies "stretching backward to perhaps the beginning of time," similar to the Allmuseri's reputation as "a remarkably *old* people" (61, original emphasis). Most important, Rutherford transcends dualism, the division of "the unity of Being," into self and nonself (65), by abandoning his habitual thoughts that separated himself from others. From this moment on, Rutherford is no longer a selfish "parasite" who is "hooked on sensation" (162, 3). His previous habitus had been a particularly pernicious version of a buffered self that has an inherent, independent existence. His new understanding replaces the buffered self, not with a reversion to a porous self within an enchanted cosmos, but with a field of profound interdependence that implies a transcendence of subject-object divisions. In this way, Rutherford remains generally within Charles Taylor's immanent frame while managing to disrupt one of its central elements, the buffered self.

During this epiphany, Rutherford's thought process also takes on characteristics of the Allmuseri language. Previously, he explained that "nouns or static substances hardly existed in their vocabulary at all" (Johnson, *Middle Passage* 77). In the same way, most of what Rutherford says that comprise his newly understood identity are actions, that is, verbs such as *touched, seen, broken*, and *passed*. Even the nouns Rutherford uses break down into processes, such as the "mosaic" that depends on the implicit act of stitching together. Furthermore, just as in the speech of the Allmuseri Ngonyama, "the objects and others he referred to flowed together like water" (77), Rutherford's long, flowing sentences embody a loss of static selfhood and a sense of identity with his surroundings. Rutherford uses a syntax of "indebtedness." This epiphany marks a point of no relapse that sets up Rutherford's happy ending. After he returns to shore, he embraces relationships and responsibilities rather than fleeing from them. He adopts an orphaned Allmuseri girl from the ship and agrees to marry Isadora, the woman whose marriage proposal drove him to sea in the first place.

Although *Middle Passage* presents an African culture with important non-African characteristics, Johnson is not simply flouting ethnography. Rather, the Allmuseri allegorize the relationship between enlightened wisdom and ignorant dualism as a temporal fall from grace. In other words, Johnson imagines a utopian past that existed before human beings developed destructive thought patterns. In this vision, the relationship between monistic and dualistic thought is not simply one of ideal versus real but also one of past versus present. Rutherford reflects that the Europeans who, according to Allmuseri lore, once belonged to the tribe, "fell . . . into the madness of multiplicity," the very place where, by enslaving them, "we were taking them" (65). Accordingly, the change Rutherford sees in the Allmuseri is ambivalent: "We had changed them . . . into what sort of men I could not imagine. . . . And of what were they now capable?" (124). Rutherford's nervousness implies that the Allmuseri, through their exposure to the violence of enslavement, may no longer be as reliably nonviolent as they once were. His fear is realized when the Allmuseri rebel, seize control of the ship, and are, in Rutherford's words, "fallen; now a part of the world of multiplicity, of *me* versus *thee*" (140, emphasis in original). In these descriptions, unity is the essential beginning; multiplicity, the contingent decline. Even though this vision is derived from Asian religions, Johnson allegorically locates this primordial beginning in Africa, the cradle of humanity.

MARTIN LUTHER KING JR. AS EASTERN SAGE IN *DREAMER*

Whereas *Middle Passage* is somewhat fantastic, *Dreamer* turns sharply toward realism by focusing on the Reverend Dr. Martin Luther King Jr., not a fictional mystical tribe, as the conveyor of Asian thought to African Americans. In *Dreamer*, Johnson's characterization of King mediates Asian wisdom to America through his enlightened activism. This is not to say that the novel ignores King's Christianity, but rather that Johnson uses King's status as a Christian figurehead as a platform for communicating Buddhist and Hindu messages. This idea is not without precedent. Various scholars have studied King's debt to Gandhian nonviolence as both a political tactic and a way of life (Mary King, T. Jackson, Nojeim). But Johnson takes King's Asian influences further than historical accounts by making concepts from Asian religions an important part of King's personal faith. This approach builds on Johnson's practice of assigning beliefs from Asian religions to African-descended mediating characters, and it is furthered to give his clearest dramatization of enlightened individualism.

In *Dreamer* King does not find realizations of emptiness and nonduality from within Christianity but gains them from his exposure to Indian religion. Johnson, portraying King's historical trip to India in 1959, describes how King comes to India "as a pilgrim" and feels "an ineffable peace, and had never felt so free" as he and his wife hear a Sanskrit chant in the distance (22). Much later, King wants to "probe deeper into their concept of Maya—the world as itself a cradle-to-crypt dream, in which all men were caught and only the blessed allowed to awaken" (224). As Gary Storhoff has noted, Johnson's Buddhification of King lends additional meanings to the novel's title. "*Dreamer*" most obviously refers to King's landmark "I Have a Dream" speech. But it also refers to the fact that, in Hinduism as well as Buddhism, the physical world is a dreamlike illusion (Storhoff 184). Furthermore, *Dreamer* imagines that Asian teachings rescue King in a moment of personal crisis, making his continued civil rights leadership possible. Thus, in this revision of history, Buddhist and Hindu ideas directly contribute to a liberal social activism that the historical King consistently connected to the Declaration of Independence.

In the novel, King's trip to India plants the seeds of profound realization that germinate only in America, where Eastern notions of ultimate nonduality come to life one night in King's kitchen. Marc Connor and William Nash recognize that Johnson rewrites King's famous kitchen experience in Buddhist terms, saying that this scene promotes "the amalgamation of various paths to spiritual, mental, and physical liberation" (xxiv). But their analysis treats Buddhism and Christianity like two colors of paint that blend equally in King. The scene is more complicated than that: In *Dreamer*, this "kitchen conversion" is the moment when King decisively brings Eastern wisdom to the US, and to African Americans in particular. Through King, Johnson does not simply blend Christianity and Buddhism: rather, he situates Christian *agape* within an overriding context of Buddhist emptiness. In his memoir *Stride Toward Freedom*, King remembers one night when his resolve to continue his public campaigns wavers, having been severely tested by violent threats. He pleads to God for help and receives a powerful answer:

> I got out of bed and began to walk the floor. Finally I went to the kitchen and heated a pot of coffee. I was ready to give up. With my cup of coffee sitting untouched before me I tried to think of a way to move out of the picture without appearing a coward. In this state of exhaustion, when my courage had all but gone, I decided to take my problem to God. With my head in my hands, I bowed over the kitchen table and prayed aloud. The words I spoke

to God that midnight are still vivid in my memory. "I am here taking a stand for what I believe is right. But now I am afraid. The people are looking for leadership, and if I stand before them without strength and courage, they too will falter. I am at the end of my powers. I have nothing left. I've come to the point where I can't face it alone."

At that moment I experienced the presence of the Divine as I had never experienced Him before. It seemed as though I could hear the quiet assurance of an inner voice saying: "Stand up for righteousness, stand up for truth, and God will be at your side forever." Almost at once my fears began to go. My uncertainty disappeared. I was ready to face anything. (134–35)

This experience, which King marked as a turning point in his career, is historically important but theologically unexceptional, appealing to standard Christian tropes of the believer's supplication and God's reassuring response. I say this not to belittle King's narrative or his devotion, but rather to highlight the contrast of Johnson's radical revision. In Johnson's version, instead of focusing on God, King has a Buddhist epiphany of nonduality. Again, I quote at length for comparison:

At last he began to pray. To whom—or what—he could not say. Not asking for anything then. Not fighting, only confessing, "Lord, I have nothing left . . ." His gaze drifted to the fragments of the cup that was no longer a cup. But where had the "cup" gone? His fist opened, disappearing into his hand. Where had his "fist" gone? Then it came quietly, unbidden. He was traveling light again, for the long, lurid dream of multiplicity and separateness, the very belief in an "I" that suffered and strained to affect the world, dissolved, and for the first time he felt like a dreamer gently roused from sleep and forgetfulness. Awake, he saw he was not the doer. How could he have ever believed otherwise? That which he'd thought practiced virtue, surrendered to vice, held degrees, opinions and elaborated theories, and traveled toward a goal was spun from a spiderweb of words, no more real than the cantels of the erstwhile cup before him. Later, he would tell reporters and his congregation the room was rayed with shadowless light, and the Lord said unto him, *Stand up for righteousness, stand up for the truth, and God will be at your side forever,* but in fact the light came from him—not without—and the *vox dei* he heard had been his own. *Not I,* he heard it whisper again in the suddenly transparent kitchen, but the father within me doeth the works. . . . *I seek not my will but the will of the Father who sent me.* (Johnson, *Dreamer* 82, original italics)

Johnson's rewrite downplays the Christian aspects of King's religious experience while adding Buddhist elements. In King's original, the coffee cup is just there, a mere prop that does not command his attention. But Johnson makes the cup an object of contemplation that leads to an experience of emptiness. By seeing the cup as "fragments that [were] no longer a cup," King realizes that the "cup" does not inherently exist but is a concept that the mind constructs. This train of thought soon extends to include himself; he too is empty of inherent existence, "no more real than the . . . cup."

As King's sense of self breaks down, the division between himself and God dissolves as well. Originally, King presupposes a separation between himself and God, humbling the former and praising the latter. When he has "nothing left" and "can't face it alone," God provides support as though He is a separate person. But in Johnson's version, King prays without an addressee, "to whom—or what—he could not say." Even though King then begins his prayer with "Lord," implying that he is talking to God, the preceding disclaimer suggests that the word has become perfunctory and the traditional Christian sense of God's separate coherence is breaking down. Then, in an act of remarkable boldness, Johnson quotes King in order to contradict him, insisting that God does not provide external support, but rather "the *vox dei* had been his own." There is an apparent contradiction in saying that the voice of divine truth is "his own" and that the self from which the voice issues is empty. This tension resolves in an Asian-derived belief in nonduality where there is no differentiation between the self, God, and external objects.

Johnson's style in this passage's reinforces the fictionalized King's realization. King's original version consists of relatively short sentences. But the sentences in Johnson's version grow progressively longer, paralleling King's expansion of consciousness. The run-on list of actions done by "that which he'd thought practiced virtue" conveys King's idea of selfhood dissolving. Like Rutherford's epiphany in *Middle Passage,* Johnson's sentences show his characters becoming open to everything by gently erasing the illusion of boundaries. In King's version, God helps him conquer fear. In Johnson's version, an epiphany of emptiness transcends fear. This realization empowers King to continue his campaigns and makes him a model from which the novel's other characters learn.

Furthermore, this passage once again portrays a transcendence of the buffered self through a Buddhist realization of nonself. In King's original version, God's voice and his deeply interior response to it preserve the buffered self. God does break in as from above, but He addresses King as an individual who receives the message and carries it forward. By contrast, Johnson's revision of King undoes the buffered self. But Johnson does not replace this buffered self with a premodern, porous self. Rather, the buffered self gives way to a Buddhist conception of phenomena as empty of selfhood and a Hindu sense of reality as ultimately undifferentiated.

Although King admired Gandhi as an ethicist and political strategist, there is no evidence that Gandhi's Hindu metaphysics superseded King's Christian convictions, as Johnson suggests they did. However, Johnson does not view his fictional King as any less Christian for his Buddhist realization. In a 2003 interview, he states, "I've always been a sincere Christian *and* a Buddhist. . . . There's no contradiction, at least not for the Buddhadharma, which emphasizes the interdependence of all things and avoids dualism" (McWilliams 296). Johnson's key phrase is "at least not for the Buddhadharma." Elsewhere, Johnson himself describes Christianity as "metaphysically dualistic," in direct contrast to Buddhism ("Sangha" 49). Therefore, to assert that there is no contradiction between Buddhism and Christianity is to already privilege Buddhism over Christianity. One may draw parallels between the two faiths, but that does not mean that they are fundamentally reconcilable. Accordingly, Johnson's Buddhist revision of King must negate King's Christian convictions, a fact that challenges Johnson's characterization of King and his attempted Christian-Buddhist synthesis more broadly. Of course, *Dreamer* is fiction, not biography, so the charge of "misrepresentation" does not straightforwardly apply here. But Johnson's creative license prompts readers to ask what factual duties a writer has in fictional portrayals of historical figures.

KING'S FRAUGHT COUNTERPART

King's main foil in *Dreamer* is Chaym Smith, a man who looks like King and has a prodigious intellect but struggles with poverty, addiction, and bitterness toward those more prosperous than he himself. In contrast to King's cogent application of Asian wisdom to American politics, *Dreamer* presents Chaym as an example of the problems of failing to connect Asian religions with liberal projects of American social progress. Only later, after much suffering and introspection, does Chaym learn to imitate King's mediation of Asian wisdom to the US through activism, thus further dramatizing the novel's emphasis on the importance of this cross-cultural adaptation. The novel's plot gains momentum when Chaym asks to be King's body double. King reluctantly agrees, and Chaym undertakes intensive theological study in case an overscheduled King needs Chaym to speak in his place. But Chaym's motivations are not to help the nonviolent movement; rather, he selfishly wishes to prove his talent as equal to King's: "I can do anything *he* does. Just watch me—and I'll fucking do it better" (112).

Both Chaym and King have spent time in Asia and learned from its faiths, but whereas King brings these philosophies to bear on black uplift in America, Chaym fails to deploy his Eastern religious training. In fact, Chaym is far more highly trained in formal Buddhist practice than King, having spent a year in a Japanese Zen temple, but King's historical consciousness makes his realizations superior in spite of his lesser knowledge of Buddhism. Chaym's term as a novice at the *Zendo* is naive escapism, not engaged insight; he recounts that "the world that hurt me so bad didn't exist no more, and I was happy" (98). But although his practice is "correct" (99), Chaym passively does what he is told rather than cultivating compassion for others. His enjoyable time abruptly ends when the head of the temple expels him on the racist grounds that "only a Japanese can experience true enlightenment" (99). Once this peaceful refuge exposes itself as tainted by racism, Chaym is devastated, and his life rapidly deteriorates. Chaym continues to collect and recite scriptures, drawing from many traditions (58–59, 95–96, 153–54), and he demonstrates formidable concentration and memorization. But his private recitations do not alleviate his problems, nor do they motivate him to serve others.

Because Chaym does not connect Asian wisdom to his cultural position as an African American, he becomes bitter when he talks about Buddhist philosophy. He defends his ability to stand in for King by saying, "Everybody's playing a role anyway, trying to act like what they're supposed to be, wearing at least one mask, probably more, and there's nothing underneath, Bishop. Just emptiness" (86). In Buddhism the notion that our personalities are habitual constructions points to the possibility of a blissful liberation from self-clinging. But Chaym sours this doctrine into a sardonic diagnosis of universal insincerity. Similarly, when supporting character Amy tries to persuade Chaym to join King's movement, he calls her inspirational family

> a fucking lie. All narratives are lies, man, an illusion. . . . As soon as you squeeze experience into a sentence—or a story—it's suspect. . . . If you want to be free, you best go beyond all that.
>
> To *what*?
>
> That's what I'm trying to figure out. (93)

In Buddhism the idea that narratives are illusory does not foreclose their use; rather, it points the way to the transcendence of time. Chaym reduces this idea to the cynical formulation that all stories are lies. And his follow-up shows that he does not know what, by contrast, could be true. Chaym's personal despair leads him to resign himself to social injustice, even suggesting that blacks deserve their second-class status in mid-twentieth-century America (65–66).

But eventually Chaym undergoes a redemptive transformation. His Buddhist training finally comes to life through his contact with African American struggle and culture. One night an angry man shoots Chaym, thinking he is King. As scholar of Buddhist American literature John Whalen-Bridge has noted, this is a turning point after which Chaym loses his bitter edge ("Waking Cain" 513–14). Chaym's unintentional act of sacrifice—in effect, taking a bullet for King—humbles him; he does not brag about his survival and no longer speaks in tirades (Johnson, *Dreamer* 153). This event, a chastening wake-up call that shocks Chaym out of his cynicism and alienation, marks the beginning of his participation in the Civil Rights movement. Soon thereafter, Chaym takes on a job doing restoration work at a church in southern Illinois. As Johnson scholar Rudolph Byrd deftly explains, this labor helps make Chaym a part of something larger than himself, connecting him to a web of history manifest in the building's capacious blend of old and new features (Byrd 181–82). But although Byrd sees continuity between Chaym's church service and his time at the Zendo, the church's inclusive architecture actually contrasts with the temple's noninclusive rigidity. The church is "a layering of lives and architectural styles based not on the principle of either/or but of adding this to that" (Johnson, *Dreamer* 179). In contrast, the temple is coldly sparse and clean, with "wooden floors polished so brightly by hand that they almost gleamed" (97). The temple's scrupulous cleanness is a symbol for its misguided emphasis on racial purity, which leads to Chaym's eventual exclusion. With these descriptions, *Dreamer* inverts conventional judgments of tidiness as superior to messiness.

The contrast between the Zendo and the church shows that Chaym gains greater spiritual realizations from the latter than the former. In effect, Chaym realizes the Buddhist wisdom of interdependence through an African American Christian context. In his recollections of his time at the temple, Chaym seems to have experienced a realization of nonself, reporting that "I wasn't even aware of an *I*" (98). But this apparent liberation from selfhood endures only while the pressures that make him feel self-conscious are absent; Chaym has not actually changed the patterns of thinking that tend toward egotism. The fragility of his freedom exposes itself when a crisis—his racist expulsion—shatters his realization.

Because Chaym's redemptive work takes place in a church, his character development seems at first to suggest a synthesis of Christianity and Buddhism. Indeed, after his gunshot injury, Chaym spends much of his time studying both Western and Eastern texts ranging from the Pentateuch to the Lotus Sutra (154). However, his transformation remains grounded in Asian philosophy. Chaym's post-gunshot notebooks are filled with transcriptions of Buddhist verses about "Enlightenment" (210). Also, according to the narrator, Matthew Bishop, Chaym's recent paintings show that "the play of colors . . . did not exist . . . outside the miracle of consciousness" (209). Matthew's interpretation is consistent with Chaym's religious training and reiterates the Buddhist and Hindu belief that phenomena are illusory projections of one's own mind.

After Chaym has worked at the church, his newfound humility and selflessness hold up even in the midst of new turmoil. The FBI blackmails Chaym into helping their efforts to sabotage King's reputation. Chaym does not say what the agents who approach him want him to do, and the novel does not make it clear whether Chaym complies or not. Shortly before Chaym disappears permanently, he meets with one of King's assistants one last time in the church and hands him a signed Commitment Blank, a promise to carry out the nonviolent ideals of the Civil Rights movement as defined by King (213). By signing the pledge he had previously rejected, Chaym aligns himself with King's application of spiritual values to social activism. Also, by asking the assistant to pray for him when he lacks the conviction to pray for himself (213), Chaym shows that in a moment of crisis he turns tentatively toward religion, not away from it as he did before. Here Chaym imitates King's mediation of Eastern wisdom to the West by making it come alive in his works.

Thus *Dreamer* suggests that one becomes enlightened not by moving to Asia permanently, but by making a pilgrimage there and then returning to improve the place of one's upbringing. For Johnson, the most highly realized people are not necessarily those whose culture invented Buddhism. And yet *Dreamer* briefly revives *Middle Passage*'s trope of ethnic descent by revealing near the end that Chaym is an Allmuseri. He is a descendant of Bakela Calhoun, the Allmuseri girl Rutherford adopts at the end of *Middle Passage* (205). If the Allmuseri fall into the delusion of dualism in *Middle Passage*, they continue to decline in both moral uprightness and numbers through generations, until Chaym is "the last of his line" (205). Why would Johnson give Chaym this ethnic pedigree when *Dreamer* is for the most part less invested than *Middle Passage* in treating Asian religion as African? The thoughts of Johnson's King help answer this question. King's great hope is that "the children of masters and slaves might realize that Race was an illusion, all children were literally—genetically—their own, and embrace one another as members of a single tribe" (84). Although King does not know it, this tribe is the Allmuseri. Because *Middle Passage* figures the Allmuseri as both a distinct tribe and the universal ancestors of humanity's spiritual potential, Chaym's distinction as an Allmuseri—and his spiritual development along implicitly Allmuseri lines—underlines, rather than undermines, the universal spiritual potential of all human beings.

More recently, Johnson has continued to connect King's ideals of equality to a Buddhist critique of race, particularly in relation to the political rise of Barack Obama. Shortly before Obama won the presidency in 2008, Johnson wrote an essay in the Buddhist magazine *Shambhala Sun* titled "The Meaning of Barack Obama." Johnson views Obama's career, as many have, as a realization of King's hope: "Whatever meaning we find is based on our deeds, our actions, and, as Martin Luther King Jr. once said, 'the content of our character.'" Johnson explicitly connects Obama's appeal as a "post-racial" politician to Asian notions of emptiness, asserting that "race is *maya*," a Sanskrit word for the illusion of "dualism." Obama's success, Johnson asserts, shows that "true excellence is colorblind." By linking Asian metaphysics with liberal colorblindness, Johnson inserts American Buddhism into contemporary critical debates about race. Although he does not name names, Johnson puts himself at odds with scholars such as W. J. T. Mitchell and Tim Wise. Citing reactions that declared Obama's election as a post-racial moment, Mitchell and Wise argue that the pursuit of colorblindness actually harms efforts to make racism visible (*Seeing Through Race, Colorblind*). Johnson thus lays the groundwork for Buddhism's entry into further discussions about the value and viability of colorblindness in the US. In Johnson's version of enlightened individualism, the putative individualism of colorblindness merges with the enlightenment of antiracist nonduality.

Chaym's Buddhist loss of bitterness speaks to these competing views of colorblindness as the reader struggles to determine whether Chaym's change of heart represents progress or passivity. Chaym learns selflessness and diligence but loses his ambitious edge. He practices patient support, not tireless activism. The novel's dark, ambiguous ending further demonstrates that Chaym's spiritual progress is not enough to stop racism's pressures on his life. King's reconfiguration as an implicit Buddhist, however, draws a clear connection between Asian realizations and political progress. The fact that Chaym's story ends before he fully solidifies his life's direction attests to how much more work there is to be done. But it does not undermine the notion, strongly suggested in *Dreamer*'s narrative, that American rights-based racial progress has a viable basis in Buddhist and Hindu doctrines of nonduality.

Chaym's transformation in *Dreamer* parallels Kate's in *Now Is the Time*. Neither character initially learns Asian religions from members of their own race, as Celie and Rutherford do. Instead, both characters learn from non-black teachers explicitly trained in Asian religions, and these teachers are out of touch with the unique challenges of people with marginalized identities. As a result of this disconnect, Chaym and Kate become disenchanted with their Buddhist practice. But they learn to see Asian traditions in a new light once they discover, with the help of more socially conscious mentors who share their African American identity, how Asian religions can speak to their own American minority status. In addition, the relationship between *Dreamer* and *Middle Passage* is similar to that between *Now Is the Time* and *The Color Purple*. Whereas *The Color Purple* and *Middle Passage* allegorically disguise Asian-inspired teachers as Africans, *Now Is the Time* and *Dreamer* explicitly acknowledge the Asian origins of these ideas.

We can thus see a change over time in how Walker and Johnson deal with channeling Asian wisdom to African Americans. An allegory of literal ancestry in their earlier work gives way to overt recognition of Asian traditions in their later work. In these texts we see an evolving sense that literal ancestry is less important, although one's ethnic group remains an indispensable reference point when engaging with Asian religions. Whether they deal with African origins or African American solidarity, Walker and Johnson emphasize ethnic identity to convey their view of Buddhism's relevance for African Americans. Their literary projects are thus a groundbreaking effort to make Asian ideals of nonduality a tool for improving America as a multiethnic society in concert with Enlightenment notions of individual and human rights. For both Walker and Johnson, the liberating potential of Asian religions makes Buddhists and Hindus the "ancestors we didn't even know we had" for African Americans (Walker, *We Are the Ones* 109). This expression of enlightened individualism is a creative effort to imagine ways of being both culturally cosmopolitan and ethnically authentic.

CHAPTER 5

Buddhist Nonself and Asian American Identity

Lan Cao's Monkey Bridge *and*
Maxine Hong Kingston's The Fifth Book of Peace

THE STORY I have told so far about American literature's adaptations of Buddhism and Hinduism has focused on how non-Asian writers have adapted relatively foreign Asian religions to the US. This perspective may seem odd given that Asian immigrants have practiced Buddhism in the US since the mid-nineteenth century, and Hinduism since around 1900 (Fields 72–73, Kurien 41–43). But except for some noteworthy Beat interactions with Japanese American Buddhists in the 1950s (Masatsugu), American literature about Asian religions has been mostly aloof from the religious life of Asian immigrant populations. In fact, there is more post-1950s evidence of European American enthusiasts interacting with Asian teachers than with Asian American practitioners.

Additionally, the selection of case studies in this book reflects the surprising fact that until recently, Asian American fiction has dealt relatively little with religion. But that is changing, as recent expressions of enlightened individualism are coming from Asian American writers working to synthesize Asian religions and American individualism. Their vision is distinct: Whereas the non-Asian writers in this study tend to focus on philosophy, the Asian American writers combine philosophy with an attention to ritual and the concrete stuff of Asian American religious life. And their influence exerts a broader impact on ideas of enlightened individualism, Asian religions in the US, and evolving ideas of American democracy.

I trace these developments in pivotal portrayals of Buddhism in Asian American fiction. Asian American writers have only recently produced a body of strongly Buddhist-inflected fiction in English—roughly over the past twenty-five years. The reasons for this are related to the dynamic history of Asian American activism, scholarship, and art. During the late 1960s and 1970s, American activists of Chinese, Japanese, Korean, and Filipino descent helped form a pan-Asian identity to fight for social and economic equality (Maeda xi, Wei 1–2). This movement had many significant accomplishments, such as establishing Asian American studies as an academic discipline (Chang 181). But this movement did not highlight religion in its activism or literature because doing so would come across as incongruously sentimental and ethereal within the movement's hardheaded, materialist orientation. As Josephine Park explains, the Asian American literary movement of the early 1970s "left out from the canon ... all those works which did not strike a note of defiance and whose literary expressions were illegible to the stated aims of the movement" of Asia American activism (17).

In the case of Asian American fiction with themes from Asian religions, these texts were not only "left out from the canon"; they were hardly being written at all. There seems to be very little Asian American fiction about Buddhism or Hinduism before the late 1980s. And what Asian American literature about Asian religions there was consisted mainly of essays and poetry (as in, for example, the early twentieth-century periodicals of the Japanese Buddhist Churches of America), and the literature was not featured in the literary wing of the Asian American movement. Moreover, while canonical classics such as Toshio Mori's *Yokohama, California*; John Okada's *No No Boy*; and Frank Chin's *The Chickencoop Chinaman* occasionally refer to Buddhism, it is not a prominent theme.

Thus, surprisingly, Buddhist themes were not part of the Asian American movement of the 1960s and 1970s even though, as Park states, "activist Asian American poets redeployed the terms of Beat enlightenment in order to usher their own culture into existence" (121). This redeployment, as it turned out, focused on cultural stereotypes and not religion. For example, the 1978 poetry collection *The Buddha Bandits Down Highway 99* (Hongo, Lau, and Inada) revisits Beat tropes of road trips and wrestles with Beat Orientalism, but in spite of its title, it does not substantially deal with Buddhism. All of this is to say that the Asian American movement was not fertile ground for Asian American Buddhist fiction to emerge.

However, the focus on secular pan-Asian solidarity that defined the Asian American movement of the 1960s and 1970s began to change after the late 1980s. The movement was so successful in establishing *Asian American* as a recognizable identity and protesting prejudice against Americans of Asian descent that it opened up more-diverse literary, critical, and cultural possibilities. In other words, the success of challenges to the imperatives of the Asian American movement was made possible by that very movement. Along these lines, in the late 1980s, Asian American studies shifted toward emphasizing difference over pan-Asian solidarity (Wu and Song xiv–xv, Xiaojing 3). In particular, Lisa Lowe's influential 1991 essay "Heterogeneity, Hybridity, Multiplicity: Marking Asian American Differences" was a turning point in the field. Here Lowe reaffirms the value of *Asian American* as an identity category for political activism. But she stresses the need to avoid essentialism by emphasizing the many differences among Asian Americans, including national origin, language, class, and other factors (28). Lowe's argument had gained considerable traction by 2000, the year in which her essay was anthologized in the important collection *Asian American Studies: A Reader* (Wu and Song xxiii). In 2003 Kandice Chuh built on Lowe's prerogative by arguing that Asian American studies should conceive of itself as a "subjectless discourse" that studies contingent social formations and not populations with inherent cohesiveness (Chuh 9). Reflecting this growing consensus, the 2010 *Asian American Studies Now: A Critical Reader,* which is a follow-up to *Asian American Studies: A Reader,* treats a difference-based approach to Asian American studies as a given (Wu and Chen xv).

This changing climate in Asian American scholarship was part of larger developments in activism and art, which fostered a proliferation of themes in Asian American literature, including, as I will discuss, Buddhism. To use terms from literary scholar Michelle Janette, a literary tradition that had been dominated by activist *tales of witness* into the 1980s began to produce more *tales of imagination.* Tales of witness draw heavily from history and personal experience and aim to "correct the record and claim a spot in the American psyche" (Janette xix). Tales of imagination, on the other hand, tend to be less polemical and more contemplative, experimental, and topically diverse. They treat "their topics with the indirections of poetry rather than the linearity of explanation" (xxii–xxv). While Janette writes specifically about Vietnamese American literature, I find her typology useful for Asian American literature more broadly. Without the particular imperatives of preceding Asian American activism, authors felt freer to undertake open-ended explorations of specific and overlooked Asian cultures and experiences. Taking inspiration from Janette's evocative terminology, I propose that Asian American tales of imagination help make space for the mythology, ethereality, ritual, and sacredness of Asian religions.

Accordingly, Buddhism began to emerge as a theme in Asian American fiction around 1989—close to when Lowe's pivotal essay appeared. This year saw the publication of Amy Tan's *The Joy Luck Club* and Maxine Hong Kingston's *Tripmaster Monkey,* two influential works that were heavily underpinned with Chinese religions. Since then, important Buddhist-themed texts by Asian American fiction writers include Russell Leong's *Phoenix Eyes* (2000), Marilyn Chin's *Revenge of the Mooncake Vixen* (2009), Julie Otsuka's *The Buddha in the Attic* (2011), and Ruth Ozeki's *A Tale for the Time Being* (2013). This proliferation shows that Asian American Buddhist fiction has come into its own.

In this chapter, I focus on two key texts of Asian American Buddhist fiction: Lan Cao's *Monkey Bridge* (1997) and Kingston's *The Fifth Book of Peace* (2003). These narratives reflect on what it means to be Asian American while also grappling with Buddhism's attempt to transcend individual and collective identities. Both writers resist and take inspiration from previous American adaptations of Asian religions. In particular, Cao reclaims Buddhism as a living tradition in defiance of Orientalist Modernism, and Kingston shows the progressive political potential of Beat-influenced Buddhism against criticisms of countercultural irresponsibility. Furthermore, these texts' divergent remembrances of the Vietnam War—which made Cao a refugee and Kingston an antiwar activist—reinforce the countercultural debts of enlightened individualism.

Both texts make an important, overlooked intervention in discussions of Asian American identity. Scholars have widely accepted Lowe's anti-essentialist priorities. However, as Asian American studies scholar Viet Thanh Nguyen points out, academic arguments for subjectlessness are often unappealing to "actually existing political subjects" who rely on identity claims for their activism (925). Cao's and Kingston's stories suggest a way around this dilemma by offering Buddhism as a cultural resource for Asian American identity. Here, Buddhist nonself becomes pivotal. The Buddhist doctrine of nonself (Sanskrit: *anātman*) states that the self is an illusory collection of parts with no central essence (McMahan 151, Rahula 51–52). According to Buddhism, by realizing the truth of nonself, one becomes free from the selfish desires that cause suffering. While Cao and Kingston do not discuss nonself explicitly, their novels portray Buddhist realizations that enable characters to embrace fluid identities, overcoming attachment to themselves and to specific groups. In *Monkey Bridge* and *The Fifth Book of Peace,* Buddhism simultaneously dissolves and celebrates Asian American identity. Buddhism critiques identity, but this very critique is a specifically Asian heritage.

Cao's *Monkey Bridge* and Kingston's *The Fifth Book of Peace* speak not only to Asian American Buddhism but also to the gap between American Buddhists of Asian and European descent. Scholarship on Buddhist practitioners in America has noted a large social division between immigrant Buddhists from Pacific Rim countries and predominately white convert Buddhists. Asian American Buddhist practice tends to involve ritual and prayer, devotional practices that many Westerners dismiss as merely "cultural." By contrast, as I have discussed, Western convert Buddhists tend to focus on analytical meditation and leave behind what they view as the cultural trappings of Asian Buddhism (Coleman 7, Seager 8–10, Prebish 57–60). There is very little interaction between these two kinds of communities, and there has even been condescending disparagement from white converts toward Asian American Buddhists. Joseph Cheah documents a tendency among Western converts to view their version of Buddhism as "true" Buddhism. This "true" Buddhism is supposedly superior to Asian Buddhism and Asian American Buddhism, dismissed as "ethnic" phenomena weighed down by superstitious cultural accretions (71–72). For all of Buddhism's emphasis on nonduality, Asian and Western Buddhist differences form a pivotal fissure within American Buddhism.

These divisions are expressions of larger trends in comparative religious history. Starting around 1500, Western Christendom underwent a process of secularization that began with "disenchantment," that is, a removal of a sense of sacred power and supernatural forces that inhabit some objects and places and not others (Taylor). These reforms did not occur elsewhere in the world (62), which means that most other religious cultures retained a sense of enchantment that American Protestantism and secular humanism alike tended to view with suspicion. Admittedly, some nineteenth-century "Protestant" reforms of Hinduism and Buddhism by Asian teachers such as Ramakrishna, Dharmapala, and Shaku Soyen gave Asian religions a more palatable face for Western intellectuals (R. King, *Orientalism*; Prothero, *White Buddhist*; Snodgrass). But these adaptations were quite different from the religions of the lay populations that immigrated to America's West Coast. Thus when Asian populations came to the US, white Americans tended to view their religions as backward and superstitious, not only because of racism, but also because these religions maintained a "primitive" sense of ritual power that Western reforms had worked against for several centuries. Recent Asian American texts try to overcome this divide between enchantment and disenchantment, creating innovative forms of embodied religion that can occupy the immanent frame of the secular West.

By dramatizing the transformative power of both Buddhist metaphysics and ritual practices, Cao's and Kingston's texts work to overcome the many barriers between white and Asian American Buddhists. As I mentioned in the first chapter, most Western writers discovered Asian religion through books, not through cultural inheritance or missionary conversions. Consequently Asian religions' presence in American fiction tends to be abstract and philosophical, a set of individual mental exercises rather than a communal practice. We see this, as I have discussed, in Ray Smith's solitary meditations on emptiness in *The Dharma Bums* (chapter 1) and Rutherford Calhoun's psychological discovery of nonduality in *Middle Passage* (chapter 4). Cao and Kingston continue to portray contemplative Buddhist breakthroughs like these. But they also depict funeral rites and food offerings, ghostly spirits and karmic consequences. In both texts, Buddhism is vividly alive. This religiosity coexists with non-Buddhist traditions of ancestor veneration, a Confucian-influenced element that is a prominent aspect of both Vietnamese and Chinese religions, especially on the household level (Ho 82). Cao's and Kingston's writing positions these practices as complements to, not distractions from, meditative quests for enlightenment and social missions of American liberal politics.

LAN CAO: INNOVATION AND RECLAMATION

Of the many waves of Asian immigration to the US, the South Asian wave is the most recent, gaining momentum only in the 1970s, just as the countercultures I previously discussed were fading. This wave included Vietnamese and Lao refugees from the Vietnam War and Cambodian refugees from the Khmer Rouge regime (Hein). In the late 1970s, the newly arrived population of Vietnamese refugees in the US was, as Cao's semiautobiographical narrator of *Monkey Bridge* states, "an awkward reminder of a war the whole country was trying to forget" (15). This tension was further embodied in the geographically symbolic fact that a principal area of Vietnamese refugee resettlement was in Falls Church, VA, just outside the US capital.

It was in this context that Lan Cao came to the US, arriving in 1975 at the age of thirteen, shortly before the fall of Saigon (Janette 166). She lived in a Vietnamese American community until graduating high school and went on to a distinguished career, not primarily as a fiction writer, but as a legal scholar. Cao's debut novel *Monkey Bridge* is not famous but is critically acclaimed, and it is, as far as I know, the first English-language Vietnam War novel by a Vietnamese American author. It is an original exploration about how Buddhist ideas can help Asian Americans, and Americans more generally, harmonize multiple identities.

While firmly rooted in the author's experiences, *Monkey Bridge*'s fictional events, ruminative pace, and de-emphasis on social grievance depart from Vietnamese testimonial literature, making it more a "tale of imagination" than a "tale of witness" (Janette xix). There are, of course, unmistakable parallels between the author and the main character, Mai, both of whom came to Falls Church, VA, in 1975 and subsequently attended Mount Holyoke College (Janette 166). But the particulars of the mother-daughter relationship in *Monkey Bridge*, and the backstory of the Nguyen family's history in Vietnam, are entirely fictional (Newton 173-74). With a skillful blend of experience and invention, Cao's artistry allows the novel to synthesize American and Vietnamese identities in creative ways, including by reclaiming Buddhism from Modernist appropriation. Despite *Monkey Bridge*'s many Buddhist references, religion as a topic has not come up in interviews with Cao (Newton, Shan), and there is no biographical evidence that Cao has practiced Buddhism. But *Monkey Bridge* is seriously concerned with the Buddhist concept of karma, and the novel's concluding move toward Buddhist nirvana attempts to reconcile Buddhist and American ideals of freedom. Cao's enlightened individualism is ambitious in its effort to join the Buddhist freedom *from* selfhood to the American freedom *to be* a fulfilled self.

The terms of this reconciliation involve a response to Modernism. As the introduction discussed, Modernism has had a great influence on Western adaptations of Buddhism and Hinduism. Josephine Park has written extensively on how Modernist poets treated Asian religions as exotic artifacts of spiritual purity, artifacts that contrast with the decadence, aimlessness, and violence of the modern West (Park, Kern). Cao is strongly influenced by Modernist poetry, but she also strives to show that Buddhism is neither simply foreign nor a mythical contrast to the decadence of the West, but a living presence that can be synthesized into the modern West. She accomplishes this through a subtle pattern of recontextualized allusions to T. S. Eliot's *The Waste Land*, which I will explore later. While the Modernists, and not the Beats or hippies, are Cao's foremost literary influences, *Monkey Bridge* also shows an awareness of antiwar countercultures in its treatment of the famous 1963 image of the self-immolating monk Thich Quang Duc, which became a global phenomenon and a focal point of American antiwar activism.

CULTURAL DIFFERENCE AND KARMA IN *MONKEY BRIDGE*

The mother-daughter relationship at the core of *Monkey Bridge* brings to life major themes of Asian American literature, particularly tension between Old World ethnic and New World American identities, the American prerogative to reinvent oneself anew and look to the future versus the Asian reverence for one's ancestors. In particular, the daughter Mai's embrace of scientific empiricism and America individualism conflicts with the mother Thanh's traditional Vietnamese religion and Confucian filial piety. Mai views her mother as superstitious, volatile, and embarrassing; Thanh sees her daughter as narrow-minded, cold, and condescending. These themes come into focus in the novel's opening chapter, when, about four years after settling in the US, Thanh is recovering from a stroke. Sitting by her hospital bed, Mai describes how Thanh is

> drumming her right fingers against her left wrist, tying a ferocious knot with the sheet corners, carrying on in her usual convoluted language about karma I could not make out. "Karma," that word alone, whose sacred formula I could not possibly know, had become her very own singular mantra. This was alien territory, very alien, even to me. (10)

Mai's allusion to Thanh's "usual convoluted language about karma" is dismissive. Her perception of Thanh's behavior as "ferocious" insinuates that Thanh's stroke has distorted her already eccentric belief in karma into a deranged obsession. Mai's language further suggests that the idea of karma itself has become foreign, "alien," to her. At this point, spiritual beliefs seem culturally distant to Mai, even when coming from her own heritage, and specifically her own mother. Mai subsequently remarks that her mother has "paranoia" and a "terrible sense of the world" (17), clinging to an unfounded, "peculiar understanding of cause and effect" (23). Mai even questions her mother's "fragile sanity" (24). For Mai, belief in karma, spirits, and the like cannot coexist with her implicit Western empiricism. In order to "sustain a new identity" in the US (39), Mai feels the need to distance herself from the traditional religious beliefs her mother embodies.

But *Monkey Bridge* comes to explore, in the pages of Thanh's journal, how these attitudes need not be opposed. Ironically, it is the older and presumably less flexible Thanh who sees compatibility where the younger, more cosmopolitan Mai does not. *Monkey Bridge* folds Thanh's journal into Mai's narrative viewpoint by having Mai discover and read it surreptitiously—which, it turns out, is exactly what Thanh wants. The pages of Thanh's diary show her to be far more articulate and self-aware than Mai initially acknowledges. In fact, Thanh thoughtfully explores the relationships between Buddhist and Western traditions. Whereas Mai separates the physical from the spiritual, Thanh unites them. Thinking of the hospital staff, Mai wonders, "How could they have known it was not muscular but karmic movements and the collapse of Heaven that frightened my mother?" (8). But in her own writing, Thanh equates Western science with karma: "No one can escape the laws of karma. . . . It's something as exact and implacable as the laws of physics" (55). Similarly, Thanh opines, "Genetics and karma, they're as intertwined as two strands of thread from the same tapestry. If you believe a pebble dropped into a pond makes circles after circles of ripples, you are a believer in the forces of karma" (169). Thanh even addresses Mai directly in her diary, insisting that "karma, my child, is nothing but an ethical, spiritual chromosome, an amalgamation of parent and child" (170). Although Thanh maintains traditionally Vietnamese customs and worldviews, she accepts Western science and views it as complementary to karma.

But Thanh's eloquent ideas about cross-cultural synthesis do not nourish her lived experience. Her life is still defined by grief and despair over a sordid family past that she hides from her daughter. Thanh wants to protect Mai from what she believes is bad karma that follows her family from one generation to the next. Eventually, Thanh commits suicide in an attempt to pay off karmic debts and give Mai a metaphysical zero balance, so to speak. Thanh's last journal entry, in effect a lengthy suicide letter that Mai discovers alongside Thanh's body, explains that Thanh had left her journal for Mai to read and filled it with a sanitized version of her family history to endear Vietnam to Mai. But the truth is a sordid tale of prostitution, revenge, and violence. Thanh's father, unable to pay a debt to his landlord after a crop failure, prostituted his wife to the landlord instead. Thanh is the illegitimate daughter of this relationship. Thanh's official father resents the class system that led to his family's predicament, and he later defects from his Southern village to become a soldier for North Vietnam. He eventually murders his former landlord, an act Thanh witnesses (249). Also, as a result of Vietnam War fighting, Thanh cannot bury her grandmother in her home village, a failure that endangers her spirit's peaceful passage, according to Vietnamese custom (251). In the US Thanh remains preoccupied with her family's monstrous accumulation of negative karma. Her suicide letter expresses relief that her death will expunge this burden.

This letter, Thanh's final journal entry, contains subtle reclamations of Buddhism from Western refraction. This happens specifically with regard to Modernist poetry, which Cao puts under creative pressure in Thanh's specific descriptions that allude to T. S. Eliot's *The Waste Land*. Thanh's diary recontextualizes Eliot's references in a way that recovers East Asian religious lineage from Western filters. In her description of her life during the Vietnam War, Thanh describes an American-run camp, built to protect the inhabitants of her village from violence, as an "unreal village" (Cao 233), a nod to Eliot's line "unreal city" (Eliot line 60, 207 in Rainey 59, 63). Thus Thanh compares London ravaged by WWI to her own village displaced by the Vietnam War. Also, Thanh powerfully repurposes Eliot when she writes about the famous self-immolation a Vietnamese monk performed as a protest against South Vietnam's anti-Buddhist policies. Thanh writes, "The monk performed the ultimate act of sacrifice and pressed his palms in prayer, a sermon of fire, his body in an erect, uncollapsable lotus position, while flames, burning, burning, orange and ocher, the color of his saffron robe, enveloped and consumed the flesh he offered as an act of supreme devotion" (Cao 253). The phrase "sermon of fire" alludes to the third section of *The Waste Land*, "The Fire Sermon." Thanh's repetition of "burning, burning" also alludes to line 308 of *The Waste Land*, "burning burning burning burning." Thanh's allusions to Eliot suggest a larger point about the history of Western literature's engagement with Asian religions. In one sense, Thanh is alluding to Eliot, who is alluding to Buddhist scripture. But in another sense, Thanh brings up Eliot in order to highlight the fact that she does not need him. Although Thanh clearly borrows Eliot's language in her description of the self-immolating monk, Thanh grew up in a Buddhist culture and would probably have known about the Buddha's fire sermon independently of Eliot. In the Buddhist text *The Fire Sermon*, the Buddha tells his audience to shun desire by comparing cravings of the senses to being on fire (Rainey 99–100). In Thanh's interpretation, the self-immolating monk has literalized the Buddha's metaphor. Furthermore, Thanh characterizes the act as an expression of religious piety, a "sacrifice," and shifts attention away from its meaning as an act of protest. Thanh alludes to the same Buddhist text as Eliot, but with a far stronger sense of Buddhist lineage. Cao thus urges readers familiar with *The Waste Land* to see the Fire Sermon not as an exotic object for Western allusion, but as a sacred text from an Asian Buddhist point of view.

Cao's complex treatment of the image of the self-immolating monk also speaks to the countercultures of the 1960s. This photograph quickly became a central image for the antiwar movement, a fact that Cao's readers would generally recognize. But Thanh gives no direct acknowledgment of the political afterlife of this image, suggesting that the image has spiritual meanings for her as a Vietnamese person, meanings that do not depend on its use by a Western antiwar movement. The monk who set himself on fire, Thich Quang Duc, meant his act primarily as a protest against the anti-Buddhist policies of the South Vietnamese government. But the antiwar movement's use of this image actively implied that Duc's self-immolation was a protest against the American war, which is an oversimplification. Although *Monkey Bridge* does not mention Beat or hippie countercultures by name, its treatment of this image works to reclaim an Asian context from images of Buddhist activity that became famous in Western media. Cao writes with an understanding that her readership's knowledge of Buddhism is likely gleaned from writers such as Jack Kerouac, Gary Snyder, and Allen Ginsberg. Cao does not base her enlightened individualism on these countercultures, but her vision of American Buddhist life also echoes many of those counterculture's priorities.

Thanh's repurposing of the image of the self-immolating monk also plays into larger motifs in the novel. The text reverses Modernist Orientalism by having a Buddhist allude to Eliot rather than the other way around. Thanh's subtle references to *The Waste Land* resonate throughout the novel, especially in its ongoing shadow motif. Thanh's engagement with Eliot casts new light on the novel's opening epigraph, taken from *The Waste Land*:

> (Come in under the shadow of this red rock),
> And I will show you something different from either
> Your shadow at morning striding behind you
> Or your shadow at evening rising to meet you;
> I will show you fear in a handful of dust. (26–30)

Just as the word *shadow* dominates this ominous passage, shadows become a motif for lurking insecurities throughout *Monkey Bridge*. For example, Mai observes a "shadow war" which one of her Vietnamese neighbors wages by rewriting her memories of her contentious husband (Cao 40). Also, Mai reflects on how Vietnamese soldiers "would turn the country into a narcotized landscape haunted by shadows" in order to "spook the invaders" (120). This motif receives a Buddhist turn when Thanh writes of "the shadows of our family's karma" (229). In this metaphor, karma is a shadow that follows oneself and one's family for indefinite generations. In a poetic gesture of empowerment, Cao uses Eliot's shadows as material for the novel's Buddhist content. Now a Buddhist context alludes to Eliot, not the other way around. By turning the tables on Modernist Orientalists like Eliot, *Monkey Bridge* works to make Buddhism not an object of exotic fascination and yearning, but a living tradition that complements Western science and individualism.

FROM KARMA AND SUFFERING TO NIRVANA AND NONSELF

Thanh's visions of cultural empowerment and synthesis, eloquent and complex though they are, do not overcome her profound isolation and shame over the traumatic events she experienced in Vietnam. Instead, it is Mai who arrives at a more hopeful vision of the future, in large part due to her ability to contemplate the ultimate release of nirvana beyond the intermediate—and, in Thanh's view, grim—workings of karma. The novel's conclusion is paradoxical and bittersweet. Ironically, it is only Thanh's suicide that instigates Mai's spiritual insights and newfound ways of inhabiting multiple identities, a change that involves a renewed appreciation for her late mother. Mai is left wondering what she could have done to be closer to her mother and prevent her from feeling hopeless (256), but she still does not allow herself to grieve, focusing instead on maintaining her composure (257).

And yet a realization breaks through at last, showing that Thanh's methods worked. Mai's epiphany enacts the idea that through Buddhist nonself, one can develop a more flexible and capacious sense of identity that allows one to be inhabited by disparate commitments simultaneously. The pivotal vision occurs during a dream Mai has on the night before she leaves for college. The religiously charged dream enables Mai to experience her grief, gain greater appreciation for her mother, and contemplate Buddhism:

> What I saw was a beautiful ladder, the same one my mother had described many times before, guarded by a secret creature with an inner light glowing through its skin, a light as faint and dormant as the faint flame of a candle glowing through a screen of silk. The creature, my mother once said, always lies with its head cradled on the first rung, waiting for a human soul to pass by to infuse it with an inner life. As the passerby makes her way up the rungs, the creature would slowly stir, following the passerby the way it has followed hundreds upon hundreds of pilgrims generations and generations before, its translucent skin becoming more and more luminous the higher it and the passerby get, making their way up each step. The creature would approximate perfection, its skin would turn lustrous, its light would shine a brilliant shine the closer it gets to the top, but only at the very top of the ladder would the climber cast no shadows and achieve what every seeker seeks through all the ages to achieve: nirvana itself. (258–59)

This passage's style implies a Buddhist sense of the illusory nature of selfhood and of phenomena in general. In a departure from the novel's lush, sensuous descriptions, this passage is strikingly vague. Cao's sensory descriptions throughout the novel apply particularly to Mai's exposure to Vietnamese religion. There are considerable details about Thanh's religious materials, such as a spirit offering of "stir-fried tripe with fresh parsley and licorice basil, lettuce leaves, coriander, cucumber wedges, and chopped chili peppers . . . on top of a brand-new yellow-lace doily" (162). Elsewhere a holyday ritual feast with Mai's and Thanh's Vietnamese friends includes "a large pot of sweet-and-sour fish soup flavored with the tanginess of ripe tamarind[,] . . . a tender slice of sweet memory" (217). In contrast to Mai's previous exposure to traditional religion, the dream passage above, the novel's most explicit appeal to religious transcendence, has the fewest ties to the physical senses. The descriptions in this passage do not convey a specific sight or sound. The only pieces of information about the "creature" are that it has a head and translucent skin; the content of its "perfection" is unspecified. The predominant phenomenon in this passage is "light," but without defined form or color.

This stylistic choice bears specific connections to Buddhist philosophy. *Nirvana* is the Sanskrit Buddhist term for the complete, permanent cessation of suffering achieved by the individual meditator. Since this transcendence is beyond all description, Buddhist writing tends to define nirvana by what it is not, rather than by what it is (Rahula 36). One who has achieved nirvana sees both oneself and all phenomena as lacking any inherent nature; all is emptiness, and therefore there is no ground for the attachments from which suffering arises (Rahula 37, H. Smith 116). Buddhism emphasizes letting go of attachment to the objects that stimulate the senses (Rahula 29). Paradoxically, "nirvana it*self*" is that which erases all sense *of* a self (emphasis added). By avoiding specific descriptions, Mai shows freedom from such attachment. Because her vision is vague on sensory details, it is therefore also culturally nonspecific. If nirvana is beyond all sensory specifics, then it cannot be tethered to a single culture. Her style imitates the unconditional quality of nirvana as theorized in the Buddhist tradition. Mai's dream thus fulfills the lesson from the Buddha's "Fire Sermon" (see Rainey 99-100).

Furthermore, Mai's dream helps her regain affection toward her mother, if only in memory, and to recuperate positive values from the concepts of karma Mai previously derided. Mai realizes that "we had inhabited the same flesh, and as I discovered that night, like the special kind of DNA which is inherited exclusively from the mother and transmitted flawlessly only to the female child—the daughter—a part of her would always pass itself through me" (Cao 259). Mai has become more receptive to Thanh's way of thinking and sees her mother's influence as something to value rather than resist. Although Mai does not specifically reference karma, this passage strongly echoes Thanh's earlier assertion that karma is a "spiritual chromosome" (170). In fact, Mai's understanding of spiritual heredity is even more personal than Thanh's. Where Thanh sees karma in "parent and child" (170), Mai more specifically genders the heredity as being from "mother" to "daughter." This gesture is both intimate and empowering, especially considering the prestige of heroines in Vietnamese lore and their attributes of strength, skill, and intelligence (Pham and Eipper 51, Newton 181). Furthermore, Mai's vision that the figure climbing the ladder "would cast no shadows" signals that Thanh's wish for Mai to "recede from the shadows of our family's karma" is fulfilled (Cao 259, 229). The belief in karma that Mai previously dismissed as "alien" and pathological now registers, on some level, as personally meaningful (11). Mai's vision of nonself allows her to integrate American and Vietnamese ways of knowing much as Thanh did, but with a more hopeful future.

After this dream sequence, the novel ends with a beginning: Mai contemplates her entrance into Mt. Holyoke College, growing in confidence that "I would follow the course of my own future" (Cao 260). But this future is uncertain. The reader does not know whether Mai pursues spirituality further or what other life choices she makes after she enters college. In a 2000 interview, Cao explains that "I only wanted to see the initial stage in which she made the decision to leave the Vietnamese community.... It really almost does not matter what she ultimately decides after that" (Newton 182). The novel's last line, a one-sentence paragraph, is "Outside, a faint sliver of what only two weeks ago had been a full moon dangled like a sea horse in the sky" (Cao 260). Just as the moon wanes, the grip of her mother and the Vietnamese community also diminishes as Mai becomes less determined by her ancestry and freer to pursue her "own future." But the beginning of Mai's independence is not an abandonment of her past. Literary scholar Jennifer Ann Ho observes that the waning moon's seahorse shape resembles the coast of Vietnam and "symbolizes the continued influence that Viet Nam and her mother will have over Mai" (100). For Ho, this influence is a healthy balance of learning to accept a complex, constantly renegotiated ethnic identity (100). Mai has learned to value her mother without feeling pressure to imitate her.

Mai's realization advances postsecular challenges to the division between religious and secular worldviews (Branch 94). Just as Thanh's diary explores the scientific resonances of her religious beliefs, Mai's inner thoughts throughout the novel conversely suggest that her own veneration for science involves elements of religious devotion. Earlier in the novel, Mai condescendingly tolerates her mother's rituals, at one point musing, "What harm could there be in a little bit of astrology?" (156). But elsewhere, Mai rationalizes her "philosophy" of self-medicating to avoid "the undomesticated world of dreams" by saying to herself, "What harm could there be in that?" (11), the same formulation she uses in her dismissal of Vietnamese rituals. Also, during a college interview, Mai steers the conversation toward her medical aspirations because, remembering what her father told her, "the physical sciences . . . are a safe, predictable arena" (129). She further likes being "as implacable and exact as the sciences my father had taught me" (163). For Mai, the sciences are accompanied by a feeling of refuge and protection. Mai's thoughts make rationalism visible as a form of faith, a source of values, not just an epistemological method. Through Mai, the reader sees how secularity, as Taylor puts it, is not what remains in the absence of religion, but is rather a "value-laden construal of agency" (565).

Mai's dream-induced realization helps her reconcile secular science with religiosity. After her climactic dream, Mai states, "As I discovered that night, like the special kind of DNA which is inherited exclusively from the mother and transmitted flawlessly only to the female child—the daughter—a part of her would always pass itself through me" (259). Here Mai refers to both DNA and a different "part" which, in the context of her dream, evokes a spiritual heritage that recuperates a positive kind of karma from Thanh's negative view. Mai begins to see that there is room in her psyche for European-scientific and Asian-spiritual impulses, and they are not so alien to each other after all.

Accordingly, although Mai's future schooling, career, and spiritual path are unknown, the text tries to establish that Mai's "American future" is also a Buddhist future (Ho 100). On the strength of a Buddhist-inspired epiphany, Mai embarks upon her college career, today's standard platform for American class mobility and self-discovery. A skeptical reader might therefore ask, Is Mai's adaptation simply a capitulation to the dominant culture that leaves Vietnamese traditions behind in favor of Western individualism and abstraction? My answer is no. As the final sentence's imagery suggests, Mai ventures into her future while still identifying as Vietnamese. In a distinctly Asian American version of enlightened individualism, Mai's American freedom of choice intersects with the Buddhist freedom of nirvana. Furthermore, Mai's glimpse of transcendence is what enables her to view these facets of her identity as flexible nodes rather than irreconcilably opposed entities. Mai's dream thus allows her to value religion in general and her mother's piety in particular. By honoring her mother without being limited by her, Mai harmonizes the Vietnamese belief in family-centered karma with American individualism and self-determination. In these ways, Mai's Buddhist epiphany allows her to successfully inhabit multiple identities. If there is no essential self, then one may wear multiple identities lightly without the ontological worry that that they are inherently incompatible or, as Chaym had brooded about in *Dreamer,* that identities are inherently deceptive. *Monkey Bridge* thus shows how Buddhist nonself can build bridges between Asian and American visions of individual roles, family ties, and ways of knowing.

MAXINE HONG KINGSTON AND "THE CHINESE RELIGION"

Cao's fictionalized account of the Vietnam War is a noteworthy example of overlooked Vietnamese American experiences. Her Asian-informed enlightened individualism also has important affinities with the work of a very different and more famous author, Maxine Hong Kingston. Whereas Cao's perspective on the Vietnam War is primarily that of a 1.5-generation refugee, the older Kingston was born in the US and was of an age where she became an antiwar activist. Yet as different as these perspectives are, both Cao and Kingston share a project of integrating Asian enlightenment and American individualism through a Buddhist framework. As I noted in the very beginning of this chapter, their Asian American approach involves an attention to Asian traditions of ritual, devotion, and materiality that is greater than other American adaptations of Asian religions. It is especially revealing to consider Kingston alongside Cao because Kingston's connection to Beat and hippie countercultures is far more direct than Cao's, and Kingston is thus ambivalently indebted to that counterculture while also striving to overcome its limitations of engaging with minority cultures.

Kingston holds an abiding affection for what she calls "the Chinese religion" of her upbringing, which encompasses Buddhism, Confucianism, and Daoism (Whalen-Bridge 180–81). Her experience is representative of Chinese tradition; recent scholarship finds that for many centuries, "syncretism became the main tendency in Chinese religious life" (Lu and Lang 202; see also Overmeyer 315–16, Barrett 531–33). What these various Chinese religious traditions share—and what Kingston refashions in her own writing—is materiality. There are shrines, statues, chants, pictures of celestial beings. Kingston, like Cao, finds room in Western Buddhism for ritual and ancestor veneration that previous adaptations have left out. Furthermore, Kingston develops this synthesis in a way that explicitly promotes liberal American ideas of individualism.

Although Kingston values "Chinese religion," her interest in Buddhism in particular is based on her engagements with American countercultures. In fact, it was her early exposure to the Beats, and not her culturally Chinese upbringing, that spurred Kingston's interest in Buddhism (Whalen-Bridge 178). In 2009 Kingston said that "what really got me was reading the Beats. Jack Kerouac and Gary Snyder. It just seemed like so much fun to be a Buddhist. Be a dharma bum!" (Carolan). Kingston's interest in Beat Buddhism eventually led her from books to personal contact: In 1984 Kingston visited China for the first time, traveling with a group of writers that included Gary Snyder, Allen Ginsberg, Toni Morrison, and Leslie Marmon Silko (Simmons xi, Skenazy 147). In 1991, Kingston attended a Buddhist retreat designed for Vietnam War veterans led by the famous Zen monk and peace activist Thich Nhat Hanh (Perry 176), whom Kingston cites as one of her major influences (Carolan). As *The Fifth Book* chronicles, Thich Nhat Hanh's meditation retreats for Vietnam veterans became Kingston's primary model for her own ongoing Vietnam Veterans Writers Workshop, where she makes a conscientious effort to integrate Buddhist and American faiths. This is an example of what Thich Nhat Hanh calls "engaged Buddhism" (Hanh, *Interbeing*), the application of Buddhist principles of compassion and emptiness to Western-enlightenment-inspired political activism.

Kingston's literary output shows a steadily increasing attention to Buddhism. She has said that her first major publication, *The Woman Warrior*

(1976), while steeped in Chinese myths, is not "a Buddhist book" (Whalen-Bridge 183). Nor does *China Men* (1980) dwell on Buddhism. A turning point comes with *Tripmaster Monkey* (1989), whose indebtedness to Buddhist sources is so complex that one scholar wrote an entire dissertation on Buddhism in just that novel (Zuo). Partly a sequel to *Tripmaster Monkey*, *The Fifth Book* is the first of Kingston's books to offer an explicit discussion of Buddhist practices adapted for American audiences. The novel began purely as a sequel to *Tripmaster Monkey*, which continued the life of *Tripmaster*'s main character, Wittman Ah Sing. However, Kingston's house was destroyed in the Oakland-Berkeley fire of 1991, and her novel-in-progress was lost. So she rewrote the novel and added reflections on her own life and work, including the story of the earlier manuscript's destruction. This image of her destroyed neighborhood, which Kingston says was a "scene that is like war" (14), instigates her to reflect further on the Vietnam War and conduct unique meditation retreats with Vietnam veterans that seek real-life reckonings with the war's legacies.

The resulting book is what Kingston has called "a nonfiction fiction nonfiction sandwich" (Schroeder 223). *The Fifth Book* has four sections. The first two, "Fire" and "Paper," are nonfictional memoirs of Kingston's loss of her manuscript in the fire and reflections on the literary context of her work. In "Paper," Kingston explains that "after the fire, I could not reenter fiction. Writing had become a treat for my own personal self" rather than something that could be directed toward helping others" (61). Kingston begins to work through this problem in the fictional third section, "Water," which is the restored and expanded narrative of Wittman's continued life. The fourth section, "Paper," returns to the realm of nonfiction with a depiction of Kingston's activities running the Vietnam Veterans Writers Workshop. In this final section, Kingston follows Wittman's trajectory toward greater selflessness. Kingston thus finds new ways to understand the value of creative writing, as I will show, in ways that join Asian and American values and identities.

FROM ESCAPISM TO ACTIVISM IN *THE FIFTH BOOK OF PEACE*

Through Wittman's character development in "Water," Kingston tries to wrest American Buddhism away from accusations of Beat frivolity while still being influenced by the Beats. As noted above, *The Fifth Book* continues Wittman's development from Kingston's *Tripmaster Monkey*. Set in late 1960s San Francisco, *Tripmaster*'s protagonist, a fifth-generation Chinese American hippie, resents Kerouac's stereotype of "little twinkling Chinese" (Kingston, *Tripmas-*

ter 69–70), but under Kerouac's influence it also recognizes everyday people as "bodhisattvas . . . like in *The Dharma Bums*" (235). In *The Fifth Book* the reader learns that after the events of *Tripmaster Monkey*, Wittman marries, has a kid, and impulsively (and, it turns out, self-defeatingly) moves his family to Hawaii in order to distance himself from the draft and the Vietnam-focused politics in the American mainland. There, Wittman makes a problematic invocation of Chinese culture to outrace, or at least to ignore, the negativity of world events during the late Vietnam era, as the following passage shows:

> Another of his vows-to-live-by was to stop reading the newspapers and listening to or watching news until the war is over. That would be news: THE WAR IS OVER. Allen Ginsberg declared the war ended already. What was being broadcast were numbers that kept getting higher, and putting you into despair so you didn't want to live. It's not good to be well informed. Being up on current events adds to the war, and makes war real. (117)

Here Wittman prefers ignorance to activism. This passage more broadly invites readers to consider Ginsberg's Buddhist- and Hindu-inspired anti-war activities, which, as I have discussed, included mass mantra chants in an attempt to change the world with divine sound waves (Hungerford 30–32). But instead of bringing positive realities into being through chant, as Ginsberg attempts, Wittman focuses on denial. One the one hand, Ginsberg's insistence on the power of supernatural language to change political realities bore no immediate, world-altering effects. On the other hand, one may reply, at least he engaged in active protests, whereas Wittman misuses Ginsberg to give himself permission to flee from activism, a withdrawal not unlike the radical inwardness promoted by anti-Beat writers like Salinger and Pirsig. Kingston's own real-life spiritual activism suggests that she is going for more a criticism of Wittman's lazy appropriation of Ginsberg rather than a direct criticism of Ginsberg himself, since Ginsberg's mantra-based activism influenced Kingston.

By invoking Ginsberg, Kingston not only reminds us of Wittman's Beat and hippie ties; she also suggests a bridge back to Wittman's namesake, Walt Whitman, who as I discussed in chapter 1, was a central influence on Ginsberg. Wittman's first name has an extra *t* and no *h*, figuring what Kingston calls the Chinese American tendency to "spell it kind of funny" (Blauvelt 79). The last name "Ah Sing" is a play on Whitman's poem "*I Sing* the Body Electric" (my emphasis; see also Park 122). Kingston explained in a 1989 interview that just as Whitman writes, "I sing the body from top to toe," she wants to "carry on in the tradition of Walt Whitman," with a particular focus on ethnicity, and "sing the Chinese American from top to toe" (Blauvelt 79, 80). The allusion to Ginsberg also calls upon Beat, and earlier Transcendentalist, valorizations of Hinduism and Buddhism (Stiles 36, 67–68, 108). Ginsberg "declared the war ended already" out of inspiration from Eastern metaphysics, which emphasize the power of mantras to change the world with their spiritual vibrations (Hungerford 37–38). Although Whitman was not Ginsberg's primary introduction to Asian religions, this affection for Eastern wisdom remained a source of affinity across time between the two poets. In Whitman's "Passage to India," the speaker generously praises India's "elder religions" (Whitman line 23). Ginsberg highlights Whitman's influence in "A Supermarket in California," calling Whitman "dear father" and "lonely old courage-teacher" (Ginsberg 144). If Whitman influenced Ginsberg, Ginsberg figuratively reciprocates by influencing the latter-day Wittman, thereby setting up a complex cultural interplay in which Wittman invokes Ginsberg but reproduces what many viewed as the countercultures' flaws and lack of responsibility.

After referring to Ginsberg, Wittman further provides a mystical justification for his escapism. He thinks that his "independent project was to work on perception. . . . Mind creates what's out there. . . . *See* the world peaceful and the war will end. Wittman had such faith from having been raised Chinese" (Kingston, *The Fifth Book* 143). This rationalization arises from Wittman's laziness (Kingston, *Tripmaster* 241). In addition, whether he knows it or not, Wittman is justifying his laziness in the metaphysics of Asian religions, which, particularly in Mahayana Buddhism and Advaita Vedanta Hinduism, teach that all phenomena are a projection of one's own mind (Deshung Rinpoche 198, Iyer 68). From this idea it follows that to change one's mind is to change the world. Yet the more immediate factor in Wittman's mind is not specifically Buddhist philosophy but a vague sense of cultural identity from "being raised Chinese," which becomes a justification for complacency.

But in a noteworthy epiphany, Wittman models a way of moving from a frivolous version of Beat Buddhism to a more productive faith. This reformed American Buddhism is still influenced by the Beats but integrates the metaphysics of emptiness with a sense of civic responsibility for social change in American traditions of democratic activism. Wittman's turning point comes from engaging more closely with Buddhism. Ennui has overtaken him; he feels as though "the bad days and nights outnumbered the good days and nights" (Kingston, *The Fifth Book* 191). He finds relief in a courtyard outside a Buddhist shrine room, where he continues to try to escape through literature, passively "waiting for a poem to come" (191). After a passerby admonishes him against naïveté (192), Wittman goes inside. Now he is "determined to learn something. The ancestors made these images out of stone to last for thousands of years. Try to read them; there must be a message." This language marks an important turning point. Rather than fleeing from knowledge (117), Wittman is "determined to learn something." And rather than pursuing the instant gratification of wishful thinking, Wittman is inspired by the statues' longevity measured in "thousands of years." Whereas Wittman's "faith from having been raised Chinese" was frivolous, Wittman now defers more seriously to the heritage of "ancestors" and their spiritual orientations. He imitates the postures and smiles of the various figures, and he "felt his attitude changing" (192). The content of this change is not clear at first, but Wittman soon comes across an antiwar protest that leads him to involvement with an AWOL sanctuary at a local church. He and his wife support this sanctuary by meeting the deserting soldiers, leading classes on literature and politics and putting on a production of Megan Terry's antiwar play *Viet Rock* (1965). Wittman is drawn to the protest by a sense of "fun-in-crowds," but this frivolous pleasure soon deepens as he "felt a joy-in-human-beings coming back to him" (193, 198). Wittman goes from being an indigent draft dodger to a selfless peace activist.

Wittman's development reflects the Buddhist teaching of nonself. In Buddhism, the individual self is a delusion that causes suffering; therefore, realizing that the self is a limiting fiction frees oneself from suffering and makes it easier to give generously to others (Milarepa, qtd. in Snyder, *Mountains* ix; Santideva 1.52; Rahula 51; McCleod). After Wittman's "attitude [changes]" in the shrine room, the narrative shifts focus away from his own thoughts and toward the testimonies of the AWOL soldiers he works with. Wittman remains the viewpoint character, but his self-clinging has left to make room for helping and getting to know the soldiers. Instead of statements like "admiration and envy coursed through Wittman" (Kingston, *The Fifth Book* 132), the narration now relies on empathetic statements like "Wittman listened to the AWOL GIs go back over their lives, figuring out how they got to be who they were and how they came to be here" (216).

The principle of nonself that characterizes Wittman's development is also emphasized in Western abstractions of Buddhism, but often to the exclusion of ritual. However, the means through which Wittman comes to the realization of nonself are concrete and sensory and thus are indebted to East Asian Buddhism. Wittman's turning point comes not through discursive argument or inner meditative absorption, but through being in a physical space of devotion vividly decorated with statues and other religious objects, a style characteristic of the Japanese Buddhism most common in Hawaii. Thus Wittman's realization of nonself bridges Western abstraction and Eastern ritualism.

Interestingly, the novel portrays Wittman's realization of Buddhist nonself as paradoxically consistent with an increased pride in his Asian heritage.

As Wittman listens to a Japanese American pastor discuss the sanctuary, the narrator declares, "Proud, proud was Wittman—a person of one's own Asian ancestry declares Peace, declares Sanctuary" (197). Buddhist nonself thus becomes a transformative aspect of Wittman's "own Asian ancestry." When Wittman takes his own lineage and its materiality more seriously, he is able to distance himself from the most problematic excesses of countercultural Buddhism while still being influenced by it. In this way, *The Fifth Book* enacts an enlightened individualism that encompasses Asian and American identities.

FORGING BUDDHISM FOR AMERICA AND BEYOND

After narrating Wittman's life in "Water," "Earth" describes Kingston's real-life work running the Vietnam Veterans Writers Workshop. I read this section as Kingston's description of her own enactment of what Wittman learns. The workshop Kingston leads seeks to make up for the incomplete work of the historical sanctuary in which the fictional Wittman participates. In a 1993 interview, after Kingston had begun the workshops, she voiced her hope that her workshops and others like them could create "a true ending to the war with Vietnam" by making a reparative community (Seshachari 196). In the workshops, which are modeled after Vietnam veterans' retreats by Thich Nhat Hanh (Schroeder 225, Carolan), Kingston links writing and Buddhism. Like Thich Nhat Hanh, Kingston leads a curriculum of Buddhist practices, including breathing meditation, walking meditation, and even eating meditation. She also invents a form of writing meditation as well. Kingston emphasizes mindfulness and ethics over doctrine and is "not trying to put anything religious over on anybody" (Kingston, *The Fifth Book* 336), but the framework for the workshop is strongly Buddhist. Not only does Kingston follow Thich Nhat Hanh, but she also invokes Avalokiteshvara, the bodhisattva of compassion, during some of the workshop's events (318, 395). This devotional act is a more markedly Asian feature than what one would expect at a typically Westernized meditation retreat.

In a complex effort to both affirm and critique the countercultures to which Kingston's Buddhist practice is indebted, Kingston deals with criticisms that she is conducting a frivolous, feel-good program. She recalls a moment during a retreat with Thich Nhat Hanh in which "a paranoid psychologist called us 'candyass Buddhists' and stomped out" (268). In response, Kingston gives evidence that writing helps veterans while at the same time she distances herself from sentimentality. One member testifies that "'writing my pain, I am writing myself back to health. . . . Poetry writing and journal writing are instruments in my healing.' *Healing*. I avoid that New Age word. It implies that something's wrong, that they're unwell, and need fixing" (264–65). It is ironic that Kingston uses the term "New Age" pejoratively, given that Asian religions' growing popularity in the US is associated with the New Age movement and, by extension, the hippie counterculture of antiwar activism (Campbell 115–16). But Kingston's skepticism toward "healing" has a Buddhist impetus, since in Buddhism, as Thich Nhat Hanh explains, a being's true nature is Buddha-nature: The practitioner clears away obscurations rather fixing inherent defects (Nhat Hanh, *Love's Garden* xv; McCleod). It remains undeniable, though, that Kingston seeks some version of "healing"; she aspires to "help [veterans] write until the stories full of explosions become quiet" (Kingston, *The Fifth Book* 314). But by distancing herself from the New Age, Kingston turns the doctrine of Buddha-nature from a seemingly unrealistic fantasy into a way of discarding unhelpful stigmas.

Ultimately, Kingston wants the Buddhist practices she adapts to be considered apart from the countercultural frivolities that the term "New Age" vaguely evokes, even though she has been heavily influenced by these movements. Kingston's aforementioned trip to Asia with major writers, including countercultural heroes Ginsberg and Snyder, is further evidence of this influence. But Kingston also justifies the value of her program in ways that reference Asian, but not American, sources such as the Heart Sutra (376), also one of Ginsberg's favorites. This dynamic is somewhat comparable to Cao's effort to write both out of and against Modernist Orientalism. While Kingston's struggles with the counterculture are ultimately less severe than Cao's challenges to Modernist Orientalism, both writers are ambivalently involved with Buddhism's relationship to Western avant-garde literary movements.

Kingston's real-life recollections in "Earth" parallel the fictional Wittman narrative, "Water," by giving Kingston a Buddhist-inspired loss of interiority similar to Wittman's. As "Earth" progresses, excerpts from the veterans' stories become so prominent that the text becomes more of a montage than a memoir. In the nonfictional first two sections of *The Fifth Book*, "Fire" and "Paper," Kingston's mind is front and center; she focuses on her traumatic experience of the fire and reflects that she is "alive because of an idea" of her own selfhood (21). In "Paper" Kingston sulks over public criticism of her writing, dismissively musing that "I'm sure the people who hate me haven't read me. They are nonreaders" (56). This defensive, I-centered persona is one that the novel deliberately undoes as it progresses. Kingston writes herself as a self-centered character who eventually benefits from Buddhist philosophy's emphasis on nonself and the compassion it supports, similarly to the way Wittman experiences such a change.

This shift from "I" to "we" is also connected to Kingston's sense of ethnic identity. In "Paper," Kingston reflects that "all over Asia, people confidently say 'we.' Each naturally speaks for all the rest of the nation family. Americans say 'I.' I can speak for no one but myself, my opinion, my point of view" (56). According to this division, to write collaboratively is to cultivate Asian mores at the expense of American ones. However, this does not mean that Kingston sees American culture as inherently opposed to Buddhist compassion. Rather, American culture can be reformed and expanded with the help of Asian religions. For instance, in "Earth," Kingston makes innovative links between Buddhist principles and the Bill of Rights. The writers' workshop includes lessons on the Five Wonderful Precepts (336), Thich Nhat Hanh's explication of five basic rules of conduct common to all Buddhists (Nhat Hanh, *For a Future* 5–7; H. Smith 107–8). The precepts are prohibitions against killing, stealing, committing sexual misconduct, uttering harmful speech, and consuming alcohol and other intoxicants. The traditional formulation of these precepts is terse and strictly negative (Indaratana 1, H. Smith 107), but Thich Nhat Hanh's version is longer and more positive, explaining what to do in addition to what not to do. Each traditional prohibition is preceded by an affirmative principle. For example, Thich Nhat Hanh sets up the precept against killing with the line "I vow to cultivate compassion and to learn the ways of protecting the lives of people, animals, and plants" (Nhat Hanh, *For a Future* 5–7). By using this version of the five precepts, Kingston carries on Thich Nhat Hanh's project of presenting Buddhist principles in positive, not merely negative, terms.

This positive turn also applies to the Bill of Rights, which Kingston explicitly connects to the Five Precepts. She reflects that "the Precepts are not too different from the Bill of Rights. You could just as well put the First Amendment into practice. Speak. Write. Assemble. Practice a religion, or not" (336). Although Kingston changes the order and leaves out the petition clause, she invites readers to notice that the First Amendment has five major provisions, the same number as the Five Wonderful Precepts and *The Fifth Book of Peace* itself.

Kingston's vision is not a radical break from Enlightenment liberalism; rather, it is an enlightened individualism that retains an investment in the founding documents of the US. Kingston tries to restore her disillusioned Vietnam veterans' damaged connection to the US by telling them that "we are wonderful products of American culture. And we have great ideas, such as the First Amendment in the Bill of Rights, which I see as rights to be *practiced*—speak, write, assemble, build a sangha. The First Amendment is prescriptive; they are our American precepts" (384). This understanding departs from American jurisprudence, which tends to view the Bill of Rights not as positive prescriptions for the people, but as negative restrictions on the power of the federal government (Brant 223–24, Davey xiii, Hickock 2). The prominence of the word *no* in the Bill of Rights, especially the First Amendment's opening, "Congress shall make no law," foregrounds what the government may not do, not what the people should or can do. This is not to say that Kingston is ignorant of this fact. Rather, Kingston deliberately reinterprets the Bill of Rights in more positive terms to empower her audience toward activism, replicate Hanh's positive teaching on the Five Precepts, and position Buddhist ideas and practices as the fulfillment of American rights-based individualism.

Although Kingston's project has specifically American stakes, she also wants to broaden the workshop students' horizons beyond the nation. Toward this end, the last meeting of the workshop takes place in Plum Village, Thich Nhat Hanh's religious headquarters located about fifty miles east of Bordeaux, France. Here, the veterans not only continue their meditation and writing but also receive teachings from Thich Nhat Hanh himself. They also get to know other Vietnamese expatriates. If, as Kingston says, "the only way I can integrate East and West is thinking about global politics or a global peace-making mission" (Simmons 164), then this event is a part of this mission. Furthermore, it realizes Kingston's goal of making new endings in real life after her postfire disillusionment with fiction.

The close of "Earth" combines aspirations for global peace with Kingston's continuing interest in her Chinese religious identity, as she passes on spiritual advice from her late mother, who died during the book's composition. Kingston declares that "if the world, time and space, and cause-and-effect accord with my mother's teachings—her Tao—then we have stopped wars years hence. We made myriads of nonwars. We have ended wars a hundred years from now" (397–98). Here, Kingston's thoughts on history take on both a historical and a mythic dimension. She combines a practical wish to prevent war with an appeal to mystical power. By linking this attitude to Daoism, Kingston shows that not only does her text promote Buddhist principles and practices; it also reaffirms her "Chinese religion" by honoring her mother's spiritual advice. Furthermore, Kingston's view of time challenges the dominant Western picture of secular time as linear, consistent, and unvarying (Taylor 54–59). This disrupts Taylor's immanent frame by reintroducing premodern ideas of sacred, malleable time that gathers and warps ordinary time (55). But for Kingston, the source for this warping of secular time is not a Christian eternity that gathers all of time (56), but the idea in Asian religions that time itself is ultimately an illusion (W. King 218–19). Kingston thus furthers her cross-cultural synthesis by imbuing her American-based activism with traditional Asian views of time.

Kingston's Buddhist vision shares crucial affinities with Mai's religious epiphanies. In *Monkey Bridge* and *The Fifth Book of Peace*, Asian American characters become more at home in America precisely by delving into their Asian religious traditions. Furthermore, they do so in ways that overcome typical differences between Asian and European American Buddhists, even as both writers critique Western adaptations of Buddhism. In both texts, devotion to one's ancestors leads characters toward, not away from, Buddhist ideals of nonself. Also, the main characters in these two texts—Mai Nguyen, Wittman, and Kingston herself—paradoxically connect Buddhism's teaching of nonself to American archetypes of free exercise of one's rights. In their narratives, Cao and Kingston use Buddhism to envision new ways of harmonizing American and Buddhist freedom—what I have been calling *enlightened individualism*—and, by extension, new ways of being Asian in America. They also use Asian practices to envision fuller ways of being Buddhist in America, ways that incorporate a more capacious balance of philosophical and material expressions of religiosity. This shared project works to bridge the divide between abstract Westernized Buddhism on the one hand and more ritualistic immigrant Buddhism on the other. Cao's and Kingston's syntheses envision a more embodied American Buddhism without simply reestablishing an enchanted world. These interventions place Cao and Kingston in the midst of ongoing transformations in transnational literature, Asian American studies, and American Buddhist communities.

POSTSCRIPT

AFTER SURVEYING an array of thematically related texts, it is fair to ask, Does enlightened individualism succeed at revitalizing American freedom through other cultures without appropriation? My overall answer is yes. This literature's admittedly problematic investments in Orientalism have diminished over time, and, as a whole, the developments I have traced are salutary and not merely appropriative. The writers in this study have established a porous, two-way relationship between American and Asian ideals. Their cross-cultural spiritual texts offer readers tools to navigate America's complex terrain of cultural difference. When writers make bold innovations such as those I discuss, debates about the ethics of cultural borrowing are inevitable and valuable. But the vision of truly humane exchanges across cultures, religions, and continents is too important to cast aside. This hope, embodied in writers from Kerouac to Kingston—and beyond—makes the risks of cross-cultural adaptation worth taking. Furthermore, the ongoing release of fiction that carries on enlightened individualism's projects, such as Alex Shakar's *Luminarium* (2011), Ruth Ozeki's *A Tale for the Time Being* (2013), and George Saunders's *Lincoln in the Bardo* (2017), suggest that this mode of writing is here to stay.

As a now-established tradition of American writing, enlightened individualism is poised to continue its trend toward greater inclusivity. From the Beats to the present, US literary perspectives on Asian religions have become steadily more diverse, a trend that is represented in the organization of this study. The belated growth of women's and minority writing on Asian religions in the US shows how unevenly lofty ideals such as nonduality can express themselves in culture. But increasingly diverse voices will help Buddhist and Hindu American literature continue to wrestle with divisions between male and female, black and white, Asian and non-Asian. This trend will promote cross-cultural engagements and further reduce the risks of appropriation.

This diversification is likely to continue with the twilight of the Vietnam War generation. Asian religions in American fiction will increasingly be taken up by younger writers for whom the Vietnam War and mid-century American countercultures were not defining personal experiences as they were for most of the writers in this study. One can already see this trend emerging in two recent anthologies of American Buddhist fiction: *Nixon under the Bodhi Tree and Other Works of Buddhist Fiction* (2004) and its sequel, *You Are Not Here and Other Works of Buddhist Fiction* (2006) (Wheeler, Kachtick). These collections feature authors of both Asian and non-Asian descent, although the latter are still a majority, and they include stories where the Vietnam War is central, peripheral, or absent. This continuing diversification is also likely to result in more attention to the devotional and material aspects of Buddhism and Hinduism, as expressed in the writers I study in the final chapter. These indicators all point to a multifaceted terrain of Asian religious adaptations that will further defy stereotypes.

Enlightened individualism is likely to become even more transnational in setting as well as theme. As the twenty-first century advances, Asian religions are poised to become even more globally important in a multipolar world. Many analysts are announcing the end of American preeminence and the rise of multiple world powers (Brzezinski 2, Zakaria 1–4). This decline of American dominance causes anxiety among many Americans, often leading them to support reactionary, xenophobic political movements. But these same trends that provoke regressive responses also offer creative and cosmopolitan opportunities. Along these lines, two of the most important rising powers are China and India, and Japan will likely remain a strong, if slightly declining, economic power as well (*Global Trends* 15). These three countries have nourished the religious traditions that figure prominently in the writers I have discussed. In this emerging multipolar context, it is likely that Asian religions will expand their presence in American fiction, and this writing will continue to call upon Buddhist and Hindu transcendence as a resource to address contemporary social issues. These narratives will become even more transnational, as already evidenced in an American's Cambodian journey in Kira Salak's excellent short story "Beheadings" (Salak 91–124) and Ozeki's *A Tale for the Time Being*, whose capacious, Zen-themed narratives move between Japan, the US, and Canada. The cultural negotiations I have discussed will increasingly find narrative and historical expression not just within US borders but also across national borders, thus further promoting more cosmopolitan and less insular modes of national identity.

These are exciting developments that have the potential to influence American culture toward greater openness to otherness and to promote humane spiritual ideals. But although I am generally supportive of these trends, I also have my doubts that the shape which enlightened individualism has taken holds together as coherently as its writers and readers may think. Thus it is important to address the limits of enlightened individualism. In many cases, the writers I study are too optimistic about completely reconciling Asian and European enlightenments. By pursuing ambitious syntheses of Asian religion and American liberalism, writers risk mishandling either or both enlightenments. They can misunderstand Asian religion, arbitrarily limit which of its aspects to consider, or exoticize it. They can also take American maxims out of context, reinterpret key liberal terms too loosely, or hold on to the rhetoric of American ideals when a more radical break from US ideologies would make more sense. For example, when Charles Johnson imagines Martin Luther King Jr. as a closeted Buddhist, he makes a tendentious revision of American history. And when Kerouac makes Buddhism into a justification for hedonistic adventurism, he flouts Buddhist philosophies of renunciation. These tensions never go away completely. At a certain point, Europe's Enlightenment of individualism and Asia's enlightenment of nonduality diverge, and enlightened individualism tends to minimize this tension too easily.

A primary reason for this dynamic is that enlightened individualism unevenly yokes the ultimate values of Buddhism and Hinduism with the provisional values of Enlightenment philosophy. In our secular age, it is easy to take for granted that Enlightenment values of democracy and individual rights are unequivocally positive, universal ideals. But these principles were conceived not as ultimate ends in themselves, like Buddhist nirvana or Hindu moksa, but rather as safeguards to protect human beings from one another's ineradicable flaws. In the US, this view is captured in James Madison's Federalist Papers, where he famously wrote in Federalist 51, "If men were angels, no government would be necessary." Therefore, as stated in Federalist 10, a key job of government is to control the "mischiefs of faction" that result from human greed and narrow-mindedness, and not to eliminate those faults themselves, because that would be impossible—or practicable only with such severe repression that "the cure would be worse than the disease." Madison's American version of Enlightenment philosophy is a coping mechanism, not a path to transcendence.

Seen in this light, there are a few courses that would better navigate this disjunction between Asian and European enlightenments. One would be to link Enlightenment ideals with a stripped-down adaptation of Asian religions that gives up on transcendence. This is the approach of Pynchon and DeLillo and, somewhat differently, of the secularized yoga and mindfulness practices that are so popular in the US today (Jain, Wilson). The idea of secular contemplation for the sake of American values has even been endorsed by a major American politician, as shown in Ohio congressman Tim Ryan's book *A Mindful Nation: How a Simple Practice Can Help Us Reduce Stress, Improve Performance, and Recapture the American Spirit* (2012). But the drawback of this approach is that the pull of transcendence will not go away, and secularized adaptations from Asian religions are not likely to be enough to answer the spiritual hunger of large numbers of people over time.

A more extreme alternative, then, would be to commit fully to Buddhist and Hindu ideals and reject American Enlightenment individualism altogether. This is obviously not a framework that would gain much popular support in the US; it would at most appeal to small numbers of disaffected Americans. But not only is this idea not feasible; it is also not desirable. Enlightenment individualism, for all its problems, has also been the basis for rights-based activism that has advanced the welfare of oppressed populations, as we have seen with abolition, women's suffrage, the Civil Rights movement, and LGBTQ rights. More broadly, Enlightenment individualism still offers powerful tools worth preserving for critiquing power and questioning social assumptions.

If Enlightenment individualism is so important, an altogether different approach, then, might be to cast one's lot with the West and give up on Asian religions as fundamentally incompatible with Enlightenment projects. This is the view of some midcentury European thinkers such as Emil Cioran, Paul Tillich, and Arthur Koestler, the latter of whom asserts that "neither yoga, Zen, not any other Asian form of mysticism has any significant advice to offer" the West (282). Unsurprisingly, I do not agree with this view; such a dismissal would be a parochial and misguided relinquishment of the resources Asian religions have to offer US cultures.

Therefore—and here I tip my hand, perhaps indecorously, as an advocate for Asian mysticism—the most coherent relationship between enlightened nonduality and Enlightenment liberalism would involve giving primacy to the former. Or, less presumptuously, *if* one assigns significant value to both Enlightenment individualism and the nondualistic philosophies of Buddhism and Hinduism, then subordinating the former to the latter makes sense. For one thing, when an ultimate system (Asian nonduality) coexists with a provisional one (Enlightenment liberalism), subordinating the latter makes the most common sense. Additionally, Asian religions have specific ways of accommodating and subordinating potentially contradictory elements that Enlightenment philosophy does not offer equivalently. I am referring specifically to the Buddhist tradition of *upaya,* or "skillful means." *Upaya* means giving audience-appropriate levels of teaching that are simplified or concessive as a way of resolving apparent contradictions in the paradoxical language common in Buddhist and Hindu philosophy (Edelstein). Enlightenment liberalism could be one of these skillful means to incorporate into Asian nonduality's repertoire. Enlightenment liberalism would, in this vision, be a tool to cultivate with care, and in the most profound epiphanies, to transcend, to remember that it is not ultimate and that there are other paths that can orient us away from an individualism that cannot but constrain the scope of our concerns.

Furthermore, this type of framework, while complex, would be a more coherent spiritual context for Enlightenment liberalism than the personal God of orthodox Christianity, which has often been an awkward copresence with the political philosophies that founded the US. As Taylor points out, this Enlightenment arose largely out of opposition to a putatively dogmatic and enslaving Christianity, and Christianity has thus long been one of Enlightenment philosophy's favorite punching bags (262, 305). In spite of Christianity's history as the dominant religion in the US, there is value in Swami Vivekananda's argument that the democratic divinity of Vedanta makes more sense for the US than the monarchical God of European Christianity.

Therefore, a fruitful direction for enlightened individualism would more decisively subordinate liberalism to Asian-inspired transcendence, more fully working through the deep differences between enlightened and Enlightenment views of freedom. This sort of development would not occur primarily by making specific laws or policies. Instead, it would proceed more humbly and patiently through the slow work of changing culture, minds, and behaviors, the sort of diffuse and hard-to-measure labor to which literature is well suited.

To briefly consider just one arena in which such a reckoning might play out, the differences between Buddhist-Hindu and American views of the good life are especially pronounced in the area of love and sex. Enlightenment liberalism is individualistic, coincides with the rise of marrying for love, and, especially in the post-1960 "Age of Authenticity," sees love and sex as crucial expressions of one's true self (Taylor 502). By contrast, Buddhism and Hinduism traditionally teach that serious spiritual advancement involves celibacy on a practical level and, even if one is not a full-time monastic, overcoming attachment to sex on a mental level.

How could these divergent views coexist in ways that both validate the quest for transcendence and affirm the self-actualization of, for instance, historically oppressed sexual minorities? To answer this question, enlightened individualism would be well served to take its cue from Engaged Buddhism, a movement that uses Asian religions as bases for promoting women's rights, poverty reduction, and democratic representation in ways that are influenced by liberalism but are not always tied to US ideologies (Queen). Doing this in relation to love and sex would mean wrestling through the tough terrain of critiquing social repression against sexual minorities while parting company with some of the strongly affirming understandings of pleasure in contemporary social movements that support these groups. Here I will briefly show three writers who address these divergences in stark ways that most Americans would find unpersuasive, followed by a final example that is conceptually more promising, but still uninspiringly discursive. I then conclude with an invitation for a bolder enlightened individualism to take on a more creative charge, using the power of narrative to more vividly explore these new possibilities for American identities.

One noteworthy thinker who has begun to tackle the relationship between Buddhist and Enlightenment notions of freedom, especially in terms of love and sex, is Suwanna Satha-Anand, a Thai scholar of Buddhist philosophy. She argues that Buddhist asceticism, combined with male dominance, has made women in Buddhist societies unfairly burdened by teachings of sexual renunciation. She thus critiques patriarchal Buddhist traditions that myopically demonize female temptation and subordinate nuns to monks. Satha-Anand's use of liberal feminist thinking allows her to selectively critique parts of Buddhist tradition while upholding others. She views Buddhism's sexism as secondary to its more essential egalitarian promotion of everyone's potential for enlightenment. But Satha-Anand is also clear where she parts ways with liberalism. Her argument is a chapter in the book *Good Sex: Feminist Perspectives from the World's Religions*. Whereas lead editor Patricia Beattie Jung celebrates "the goodness of women's sexual delight" (77), Buddhism teaches that sexual desire, regardless of gender, is ultimately a "problem" (Satha-Anand 116). Thus, for Satha-Anand, sexual equality would mean critiquing sex equally for both men and women, not unambiguously uplifting female sexuality. This idea puts Satha-Anand at odds with the sex-positive enlightened individualism of Alice Walker, for instance, and, more broadly, as Satha-Anand understatedly notes, with "some feminists in the liberal West" (116). In the introduction, the editors frankly acknowledge the "real and deep differences among us" (Jung et al. xviii), and this is one of them. Satha-Anand begins to explore these differences and clarifies some philosophical foundations for a Buddhist feminism, but she leaves open more immediate questions of how her priorities would play out in day-to-day human conduct.

In order to deal more fully with these differences, someone who takes both liberal progressivism and Asian transcendence seriously would still need an understanding of the role of love and sex in one's spiritual development that is in conversation with liberal notions of identity. We see a thoughtful, if controversial, effort to do this from José Cabezón, who is a professor of Tibetan Buddhist Studies, a gay man, and a former Buddhist monk. He argues that "anyone who is seriously following the Mahayana Buddhist path would have to be committed to various forms of social liberation, including gay liberation" (Edelstein). This activist stance resonates with progressive liberal notions of universal rights and social justice, and Cabezón grounds it in Buddhist metaphysics of "emptiness . . . *beyond* gender and sexual orientation distinctions" (emphasis in original).

But while Cabezón's commitment to Buddhist emptiness supports social engagement, it also leads him away from the gay liberation movement's unequivocal celebration of sexual pleasure. According to Cabezón, insight into nonduality entails overcoming attachment to sex, which means that for the devoted seeker, "sexual activity must be diminished or curtailed," even if not through complete celibacy. In Cabezón's view, this means that in practice, "there is a kind of responsible sexuality that Buddhism calls for that commits Buddhists to keeping their sexuality within bounds," adding that "I'm far from being celibate at this stage in my life. But I still hold celibacy as an ideal." Therefore, Cabezón does not support the notion, which he describes as prevalent in contemporary gay liberation movements, that "sexual self-expression is essential to being a gay person." Some of Cabezón's comments, if taken out of context, could easily be misinterpreted as a restatement of dodgy anti-LGBTQ claims to accept gay people but simply be opposed to gay sex. But in my understanding, Cabezón's theories work toward an alternative, robust framework of antidiscrimination in which people respect identity differences, not as objects of pride in and of themselves, but as benign variations that are all equally workable starting points toward a path of absolute transcendence.

It is one thing to highlight academics who patiently navigate the ambivalences I have touched on here without seeing themselves as shapers of public opinion. But it is another to consider how such ideas would reach a broader audience. How would an American mass readership reckon with these tensions? We have a window into an answer in the Tibetan Lama Yongey Mingyur Rinpoche, a Nepali-born teacher with a large Western audience. His book *The Joy of Living* (2007) is a part of the blossoming literature of Buddhist self-help, itself a cross-cultural synthesis of genres. Some popular books in this genre greatly cater to American sensibilities and deemphasize tough-sell Buddhist concepts like emptiness and renunciation, as with much of the work of Sharon Salzberg and Thich Nhat Hanh. But Mingyur Rinpoche chooses to deal explicitly with the fissures between liberal attachments and mystical transcendence. In a key passage from *The Joy of Living*, Mingyur Rinpoche aims at no less a target than love itself:

> Recently, a student of mine told me that he thought "loving-kindness" and "compassion" were cold terms. They sounded too distant and academic, too much like an intellectual exercise in feeling sorry for people. "Why," he asked, "can't we use a simpler, more direct word, like 'love'?"
>
> There are a couple of good reasons why Buddhists use the terms "loving-kindness" and "compassion" instead of a simpler one like "love." Love, as a word, is so closely connected with the mental, emotional, and physical responses associated with desire that there's some danger in associating this aspect of opening the mind with reinforcing the essentially dualistic delusion of self and other. "I love *you*," or "I love *that*." There's a sense of dependence on the beloved object, and an emphasis on one's personal benefit in loving and being loved. Of course, there are examples of love, such as the connection between a parent and child, that transcend personal benefit to include the desire to benefit another. (173, original emphasis)

Translation is one of the most vexed aspects of cross-cultural adaptations. I noted early on how the word *enlightenment* as a translation for *bodhi* lent the term meanings that were not present before, meanings that helped enlightened individualism take shape. Here, *love* is another candidate word Mingyur Rinpoche wrestles with. English does not distinguish, as Greek does, between *eros* (erotic love) and *agape* (compassionate charity). The Buddhist intellectual tradition privileges the latter over the former to such an extent that a good translation would strive to avoid confusion. Thus, when Mingyur Rinpoche concedes examples of love that do go beyond personal benefit, he pointedly omits romantic love. Parents, as Mingyur Rinpoche sees it, love their children in a way based on giving more than receiving, whereas romantic love is too intense and associated with craving to be a guide for compassion. Rinpoche criticizes the Western valorization of love without a sense of defiance or harshness, just a clear affirmation of where his teaching must diverge from individualist ideologies. Mingyur Rinpoche adapts to Western students by using their language, but without altering his tradition's emphasis on renunciation and transcendence. Given his popularity—his book was on the *New*

York Times bestseller list and his Buddhist centers are quite popular—maybe there is room for these ideas to gain some traction after all.

Nevertheless, the three perspectives I have just sketched would be, I think, fantastically unpersuasive to all but a tiny subset of Americans. Satha-Anand, Cabezón, and Mingyur Rinpoche come across as generally antisex, which is an automatic deal-breaker for most Americans. These three writers do not concretely consider how love and sex can play a positive role in one's spiritual development, even if one's ultimate aim were to free oneself from the self-based attachments that the distinctive intensities of love and sex imply. Someone who does undertake such a consideration is social worker and Tibetan Buddhist lay practitioner Robert Sachs, as shown in his book *The Passionate Buddha: Wisdom on Intimacy and Enduring Love* (2002). Sachs recognizes that there is not much traditional guidance in Asian religions, beyond a few thinly justified rules, for sexual conduct for laypeople, much less Westerners in particular. Seeking to fill this gap, Sachs argues that even when prioritizing Asian principles of nonduality, "we need not deny our passionate nature" (17).

But neither does Sachs compromise on Buddhist nonattachment. Rather, Sachs creatively extends an aphorism by Gampopa, a twelfth-century founder of one of the major schools of Tibetan Buddhism, as follows: "'It is the sign of a superior man [sic] that he treat all with equanimity yet still has a few good friends.' Thus, Gampopa encourages us to identify with our absolute, unconditional loving nature while recognizing our personal preferences, our tendencies toward greater affinity with certain people" (3, see also Karthar). Sachs then extends this idea beyond friendship to include romantic love, something Gampopa did not do. Sachs argues that instead of pursuing romantic love in a self-centered manner, we can channel this love using Buddhist techniques so that "the love and affection we feel toward our partner and the specialness of our bond begin to expand into a *universal love and compassion* that has no bounds" (26, emphasis in original).

In making this argument, Sachs acknowledges the strong appeal of romantic love in the West without capitulating to it; he cautions that "I don't mean to simplify love as the answer" (3). But through this deft explication, Sachs is still willing to use the word *love* with its romantic associations in a way that Mingyur Rinpoche is not. While Sachs's methodical, expository approach may not capture the imagination, his synthesis does more justice, in my view, than many previous treatments to the potential of enlightened individualism.

As the above examples suggest, enlightened individualism's potential to address the philosophical chasms between the two enlightenments more trenchantly depends on complicated trade-offs between audience accommodation and cross-cultural precision. Would enlightened individualism do the most good by continuing its present course of reforming American individualism while rhetorically validating its traditional ideals? This approach would ensure enlightened individualism's ongoing appeal in this country, where patriotic idealism is a perennial key to mainstream acceptance. Or would it be better to take a more pointed, difference-based approach like those of Satha-Anand, Cabezón, and Mingyur Rinpoche, who privilege a notion of absolute enlightenment over and above American individualism, and indeed over and beyond any kind of individualism whatsoever? This view, while more philosophically precise, might not gain as much influence in the US as the model of enlightened individualism I have traced in these pages. Or does Sachs provide the most promising basis for bridging Eastern and Western enlightenments without bowdlerizing the values of either? Reasonable people will disagree. But here it is important to remember that literature is additive, not a series of either-or choices. The accommodating synthesis of mainstream enlightened individualism could coexist with a more difference-based approach. Given that today's cultural norms would have seemed unthinkable centuries ago, there is no telling how influential such new streams could one day become.

What, then, would the realization of a more radical enlightened individualism look and feel like in lived, social experience? This question reaches the limit of Satha-Anand's, Cabezón's, Mingyur Rinpoche's, and even Sachs's writings because their mode of expression is more discursive than creative. A key assumption in the background of this book has been that the religious imagination needs more than arguments to vividly grasp what a particular kind of religiosity or spirituality would be like. Along these lines, Kerouac's Buddhist writing has inspired many self-declared dharma bums; Walker's stories of nondual epiphanies have led to real-life journeys of social and spiritual liberation; Kingston's writing workshops—and her writing about her writing workshops—have fostered new forms of writing and meditation. Future creative writings will do the same, and to what extent they will take up the ideas I have briefly set forth in closing remains to be seen. Either way, the direction will matter. What is clear is that, in the US, it has been largely through the visionary enactments of fiction and poetry that Buddhist- and Hindu-inspired paths have taken life, and the future of enlightened individualism will be no different.

WORKS CITED

"About JKS." *Naropa University*, http://www.naropa.edu/academics/jks/about.php. Accessed 2 July 2013.

Adams, Tim. "Robert Pirsig: The Interview." *The Guardian*, 18 Nov. 2006, https://www.theguardian.com/books/2006/nov/19/fiction. Accessed 29 Nov. 2016.

Ahlstrom, Sydney. *A Religious History of the American People*. Vail-Ballou Press, 1972.

Aitken, Robert. "*The Cloud of Unknowing* and the Mumonkan: Christian and Buddhist Meditation Methods." *Buddhist-Christian Studies*, no. 1, 1981, pp. 87–91.

Appiah, Kwame Anthony. *Cosmopolitanism: Ethics in a World of Strangers*. W. W. Norton, 2006.

Apter, Emily. "On Oneworldedness; Or Paranoia as a World System." *American Literary History*, vol. 18, no. 2, 2006, pp. 365–89. *JSTOR*, www.jstor.org/stable/3876711. Accessed 26 Apr. 2018.

Archer, John. "The Resilience of Myth: The Politics of the American Dream." *Traditional Dwellings and Settlements Review*, vol. 25, no. 2, 2014, pp. 7–21. *JSTOR*, www.jstor.org/stable/24347714. Accessed 15 Aug. 2016.

Arnold, Edwin. *The Light of Asia, or, The Great Renunciation*. 1879. 28th ed. London: Trübner & Co., 1885.

Aronowitz, Afred G. "The Yen for Zen." *Big Sky Mind*, ed. Carole Tonkinson. Riverhead Books, 1995, pp. 80–83.

Astin, Alexander W., Helen S. Astin, and Jennifer A. Lindholm. *Cultivating the Spirit: How College Can Enhance Students' Inner Lives*. John Wiley & Sons, 2011.

Austin, Mary. "The Conversion of Ah Lew Sing." *Overland Monthly*, no. 30, 1897, pp. 307–12.

Bardach, Ann Louise. "How Yoga Won the West." *New York Times*, 1 Oct. 2011, http://www.nytimes.com/2011/10/02/opinion/sunday/how-yoga-won-the-west.html?_r=1&scp=1&sq=sunday%20review%20yoga&st=cse. Accessed 1 July 2013.

Barrett, T. H. "Chinese Religion in English Guise: The History of an Illusion." *Modern Asian Studies*, vol. 39, no. 3, 2005, pp. 509–33. *JSTOR*, www.jstor.org/stable/3876584. Accessed 23 Apr. 2018.

Barth, John. *The End of the Road*. 1958. Avon Books, 1964.

Bell, Bernard W. *Bearing Witness to African American Literature: Validating and Valorizing Its Authority, Authenticity, and Agency*. Wayne State University Press, 2012.

Bell, Sandra. "'Crazy Wisdom,' Charisma, and the Transmission of Buddhism to the United States." *Nova Religio: The Journal of Alternative and Emergent Religions*, vol. 2, no. 1, 1998, pp. 55–75. *JSTOR*, www.jstor.org/stable/10.1525/nr.1998.2.1.55. Accessed 23 Apr. 2018.

Bellow, Saul. *Mr. Sammler's Planet*. Viking, 1970.

Bernstein, Carl and Bob Woodward. *All the President's Men*. Simon & Schuster, 1974.

The Bhagavad-Gita. Trans. Swami Nikhilananda. 1944. Ramakrishna-Vivekananda Center, 1952.

Blauvelt, William Satake. "Talking with the Woman Warrior." Interview with Maxine Hong Kingston. 1989. *Conversations*, ed. Paul Skenazy and Tera Martin, pp. 77–85.

Blavatsky, Helena Petrovna. *Isis Unveiled: A Master-Key to the Mysteries of Ancient and Modern Science and Theology*. New York: Carton Press, 1877.

Branch, Lori. "Postsecular Studies." *The Routledge Companion to Literature and Religion*, ed. Mark Knight. Routledge, 2016, pp. 91–101.

Brant, Irving. *The Bill of Rights: Its Origin and Meaning*. Bobbs-Merrill, 1965.

Brunk, Conrad G. and James O. Young. "'The Skin Off Our Backs': Appropriation of Religion." *The Ethics of Cultural Appropriation*, ed. James Young and Conrad Brunk. Blackwell, 2012, pp. 93–114.

Bryan, James E. "Salinger's Seymour's Suicide." *College English*, vol. 24, no. 3, 1962, pp. 226–29. *JSTOR*, www.jstor.org/stable/373294. Accessed 23 Apr. 2018.

Brzezinski, Zbigniew. *Strategic Vision: American and the Crisis of Global Power*. Basic Books, 2012.

Burroughs, William and Allen Ginsberg. *The Yage Letters*. 1963. City Lights Books, 1975.

Buswell, Robert E. and Donald S. Lopez. "One Way to Nirvana: It's Not Just the Buddha Way That's Different—The Buddhist Mountaintop Is Different, Too." *Tricycle*, 3 Jul. 2014, https://tricycle.org/trikedaily/one-way-nirvana. Accessed 7 June 2016.

Byrd, Rudolph P. *Charles Johnson's Novels: Writing the American Palimpsest*. Indiana University Press, 2005.

Camire, Dennis. "Buddhist Congresswoman Sworn In, Urges Tolerance." *The Buddhist Channel*, 6 Jan. 2007, http://www.buddhistchannel.tv/index.php?id=60,3603,0,0,1,0#.Ucymj9gcois. Accessed 27 June 2013.

Campbell, Colin. *The Easternization of the West: A Thematic Account of Cultural Change in the Modern Era*. Paradigm, 2007.

Cao, Lan. *Monkey Bridge*. Viking, 1997.

Carlson, Thomas A. "Locating the Mystical Subject." *Mystics: Presence and Aporia*, ed. Michael Kesslar and Christian Sheppard. University of Chicago Press, 2003, pp. 207–38.

Carolan, Trevor. "'And so make peace...': Talking Story with Maxine Hong Kingston." *Kyoto Journal*, no. 72, 2009, pp. 53–55, http://www.kyotojournal.org/kjback/72/And%20so%20make%20peace.html. Accessed 1 July 2013.

Carus, Paul. "Karma: A Story of Buddhist Ethics." Open Court, 1894. *Google Books*, https://play.google.com/books/reader?id=Pf8QAAAAYAAJ&printsec=frontcover&pg=GBS.PR3. Accessed 23 Apr. 2018.

Casanova, José. "A Secular Age: Dawn or Twilight?" *Varieties of Secularism in a Secular Age*, ed. Michael Warner, Jonathan VanAntwerpen, and Craig Calhoun. Harvard University Press, 2010, pp. 265–81.

Cather, Willa. "The Conversion of Sum Loo." 1900. *Willa Cather's Collected Short Fiction: 1892–1912*, ed. Virginia Faulkner. University of Nebraska Press, 1965, pp. 323–31.

Chang, Mitchell J. "Expansion and Its Discontents: The Formation of Asian American Studies Programs in the 1990s." *Journal of Asian American Studies*, vol. 2, no. 2, 1999, pp. 181–206. Project MUSE, doi:10.1353/jaas.1999.0016. Accessed 26 Apr. 2018.

Cheah, Joseph. *Race and Religion in American Buddhism: White Supremacy and Immigrant Adaptation*. Oxford University Press, 2011.

Cheng, Chung-ying. "Onto-Epistemology of Sudden Enlightenment in Chan Buddhism." *Chung-Hwa Buddhist Journal*, vol. 13, no. 2, 2000, pp. 585–611. National Taiwan University Library, http://ccbs.ntu.edu.tw/FULLTEXT/JR-BJ001/93616.htm. Accessed 23 Apr. 2018.

Chin, Frank. *The Chickencoop Chinaman*. University of Washington Press, 1972.

———. *The Chickencoop Chinaman / The Year of the Dragon: Two Plays*. University of Washington Press, 1981.

Chin, Marilyn. *Revenge of the Mooncake Vixen*. New York: W. W. Norton, 2009.

Chinitz, David E. *Which Sin to Bear? Authenticity and Compromise in Langston Hughes*. Oxford University Press, 2013.

Chödrön, Pema. *When Things Fall Apart: Heart Advice for Difficult Times*. Shambhala Publications, 1997.

Chödrön, Pema and Alice Walker. "Good Medicine for This World: Alice Walker and Pema Chödrön in Conversation." *Shambhala Sun*, Jan. 1999, http://www.shambhalasun.com/index.php?option=content&task=view&id=1929. Accessed 2 July 2013.

Chuh, Kandice. *Imagine Otherwise: On Asian Americanist Critique*. Duke University Press, 2003.

Cioran, E. M. *The Temptation to Exist*. 1968. Trans. Richard Howard. University of Chicago Press, 1986.

Clausen, Christopher. "Sir Edwin Arnold's *The Light of Asia* and its Reception." *Literature East and West*, vol. 17, 1973, pp. 174–91.

The Cloud of Unknowing. Trans. Ira Progoff. Delta, 1957.

Coale, Samuel Chase. *Paradigms of Paranoia: The Culture of Conspiracy in Contemporary American Fiction*. University of Alabama Press, 2005.

Coleman, James William. *The New Buddhism: The Western Transformation of an Ancient Tradition*. Oxford University Press, 2001.

Collins, Wilkie. *The Moonstone*. 1868. Oxford University Press, 1999.

Comeaux, Malcolm. "'Caniques': Marbles and Marble Games as Played in South Louisiana at Mid-Twentieth Century." *Louisiana History: The Journal of the Louisiana Historical Association*, vol. 52, no. 3, 2011, pp. 324–56. JSTOR, www.jstor.org/stable/23074708. Accessed 9 Mar. 2018.

Conner, Marc. "To Utter the Holy: The Metaphysical Romance of *Middle Passage*." *Charles Johnson: The Novelist as Philosopher*, ed. Marc Conner and William Nash. University of Mississippi Press, 2007, pp. 57–80.

"Conversations: Maxine Hong Kingston." *Waterbridge Review*, May 2004, http://www.waterbridgereview.org/052004/cnv_kingston_p1.php. Accessed 1 July 2013.

Corelli, Marie. *A Romance of Two Worlds*. London: Richard Bentley and Son, 1887.

Coupe, Laurence. *Beat Sound, Beat Vision: The Beat Spirit and Popular Song*. Manchester University Press, 2007. JSTOR, www.jstor.org/stable/j.ctt155jcvn.6. Accessed 2 Mar. 2018.

Cowart, David. *Thomas Pynchon and the Dark Passages of History*. Athens: University of Georgia Press, 2012. *Project MUSE*, http://muse.jhu.edu/book/13080. Accessed 23 Apr. 2018.

Cunningham, Lawrence C. "St. John of the Cross, Mystic of Light." *America: The National Catholic Review*, 30 Jan. 2006, http://americamagazine.org/issue/558/article/st-john-cross-mystic-light. Accessed 20 May 2013.

Das, Lama Surya. Foreword. *You Are Not Here and Other Works of Buddhist Fiction*, ed. Kieth Kachtick. Wisdom Publications, 2006, pp. vii–x.

Davey, Joseph Dillon. *The Bill of Rights Today: Constitutional Limits on the Powers of Government*. University Press of America, 2008.

DeLillo, Don. *Americana*. 1971. Penguin, 1989.

———. *Mao II*. Penguin, 1991.

———. *The Names*. 1982. Vintage, 1989.

———. *Running Dog*. 1978. Vintage, 1989.

———. *Underworld*. Simon & Schuster, 1997.

———. *White Noise*. Penguin, 1985.

Deshung Rinpoche. *The Three Levels of Spiritual Perception: A Commentary on the Three Visions*. 2nd ed. Trans. Jared Rhoton. Wisdom Publications, 2003.

The Dhammapada: A Collection of Verses. Trans. Max Müller. Champaign, Ill: Project Gutenberg, n.d. *eBook Collection (EBSCOhost)*, search.ebscohost.com/login.aspx?direct=true&db=nlebk&AN=2009676. Accessed. 19 Aug. 2016.

Dickstein, Morris. *Gates of Eden: American Culture in the Sixties*. 1977. Liveright Publishing, 2015.

Dimock, Wai Chee. *Through Other Continents: American Literature across Deep Time*. Princeton University Press, 2006.

Donner, Frank J. *The Age of Surveillance: The Aims and Methods of America's Political Intelligence System*. Vintage, 1981.

Dreiser, Theodore. *The Stoic*. World Publishing, 1947.

D'Souza, Rudolf V. *The Baghavadgita and St. John of the Cross: A Comparative Study of the Dynamism of Spiritual Growth in the Process of God-Realization*. Gregorian University Press, 1996.

DuBois, W.E.B. *Dark Princess: A Romance*. 1928. Oxford University Press, 2014.

Eburne, Jonathan. "Trafficking in the Void: Burroughs, Kerouac, and the Consumption of Otherness." *Modern Fiction Studies*, vol. 43, no. 1, 1997, pp. 53–92. *Project MUSE*, doi: 10.1353/mfs.1997.0005. Accessed 24 Apr. 2018.

Eddins, Dwight. *The Gnostic Pynchon*. Indiana University Press, 1990.

Edelstein, Amy. "Dr. José Cabezón on Gay Buddhist Ethics & Gender Identity." Interview with José Cabezón. *Amy Edelstein*, 15 Dec. 2012, http://amyedelstein.com/gay-buddhist-ethics. Accessed 16 Feb. 2017.

Egan, Jim. *Oriental Shadows: The Presence of the East in Early American Literature*. The Ohio State University Press, 2011.

Eliot, T.S. *The Annotated* Waste Land *with Eliot's Contemporary Prose*. 2nd ed. Ed. Lawrence Rainey. Yale University Press, 2005.

Ellsberg, Daniel. *Secrets: A Memoir of Vietnam and the Pentagon Papers*. Penguin Books, 2002.

Emerson, Ralph Waldo. "Nature." *The Norton Anthology of American Literature: Shorter Seventh Edition*, vol. 1, *Beginnings to 1865*, ed. Nina Baym et al. W. W. Norton, 2008, pp. 488–519.

———. *Self-Reliance.* Thomas Y. Crowell Company, 1911. *HathiTrust,* https://catalog.hathitrust.org/Record/100604116. Accessed 4 May 2018.

Eperjesi, John R. *The Imperialist Imaginary: Visions of Asia and the Pacific in American Culture.* Dartmouth College Press, 2005.

Evans-Wentz, W. Y, trans. *The Tibetan Book of the Dead: Or, the After-Death Experiences on the Bardo Plane, according to Lama Kazi Dawa-Samdup's English Rendering.* 3rd ed. Oxford University Press, 1960.

Even Cowgirls Get the Blues. Dir. Gus Van Sant. Perf. Uma Thurman, Pat Morita, and John Hurt. New Line Cinema, 1993.

Eversley, Shelly. *The Real Negro: The Question of Authenticity in Twentieth-Century African American Literature.* Routledge, 2004.

"Facts at a Glance." *Naropa University,* http://www.naropa.edu/about-naropa/facts-at-a-glance.php. Accessed 4 June 2013.

"Faith on the Hill: The Religious Composition of the 113th Congress." *The Pew Forum on Religion and Public Life,* 16 Nov. 2012, http://www.pewforum.org/Government/Faith-on-the-Hill-The-Religious-Composition-of-the-113th-Congress.aspx#first. Accessed 1 July 2013.

Fargo, Matt. *Dirty Japanese: Everyday Slang from "What's Up?" to "F*%$ Off!"* Ulysses Press, 2007.

Fauré, Bernard. *The Red Thread: Buddhist Approaches to Sexuality.* Princeton University Press, 1998.

Favor, J. Martin. *Authentic Blackness: The Folk in the New Negro Renaissance.* Duke University Press, 1999.

Ferretter, Luke. "Religious Pluralism and the Beats." *The Routledge Companion to Literature and Religion,* ed. Mark Knight. Routledge, 2016, pp. 410–21.

Fields, Rick. *How the Swans Came to the Lake: A Narrative History of Buddhism in America.* Shambhala, 1981.

Fishkin, Shelly Fisher. "Crossroads of Cultures: The Transnational Turn in American Studies—Presidential Address to the American Studies Association, November 12, 2004." *American Quarterly,* vol. 57, no.1, 2005, pp. 17–57. *JSTOR,* www.jstor.org/stable/40068248. Accessed 24 Apr. 2018.

Fluck, Winifried, Donald E. Pease, and John Carlos Rowe. *Re-Framing the Transnational Turn in American Studies.* Dartmouth College Press, 2011.

Foner, Eric. "The Contested History of American Freedom." *The Pennsylvania Magazine of History and Biography,* vol. 137, no. 1, 2013, pp 13–31.

Forster, E. M. *A Passage to India.* 1924. Penguin, 1989.

Freud, Sigmund. *The Uncanny.* 1899. Trans. David McClintock. Penguin Books, 2003.

Friend, Tad. "Lenny Again." *The New Yorker,* 24 Jan. 2011, http://www.newyorker.com/talk/2011/01/24/110124ta_talk_friend. Accessed 20 May 2013.

Gaddis, William. *The Recognitions.* Harcourt, Brace and Co., 1955.

Giamo, Benedict. *Enlightened Attachment: Jack Kerouac's Impermanent Buddhist Trek. Religion & Literature,* vol. 35, no. 2/3, 2003, pp. 173–206. *JSTOR,* www.jstor.org/stable/40059920. Accessed 24 Apr. 2018.

Giles, Todd. "upsidedown like fools: Jack Kerouac and the Struggle for Enlightenment." *Texas Studies in Literature and Language,* vol. 53, no. 2, 2011, pp. 179–206. *JSTOR,* www.jstor.org/stable/23020766. Accessed 24 Apr. 2018.

Ginsberg, Allen. *Collected Poems 1947–1997*. HarperCollins, 2006.

Global Trends 2030: Alternative Worlds. National Intelligence Council, Dec. 2012, www.dni.gov/files/documents/GlobalTrends_2030.pdf. Accessed 8 July 2013.

Goddard, Dwight. *A Buddhist Bible*. 1938. Beacon Press, 1994.

Goldberg, Philip. *American Veda: From Emerson and the Beatles to Yoga and Meditation: How Indian Spirituality Changed the West*. Harmony Books, 2010.

Goodman, Russell B. "East-West Philosophy in Nineteenth-Century America: Emerson and Hinduism." *Journal of the History of Ideas*, vol. 51, no. 4, 1990, pp. 625–45. JSTOR, www.jstor.org/stable/2709649. Accessed 24 Apr. 2018.

Grace, Nancy. *Jack Kerouac and the Literary Imagination*. Palgrave Macmillan, 2007.

Gray, Timothy. *Gary Snyder and the Pacific Rim: Creating Counter-Cultural Community*. University of Iowa Press, 2006.

Greene, Laurence S. The Perennial Philosophy in J. D. Salinger's *Franny and Zooey* and Other Works: A Study in the Structural Embodiment of Mysticism and Eastern Philosophy in the World of Salinger's Later Fiction. Honors Thesis. Florida State University, 1983.

Griffin, Merv. Interview with Maharishi Mahesh Yogi. *Merv Griffin*, 1975, http://www.youtube.com/watch?v=Nkyh9i_j9Ls. Accessed 1 July 2013.

Griswold, Jerry. "Japan as American Theme Park: Kerouac's *Dharma Bums et seq*." *Seuils et Traverses: Enjeux de l'écriture du voyage*, ed. Jean-Yves Le Disez. Versailles: Université de Versailles-Saint-Quentin-en-Yvelines, 2002, pp. 141–50.

Gruesser, John. *Black on Black: Twentieth-Century African American Writing about Africa*. University Press of Kentucky, 2000.

Gupta, Sri Mahendra Nath. *The Gospel of Sri Ramakrishna*. Trans. Swami Nikhilananda. Sri Ramakrishna Math, 1932. *Ramakrishna Math and Ramakrishna Mission*, www.vedanta-nl.org/GOSPEL.pdf. Accessed 29 Nov. 2016.

Gyatso, Tenzin (H. H. the 14th Dalai Lama). *Beyond Religion: Ethics for a Whole World*. Houghton Mifflin, 2011.

———. *How to Practice: The Way to a Meaningful Life*. Trans. Jeffrey Hopkins. Atria Books, 2002.

Haggard, H. Rider. *Ayesha: The Return of She*. London: Ward Lock, 1905.

Hall, Stuart. "Cultural Identity and Diaspora." *Identity: Community, Culture, Difference*, ed. Jonathan Rutherford. Lawrence, and Wishart, 1990, pp. 222–37.

Hamar, Imre. "Buddhism and the Dao in Tang China: The Impact of Confucianism and Daoism on the Philosophy of Chengguan." *Acta Orientalia Academiae Scientiarum Hungaricae*, vol. 52, no. 3–4, 1999, pp. 283–92. JSTOR, www.jstor.org/stable/43391396. Accessed 2 Feb. 2017.

Hayes, Stephen K. *The Ninja and Their Secret Fighting Art*. Tuttle Publishing, 1981.

Hayward, Jeremy. *Warrior-King of Shambhala: Remembering Chögyam Trungpa*. Wisdom Publications, 2007.

He, Yuemin. "Gary Snyder's Selective Way to *Cold Mountain*: Domesticating Han Shan." *The Emergence of Buddhist-American Literature*, ed. John Whalen-Bridge and Gary Storhoff. State University of New York Press, 2009, pp. 45–62.

Hein, Jeremy. *From Vietnam, Laos, and Cambodia: A Refugee Experience in the United States*. Twayne Publishers, 1995.

Henricks, Robert G., ed. and trans. *The Poetry of Han Shan: A Complete, Annotated Translation of Cold Mountain*. State University of New York Press, 1990.

Herberg, Will. *Protestant, Catholic, Jew.* University of Chicago Press, 1960.

Hergesheimer, Joseph. *Java Head.* Knopf, 1918.

Herrigel, Eugen. *Zen in the Art of Archery.* Trans. R. F. C. Hull. Introduction by D. T. Suzuki. Pantheon Books, 1953.

Heuman, Linda. "A Right to the Dharma: An Interview with Myokei Caine-Barrett, Shonin." *Tricycle,* Fall 2011, http://blog.tricycle.com/feature/right-dharma?page=0,1. Accessed 8 July 2013.

Hickock, Eugene W. Jr. *The Bill of Rights: Original Meaning and Current Understanding.* University Press of Virginia, 1991.

Hijiya, James A. "The *Gita* of J. Robert Oppenheimer." *Proceedings of the American Philosophical Society,* vol. 144, no. 2, 2000, pp. 123–67. *JSTOR,* www.jstor.org/stable/1515629. Accessed 24 Apr. 2018.

Hiltebeitel, Alf. *Dharma: Its Early History in Law, Religion, and Narrative.* Oxford University Press, 2011.

Hilton, James. *Lost Horizon.* Pocket Books, 1933.

Ho, Jennifer Ann. *Consumption and Identity in Asian American Coming of Age Novels.* Routledge, 2005.

Hoffman, Renée and Darrell Steffensmeier. "Attitudes and Behavior Toward Hippies: a Field Experiment Accompanied by Home Interviews." *The Sociological Quarterly,* vol. 16, no. 3, 1975, pp. 393–400.

Hofstadter, Richard. *The Paranoid Style in American Politics and Other Essays.* Harvard University Press, 1996.

Honda, Masaaki. "*The Cloud of Unknowing* and the Logic of 'Not-Two.'" *Buddhist-Christian Studies,* vol. 1, 1981, pp. 93–96. *JSTOR,* www.jstor.org/stable/1390105. Accessed 24 Apr. 2018.

Hongo, Garret Kaoru, Alan Chong Lau, and Lawson Fusao Inada. *The Buddha Bandits Down Highway 99.* Buddhahead Press, 1978.

Hoover, Herbert. *American Individualism.* Doubleday, 1922, *Internet Archive,* https://archive.org/details/americanindividoohoovgoog. Accessed 24 Feb. 2017.

Hoyser, Catherine and Lorena Laura Stokey. *Tom Robbins: A Critical Companion.* Greenwood Press, 1997.

Huang, Su-chun. "A Hua-Yen Buddhist Perspective of Gary Snyder." *Tamkang Review: A Quarterly of Comparative Studies between Chinese and Foreign Literatures,* vol. 22, no. 2, 1989, pp. 195–216.

Hungerford, Amy. *Postmodern Belief: American Literature and Religion since 1960.* Princeton University Press, 2010.

Huxley, Aldous. *The Perennial Philosophy.* 1945. Books for Libraries Press, 1972.

Immerman, Richard H. *Empire for Liberty: A History of American Imperialism from Benjamin Franklin to Paul Wolfowitz.* Princeton University Press, 2012.

Indaratana, Maha Thera. *Vandana: The Album of Pali Devotional Chanting and Hymns.* Inward Path Publisher, 2002, *Buddha Dharma Education Association, Inc.,* www.buddhanet.net/pdf_file/vandana02.pdf. Accessed 7 June 2016.

Ives, Colta. "Japonisme." *Heilbrunn Timeline of Art History. The Metropolitan Museum of Art,* Oct. 2004, http://www.metmuseum.org/toah/hd/jpon/hd_jpon.htm. Accessed 10 July 2013.

Iwamura, Jane Naomi. *Virtual Orientalism: Asian Religions and American Popular Culture.* Oxford University Press, 2011.

Iyer, Venkatarama. *Advaita Vedanta: According to Samkara.* Asia Publishing House, 1964.

Jackson, Carl T. "The Counterculture Looks East: Beat Writers and Asian Religion." *American Studies,* vol. 29, no. 1, 1988, pp. 51–70. *JSTOR,* www.jstor.org/stable/40642254. Accessed 24 Apr. 2018.

Jackson, Thomas. *From Civil Rights to Human Rights: Martin Luther King, Jr., and the Struggle for Economic Justice.* University of Pennsylvania Press, 2007.

Jain, Andrea. *Selling Yoga: From Counterculture to Pop Culture.* Oxford University Press, 2014.

James, William. *The Varieties of Religious Experience.* 1902. Library of America Paperback Classics, 2010.

Jameson, Fredric. *Postmodernism: Or, the Cultural Logic of Late Capitalism.* Duke University Press, 1991.

Janette, Michele, ed. Introduction. *My Viet.* University of Hawai'i Press, 2011.

Johnson, Charles. *Dreamer.* Scribner, 1998.

———. Foreword. "Nixon," ed. Kate Wheeler, pp. vii–x.

———. "The Meaning of Barack Obama." *Shambhala Sun,* Nov. 2008, http://www.shambhalasun.com/index.php?option=com_content&task=view&id=3266&Itemid=244. Accessed 29 May 2013.

———. *Middle Passage.* Scribner, 1990.

———. *Oxherding Tale.* Scribner, 1982.

———. "A Sangha by Another Name." *Turning the Wheel: Essays on Buddhism and Writing.* Scribner, 2003, pp. 46-57.

———. *Turning the Wheel: Essays on Buddhism and Writing.* Scribner, 2003.

Johnson, E. Patrick. *Appropriating Blackness: Performance and the Politics of Authenticity.* Duke University Press, 2003.

Johnson, Sheila K. *The Japanese through American Eyes.* Stanford University Press, 1988.

Johnston, Allan. "Some of the Dharma: The Human, the Heavenly, and the 'Real Work' in the Writings of Gary Snyder." *Writing as Enlightenment: Buddhist American Literature into the Twenty-First Century,* ed. John Whalen-Bridge and Gary Storhoff. State University of New York Press, 2011, pp. 71–88.

Jung, Patricia Beattie. "Sanctifying Women's Pleasure." *Good Sex: Feminist Perspectives from the World's Religions,* ed. Patricia Beattie, Mary E. Hunt, and Radhika Balakrishnan, pp. 77–95. Rutgers University Press, 2001.

Jung, Patricia Beattie, Mary E. Hunt, and Radhika Balakrishnan, eds. Introduction. *Good Sex: Feminist Perspectives from the World's Religions.* Rutgers University Press, 2001.

Junghare, Indira Y. "Hindu Spirituality: A Theory for Everything." *The International Journal of Religion and Spirituality in Society,* vol. 6, no. 3, 2016, pp. 13–27. Academic Search Ultimate, http://search.ebscohost.com.proxy2.library.illinois.edu/login.aspx?direct=true&db=asn&AN=116347146. Accessed 24 Apr. 2018.

Kabat-Zinn, Jon. *Full Catastrophe Living: Using the Wisdom of Your Body and Mind to Face Stress, Pain, and Illness.* 2nd ed. Bantam, 2013.

Kachtick, Keith, ed. *You Are Not Here and Other Works of Buddhist Fiction.* Wisdom Publications, 2006.

Kapleau, Philip. *The Three Pillars of Zen: Teaching, Practice, and Enlightenment.* Anchor, 1989.

The Karate Kid. Dir. John G. Avildsen. Perf. Ralph Maccio, Pat Morita. Columbia, 1984.

Karthar Rinpoche, Khenpo. *The Instructions of Gampopa: A Precious Garland of the Supreme Path.* Snow Lion, 1996.

Kauffman, Linda. "The Wake of Terror: Don DeLillo's 'In the Ruins of the Future,' 'Baader-Meinhoff,' and *Falling Man*." *Modern Fiction Studies*, vol. 54, no. 2, 2008, pp. 353–77. *Project MUSE*, doi:10.1353/mfs.0.0010. Accessed 24 Apr. 2018.

Kern, Robert. *Orientalism, Modernism, and the American Poem.* Cambridge University Press, 1996.

Kerouac, Jack. *The Dharma Bums.* 1958. Introduction by Ann Douglas. Penguin, 2006.

———. *Mexico City Blues.* Grove Press, 1959.

———. *On the Road.* Penguin, 1955.

———. *The Scripture of the Golden Eternity.* Totem Press, 1960.

———. *Some of the Dharma.* 1956. Foreword by John Sampas. Ed. David Stanford. Viking, 1997.

King, Mary E. *Mahatma Gandhi and Martin Luther King, Jr.: The Power of Nonviolent Action.* UNESCO Publishing, 1999.

King, The Reverend Dr. Martin Luther Jr. *Stride toward Freedom: The Montgomery Story.* Harper & Row, 1958.

King, Richard. *Indian Philosophy: An Introduction to Hindu and Buddhist Thought.* Edinburgh University Press, 1999.

———. *Orientalism and Religion: Post-Colonial Theory, India and the "Mystic East."* Routledge, 1999.

King, Winston L. "Time Transcendence-Acceptance in Zen Buddhism." *Journal of the American Academy of Religion*, vol. 36, no. 3, 1968, pp. 217–28. *JSTOR*, www.jstor.org/stable/1460969. Accessed 2 Feb. 2017.

Kingston, Maxine Hong. *China Men.* Knopf, 1980.

———. *The Fifth Book of Peace.* Knopf, 2003.

———. *Tripmaster Monkey: His Fake Book.* Knopf, 1989.

———. *The Woman Warrior: Memoirs of a Girlhood among Ghosts.* Knopf, 1976.

Kipling, Rudyard. *Kim.* 1902. Doubleday, Page & Company, 1922.

Knight, Peter. *Conspiracy Culture: From Kennedy to* The X Files. Routledge, 2000.

———. "Everything Is Connected: *Underworld*'s Secret History of Paranoia." *Modern Fiction Studies*, vol. 45, no. 3, 1999, pp. 811–36. *Project MUSE*, doi:10.1353/mfs.1999.0052. Accessed 26 Apr. 2018.

Koestler, Arthur. *The Lotus and the Robot.* Hutchinson, 1960.

Kohn, Robert E. "Buddhist Duality in William Gaddis's *Carpenter's Gothic*." *Critique: Studies in Contemporary Fiction*, vol. 45, no. 4, 2004, pp. 421–32. *MLA International Bibliography*, http://search.ebscohost.com.proxy2.library.illinois.edu/login.aspx?direct=true&db=mzh&AN=2004532006. Accessed 24 Apr. 2018.

———. "The Merging of Tantric Buddhism and l'extase tantrique in John Hawkes's *The Passion Artist*." *Critique: Studies in Contemporary Fiction*, vol. 47, no. 2, 2006, pp. 147–64. *MLA International Bibliography*, doi:10.3200/CRIT.47.2.147-166. Accessed 24 Apr. 2018.

———. "Seven Buddhist Themes in *The Crying of Lot 49*." *Religion and Literature*, vol. 35, no. 1, 2003, pp. 73–96.

———. "Tibetan Buddhism in Don DeLillo's Novels: The Street, The Word and The Soul." *College Literature*, vol. 38, no. 4, 2011, pp. 156–80. *JSTOR*, www.jstor.org/stable/41302893. Accessed 24 Apr. 2018.

Konstantinou, Lee. *Cool Characters: Irony and American Fiction*. Harvard University Press, 2016.

Krebs, Stefan. "Dial Gauge versus Senses 1–0: German Car Mechanics and the Introduction of New Diagnostic Equipment, 1950–1980." *Technology and Culture*, vol. 55, no. 2, 2014, pp. 354–89. *Project MUSE*, doi:10.1353/tech.2014.0034. Accessed 26 Apr. 2018.

Kurien, Prema A. *A Place at the Multicultural Table: The Development of an American Hinduism*. Rutgers University Press, 2007.

Lauret, Maria. *Alice Walker*. 2000. 2nd ed. Palgrave Macmillan, 2011.

Lawlor, William. "A Compact Guide to Sources for Teaching the Beats." *College Literature*, vol. 27, no. 1, 2000, pp. 232–255.

Leary, Timothy, Ralph Metzner, and Richard Alpert. *The Psychedelic Experience: A Manual Based on* The Tibetan Book of the Dead. Kensington Publishing Corp., 1964.

LeClair, Thomas. "An Interview with Don DeLillo." 1982. *Conversations with Don DeLillo*, ed. Thomas DePietro. University of Mississippi Press, 2005, pp. 3–15.

Leong, Russell. *Phoenix Eyes and Other Stories*. University of Washington Press, 2000.

Levin, Amy K. *Africanism and Authenticity in African-American Women's Novels*. University Press of Florida, 2003.

Lipka, Michael. "5 facts about the Pledge of Allegiance." *Pew Research Center*, 4 Sept. 2013, http://www.pewresearch.org/fact-tank/2013/09/04/5-facts-about-the-pledge-of-allegiance. Accessed 27 Jan. 2017.

Lister, Rachel. *Alice Walker:* The Color Purple. Palgrave Macmillan, 2010.

Little, Jonathan. *Charles Johnson's Spiritual Imagination*. University of Missouri Press, 1997.

———. "From the Comic Book to the Comic: Charles Johnson's Variations on Creative Expression." *African American Review*, vol. 30, no. 4, 1996, pp. 579–601. *JSTOR*, http://www.jstor.org/stable/3042512. Accessed 21 May 2018.

Llewelyn, Robert. "The Treatment of Distractions in Zen and *The Cloud of Unknowing*." *14th Century English Mystics Newsletter*, vol. 7, no. 2, 1981, pp. 61–76. *JSTOR*, www.jstor.org/stable/20716332. Accessed 24 Apr. 2018.

Lohr, Steve. "Maybe Japan Was Just a Warm-Up." *New York Times*, 21 Jan. 2011, http://www.nytimes.com/2011/01/23/business/23japan.html?pagewanted=all&_r=0. Accessed 20 May 2013.

Lopez, Donald. *The Heart Sutra Explained: Indian and Tibetan Commentaries*. State University of New York Press, 1988.

Lott, Deshae E. "'All things are different appearances of the same emptiness': Buddhism and Jack Kerouac's Nature Writings." In *Reconstructing the Beats*, ed. Jennie Skerl, New York: Palgrave Macmillan, 2004, pp. 169–85.

Lowe, Lisa. "Heterogeneity, Hybridity, Multiplicity: Marking Asian American Differences." *Diaspora: A Journal of Transnational Studies*, vol. 1, no. 1, 1991, pp. 22–44.

Loy, David. "The Mahayana Deconstruction of Time." *Philosophy East and West*, vol. 36, no. 1, 1986, pp. 13–23. *JSTOR*, www.jstor.org/stable/1398505. Accessed 24 Apr. 2018.

———. "A Zen Cloud? Comparing Zen 'Koan' Practice with *The Cloud of Unknowing*." *Buddhist-Christian Studies*, vol. 9, 1989, pp. 43–60. *JSTOR*, www.jstor.org/stable/1390000. Accessed 24 Apr. 2018.

Lu, Yunfeng and Graeme Lang. "Beyond Exclusive Religions: Challenges for the Sociology of Religion in China." *Social Sciences in China*, vol. 31, no. 1, 2010, pp. 198–216. *SocINDEX*, doi:10.1080/02529200903565178. Accessed 26 Apr. 2018.

Lustbader, Eric Van. *The Miko*. Fawcett, 1984.

———. *The Ninja*. M. Evans & Co., 1980.

Lutz, R. C. "Japanese Trade with the United States." *Historical Encyclopedia of American Business*, ed. Richard L. Wilson. Salem Press, 2009, http://salempress.com/store/samples/american_business/american_business_japanese.htm. Accessed 15 July 2013.

Lyotard, Jean-François. *The Postmodern Condition: A Report on Knowledge*. 1979. Trans. Geoff Bennington and Brian Massumi. University of Minnesota Press, 1999.

Madison, James. Federalist 10, 1787, and Federalist 51, 1788. *The Federalist Papers*, https://www.congress.gov/resources/display/content/The+Federalist+Papers. Accessed 16 Feb. 2017.

Maeda, Daryl. *Chains of Babylon: The Rise of Asian America*. University of Minnesota Press, 2009.

Maher, Paul. *Kerouac: The Definitive Biography*. Taylor Trade Publishing, 2004.

Mahesh Yogi, Maharishi. *Science of Being and Art of Living: Transcendental Meditation*. Meridian, 1963.

Marcus, George E. Introduction. *Paranoia within Reason: A Casebook on Conspiracy as Explanation*, ed. George E. Marcus. University of Chicago Press, 1999, pp. 1–12.

Martinez, Manuel Luis. *Countering the Counterculture: Rereading Postwar American Dissent from Jack Kerouac to Tomás Rivera*. University of Wisconsin Press, 2003.

Marvin, Thomas F. "'Preachin' the Blues: Bessie Smith's Secular Religion and Alice Walker's *The Color Purple*." *African American Review*, vol. 28, no. 3, 1994, pp. 411–21. *JSTOR*, www.jstor.org/stable/3041977. Accessed 24 Apr. 2018.

Masatsugu, Michael K. "'Beyond This World of Transiency and Impermanence': Japanese Americans, Dharma Bums, and the Making of American Buddhism during the Cold War Years." *Pacific Historical Review*, vol. 77, no. 3, 2008, pp. 423–51. *JSTOR*, doi: 10.1525/phr.2008.77.3.423. Accessed 24 Apr. 2018.

Masci, David and Michael Lipka. "Americans may be getting less religious, but feelings of spirituality are on the rise." *Pew Research Center*, 21 Jan. 2016, http://www.pewresearch.org/fact-tank/2016/01/21/americans-spirituality/. Accessed 7 Aug. 2018.

Mason, Alpheus T. "American Individualism: Fact and Fiction." 1952. *The American Political Science Review*, vol. 46, no. 1, 1952, pp. 1–18. *JSTOR*, doi:10.2307/1950759. Accessed 15 Aug. 2016.

McCleod, Melvin. "This Is the Buddha's Love." Interview with Thich Nhat Hanh. *Shambhala Sun*, March 2006, http://www.shambhalasun.com/index.php?option=content&task=view&id=288. Accessed 1 July 2013.

McCloud, Sean. *Making the American Religious Fringe: Exotics, Subversives, and Journalists, 1955–1993*. University of North Carolina Press, 2004.

McClure, John. *Partial Faiths: Postsecular Fiction in the Age of Pynchon and Morrison.* University of Georgia Press, 2007.

McHale, Brian. *Constructing Postmodernism.* New York: Routledge, 1992.

McMahan, David L. *The Making of Buddhist Modernism.* Oxford University Press, 2008.

McMahon, Darrin. *Happiness: A History.* Grove Press, 2006.

McWilliams, Jim, ed. *Passing the Three Gates: Interviews with Charles Johnson.* University of Washington Press, 2004.

Merton, Thomas. *The Ascent to Truth.* Harvest Books, 1951.

Miles, Jeffrey. "Making It to Cold Mountain: Han Shan in *The Dharma Bums.*" *Essays on the Literature of Mountaineering,* ed. Armand E. Singer. West Virginia University Press, 1982.

Miller, Andrea. "Wisdom of the Rebels." Interview with Tom Robbins. *Conversations,* ed. Liam O. Purdon and Beef Torrey, pp. 151–56.

Mingyur Rinpoche, Yongey. *The Joy of Living: Unlocking the Secret and Science of Happiness.* Harmony Books, 2007.

"Mission." *Dharma Academy of North America (DANAM). DANAM,* www.danam-web.org. Accessed 22 Sept. 2016.

Mitchell, W. J. T. *Seeing through Race.* Harvard University Press, 2012.

Molloy, Seán. "Escaping the Politics of the Irredeemable Earth: Anarchy and Transcendence in the Novels of Thomas Pynchon." *Theory and Event,* vol. 13, no. 3, 2010. *Project MUSE,* doi:10.1353/tae.2010.0004. Accessed 24 Apr. 2018.

Morgan, Edward P. *What Really Happened to the 1960s: How Mass Media Culture Failed American Democracy.* University Press of Kansas, 2010.

Mori, Toshio. *Yokohama, California.* 1949. University of Washington Press, 1985.

Morinaga, Maki Isaka. *Secrecy in Japanese Arts: "Secret Transmission" as a Mode of Knowledge.* Palgrave Macmillan, 2005.

Murphy, Patrick D. *A Place for Wayfaring: The Poetry and Prose of Gary Snyder.* Oregon State University Press, 2000.

Nash, William R. *Charles Johnson's Fiction.* University of Illinois Press, 2003.

———. "A Conversation with Charles Johnson," *Passing,* ed. Jim McWilliams, pp. 214–35.

Newton, Pauline. "'Different Cultural Lenses': An Interview with Lan Cao, October 24, 2000," *Transcultural Women of Late-Twentieth-Century U.S. American Literature,* ed. Pauline Newton, Ashgate, 2005, pp. 173–84.

Nguyen, Viet Thanh. "Refugee Memories and Asian American Critique." *Positions: East Asia Cultures Critique,* vol. 20, no. 3, 2012, pp. 911–42. *Project MUSE,* muse.jhu.edu/article/483984. Accessed 24 Apr. 2018.

Nhat Hanh, Thich. *For a Future to Be Possible: Buddhist Ethics for Everyday Life.* Parallax Press, 1993.

———. Foreword. *Love's Garden: A Path to Mindful Relationships,* ed. Peggy Rowe-Ward and Larry Ward. Parallax Press, 2008, pp. xiii–xxii.

———. *Interbeing: Fourteen Guidelines for Engaged Buddhism.* 3rd ed. Parallax Press, 1987.

———. *The Miracle of Mindfulness: An Introduction to Meditation.* Trans. Mobi Ho. Beacon Press, 1975.

Nojeim, Michael J. *Gandhi and King: The Power of Nonviolent Resistance.* Praeger, 2004.

Northrop, W. S. C. *The Meeting of East and West: An Inquiry Concerning World Understanding.* 1946. Macmillan, 1966.

O'Bryan, Michael. "In Defense of *Vineland*: Pynchon, Anarchism, and the New Left." *Twentieth Century Literature*, vol. 62, no. 1, Mar. 2016, pp. 1–31. *MLA International Bibliography*, 10.1215/0041462X-3485002. Accessed 24 Apr. 2018.

Odin, Steve. *Artistic Detachment in Japan and the West: Psychic Distance in Comparative Aesthetics.* University of Hawaiʻi Press, 2001.

Okada, John. *No No Boy.* 1957. University of Washington Press, 1979.

Oppert, Gustav. *On the Weapons, Army Organization, and Political Maxims of the Ancient Hindus, With Special Reference to Gunpowder and Firearms.* London: Messrs. Trübner & Co., 1880.

Otsuka, Julie. *The Buddha in the Attic.* Knopf, 2011.

Overmeyer, Daniel L. et al. "Chinese Religions—The State of the Field Part II: Living Religious Traditions: Taoism, Confucianism, Buddhism, Islam and Popular Religion." *The Journal of Asian Studies*, vol. 54, no. 2, 1995, pp. 314–21. *JSTOR*, doi: 10.2307/2058738. Accessed 24 Apr. 2018.

Oxford English Dictionary. "Adept." *Oxford English Dictionary Online*, http://www.oed.com.proxy-um.researchport.umd.edu. Accessed 18 March 2013.

Ozeki, Ruth. *A Tale for the Time Being: A Novel.* Penguin, 2013.

Panish, Jon. "Kerouac's *The Subterraneans*: A Study of 'Romantic Primitivism.'" *MELUS*, vol. 19, no. 3, 1994, pp. 107–23. *JSTOR*, www.jstor.org/stable/467875. Accessed 24 Apr. 2018.

Park, Josephine Nock-Hee. *Apparitions of Asia: Modernist Form and Asian American Poetics.* Oxford University Press, 2008.

Perry, Donna. "Maxine Hong Kingston." Interview. 1991. *Conversations*, ed. Paul Skenazy and Tera Martin, 168–88.

Petrus, Stephen. "Rumblings of Discontent: American Popular Culture and its Response to the Beat Generation, 1957-1960." *Studies in Popular Culture*, vol. 20, no. 1, 1997, pp. 1–17.

Pham, Quynh Phuong and Chris Eipper. "Mothering and Fathering the Vietnamese: Religion, Gender, and National Identity." *Journal of Vietnamese Studies*, vol. 4, no. 1, 2009, pp. 49–83. *MLA International Bibliography*, doi:10.1525/vs.2009.4.1.49. Accessed 24 Apr. 2018.

Pintak, Lawrence. "'Something Has to Change': Blacks in American Buddhism." *Shambhala Sun*, Sept. 2001, http://www.shambhalasun.com/index.php?option=com_content&task=view&id=1741&Itemid=0. Accessed 10 July 2013.

Pirsig, Robert. *Zen and the Art of Motorcycle Maintenance.* 1974. Bantam, 1976.

Porter, Katherine Anne. *Mae Franking's* My Chinese Marriage: *An Annotated Edition*, ed. Holly Franking. University of Texas Press, 1991.

Porush, David. "'Purring into Transcendence': Pynchon's Puncutron Machine." *The Vineland Papers: Critical Takes on Pynchon's Novel*, ed. Geoffrey Green et al. Dalkey Archive Press, 1994.

Prebish, Charles S. *Luminous Passage: The Practice and Study of Buddhism in America.* University of California Press, 1999.

Prothero, Stephen. "A *Hindu Moment* for Congress." *USA Today*, 3 Jan. 2013, http://www.usatoday.com/story/opinion/2013/01/03/hindu-tulsi-gabbard-congress/1808127. Accessed 27 June 2013.

———. Introduction. *Big Sky Mind,* ed. Carole Tonkinson, pp. 1–20.

———. "On the Holy Road: The Beat Movement as Spiritual Protest." *Harvard Theological Review,* vol. 84, no. 2, 1991, pp. 205–22. *MLA International Bibliography,* doi: 10.1017/S0017816000008166. Accessed 26 Apr. 2018.

———. *The White Buddhist: The Asian Odyssey of Henry Steel Olcott.* Indiana University Press, 1996.

Purdon, Liam O. and Beef Torrey, eds. *Conversations with Tom Robbins.* University of Mississippi Press, 2011.

———. Introduction. *Conversations,* ed. Liam O. Purdon and Beef Torrey, pp. i–xxviii.

———. "A Literary Conversation with Tom Robbins." 2009. *Conversations,* ed. Liam O. Purdon and Beef Torrey, pp. 164–88.

Pynchon, Thomas. *The Crying of Lot 49.* Harper, 1965.

———. *Vineland.* Little, Brown, 1990.

Queen, Christopher S., ed. *Engaged Buddhism in the West.* Wisdom Publications, 2000.

Rahula, Walpola. *What the Buddha Taught.* Foreword by Paul Demieville. Grove Press, 1974.

Rainey, Lawrence, ed. *The Annotated* Waste Land *with Eliot's Contemporary Prose.* 2nd ed. Yale University Press, 2005.

Rambachan, Anantanand. *The Advaita Worldview: God, World, and Humanity.* State University of New York Press, 2006.

Ranchan, Som P. *An Adventure in Vedanta: J. D. Salinger's the Glass Family.* South Asia Books, 1990.

Rentilly, J. "It Takes a Villa." Interview with Tom Robbins. *Conversations,* ed. Liam O. Purdon and Beef Torrey, pp. 122–28.

Robbins, Tom. "In Defiance of Gravity." Wild Ducks Flying Backward: *The Short Writings of Tom Robbins.* Bantam Dell, 2005, pp. 175–87.

———. *Even Cowgirls Get the Blues.* Bantam, 1977.

———. *Tibetan Peach Pie: A True Account of an Imaginative Life.* New York: HarperCollins, 2014.

———. *Villa Incognito.* New York: Bantam, 2003.

Rosen, Elizabeth. "Lenny Bruce and His Nuclear Shadow Marvin Lundy: Don DeLillo's Apocalyptists Extraordinaire." *Journal of American Studies,* vol. 40, no. 1, 2007, pp. 97–112. *MLA International Bibliography,* doi: 10.1017/S0021875806000764. Accessed 24 Apr. 2018.

Roszak, Theodore. *The Making of a Counter Culture: Reflections on the Technocratic Society and Its Youthful Opposition.* University of California Press, 1969.

Rushdy, Ashraf. "Charles Johnson's Way to a Spiritual Literature." *African American Review,* vol. 43, no. 2–3, 2009, pp. 401–12. *JSTOR,* www.jstor.org/stable/41328617. Accessed 24 Apr. 2018.

Ryan, Tim. *A Mindful Nation: How a Simple Practice Can Help Us Reduce Stress, Improve Performance, and Recapture the American Spirit.* Hay House, 2012.

Sachs, Robert. *The Passionate Buddha: Wisdom on Intimacy and Enduring Love.* Inner Traditions, 2002.

Said, Edward. *Orientalism.* Vintage, 1979.

Sakya Trizin, H. H. *Entry into the Adamantine.* Grey Earth, 2010.

Salak, Kira. "Beheadings." *"Nixon,"* ed. Kate Wheeler, 91–124.

Salinger, J. D. *Franny and Zooey*. Little, Brown, 1961.

———. Letter to Swami Adiswarananda. 26 Dec. 1975. *Ramakrishna-Vivekananda Center of New York*, http://www.ramakrishna.org/activities/Salinger/Salinger.htm. Accessed 29 Nov. 2016.

———. "A Perfect Day for Bananafish." 1947. *Nine Stories*. 1953. Bantam, 1981.

———. *Raise High the Roofbeam, Carpenters* and *Seymour—An Introduction*. Little, Brown, 1959.

———. "Teddy." *Nine Stories*. 1953. Bantam, 1981.

Salzberg, Sharon. *Real Happiness: The Power of Meditation: A 28-Day Program*. Workman Publishing Company, 2010.

Sampas, John. Kerouac, *Some of the Dharma*, Foreword. pp. viii.

Samuel, Geoffrey. "Buddhism and the State in Eighth Century Tibet." *Tibet, Past and Present: Religion and Secular Culture in Tibet: Tibetan Studies II*, ed. Henk Blezer. Brill, 2002, pp. 1–20.

Santideva. *Bodhicaryavatara*. Trans. Kate Crosby and Andrew Skilton. Oxford University Press, 1995.

Satha-Anand, Suwanna. "Buddhism on Sexuality and Enlightenment." *Good Sex*, ed. Patricia Beattie, Mary E. Hunt, and Radhika Balakrishnan, pp. 113–24.

Savvas, Theophilus. *American Postmodernist Fiction and the Past*. Palgrave Macmillan, 2011.

Schmidt, Leigh Eric. *Restless Souls: The Making of American Spirituality*. HarperCollins, 2005.

Schneck, Peter. "'The Great Secular Transcendence': Don DeLillo and the Desire for Numinous Experience." *Terrorism, Media, and the Ethics of Fiction*, ed. Peter Schneck and Philipp Schweighauser, Continuum, 2010, pp. 204–19.

Schroeder, Eric J. "As Truthful as Possible: An Interview with Maxine Hong Kingston." 1996. *Conversations*, ed. Paul Skenazy and Tera Martin, pp. 215–28.

Schueller, Malini Johar. *U.S. Orientalisms: Race, Nation, and Gender in Literature, 1790–1890*. University of Michigan Press, 1998.

Schultz, Bud and Ruth Schultz. *The Price of Dissent: Testimonies to Political Repression in America*. Berkeley: University of California Press, 2001.

Schwartz, Arthur. "For Seymour: With Love and Judgment." *Wisconsin Studies in Contemporary Literature*, vol. 4, no. 1, 1963, pp. 88–99. JSTOR, www.jstor.org/stable/1207187. Accessed 24 Apr. 2018.

Seager, Richard Hughes. *Buddhism in America*. Columbia University Press, 1999.

Sedgwick, Eve. *Touching, Feeling: Affect, Pedagogy, Performativity*. Duke University Press, 2003.

Selzer, Linda Ferguson. "Black American Buddhism: History and Representation." *Writing as Enlightenment: Buddhist American Literature into the Twenty-First Century*, ed. John Whalen-Bridge and Gary Storhoff. State University of New York Press, 2011, pp. 37–68.

———. *Charles Johnson in Context*. University of Massachusetts Press, 2009.

———. "Race and Domesticity in *The Color Purple*." *African American Review*, vol. 29, no. 1, 1995, pp. 67–82. MLA International Bibliography, doi:10.2307/3042429. Accessed 24 Apr. 2018.

Senzaki, Nyogen and Paul Reps, eds. *Zen Flesh, Zen Bones: A Collection of Zen and Pre-Zen Writings*. Tuttle Publishing, 1957.

Seshachari, Neila C. "Reinventing Peace: Conversations with *Tripmaster* Maxine Hong Kingston." 1993. Interview. *Conversations*, ed. Paul Skenazy and Tera Martin, pp. 192–214.

Shan, Te-Hsing. "Crossing Bridges into the Pasts: Reading Lan Cao's *Monkey Bridge*." *Chang Gung Journal of Humanities and Social Sciences*, vol. 3, no. 1, 2010, pp. 19–44. www.cgjhsc.cgu.edu.tw/data_files/3-1%2002.pdf. Accessed 14 Aug. 2018.

Siderits, Mark and Shoryu Katsura, trans. *Nagarjuna's Middle Way: Mulamadhyamakakarika*. Somerville, MA: Wisdom Publications, 2013.

Sielke, Sabine and Christian Kloeckner. Introduction. *Orient and Orientalisms in US-American Poetry and Poetics*, ed. Sabine Sielke and Christian Koeckner. Peter Lang, 2009, pp. 9–32.

Simcikova, Karla. "Life and Its Survival: Walker's New Religion in *Now Is the Time to Open Your Heart*." *Cuadernos de Literatura Inglesa y Norteamericana*, vol. 9, no.1–2, 2006, pp. 37–46.

Simmons, Diane. *Maxine Hong Kingston*. Twayne Publishers, 1999.

Singh, Sukhbir. "Time, War and the Bhagavad Gita: A Rereading of Kurt Vonnegut's *Slaughterhouse-Five*." *Comparative Critical Studies*, vol. 7, no. 1, 2010, pp. 83–103. MLA International Bibliography, doi: 10.3366/E1744185409000962. Accessed 24 Apr. 2018.

Skenazy, Paul. "Kingston at the University." Interview with Maxine Hong Kingston. 1989. *Conversations*, ed. Paul Skenazy and Tera Martin. pp. 118–58.

Skenazy, Paul and Tera Martin, eds. *Conversations with Maxine Hong Kingston*. University Press of Mississippi, 1998.

Slawenski, Kenneth. "Holden Caulfield's Goddam War." *Vanity Fair*, 20 Jan. 2011, http://www.vanityfair.com/culture/2011/02/salinger-201102. Accessed 2 Feb. 2017.

Slawson, David A. *Secret Teachings in the Art of Japanese Gardens: Design Principles, Aesthetic Values*. Kodansha USA, 1991.

Smith, Huston. *The World's Religions*. HarperCollins, 1991.

Smith, Kyle. "A Separate Piece." *People Magazine*, vol. 48, no. 4, 1997, http://www.people.com/people/archive/article/0,,20122768,00.html. Accessed 7 July 2013.

Smithers, Stuart. "Some of the Dharma." Book Review. *Tricycle*, Spring 1998, https://tricycle.org/magazine/some-dharma. Accessed 11 Mar. 2018.

Snodgrass, Judith. *Presenting Japanese Buddhism to the West: Orientalism, Occidentalism, and the Columbian Exposition*. The University of North Carolina Press, 2003.

Snyder, Gary. *Cold Mountain Poems: Twenty-Four Poems by Han Shan*. 1958. Counterpoint, 2013.

———. "The Etiquette of Freedom." *The Practice of the Wild*. North Point Press, 1990, pp. 3–24.

———. *Mountains and Rivers without End*. Counterpoint, 1996.

———. "Notes on the Beat Generation." *A Place in Space: Ethics, Aesthetics, and Watermarks*. Counterpoint, 1995, pp. 7–13.

———. Riprap and Cold Mountain Poems. Four Seasons, 1977.

———. "Smokey the Bear Sutra." 1969. *Working the Woods, Working the Sea: An Anthology of Northwest Writing*, ed. Finn Wilcox and Jerry Gorsline. Empty Bowl Press, 1986, pp. 241–44.

Soyen, Shaku. *Sermons of a Buddhist Abbot*. Trans. D. T. Suzuki. Open Court, 1906. *Terebess Online*, http://terebess.hu/zen/mesterek/Sermons-of-A-Buddhist-Abbot.pdf. Accessed 20 Feb. 2017.

Spivak, Gayatri Chakravorty. *In Other Worlds: Essays in Cultural Politics*. Methuen, 1987.

Stalling, Jonathan. *Poetics of Emptiness: Transformations of Asian Thought in American Poetry*. Fordham University Press, 2010.

Stiles, Bradley J. *Emerson's Contemporaries and Kerouac's Crowd: A Problem of Self-Location*. Associated University Press, 2003.

Storhoff, Gary. *Understanding Charles Johnson*. University of South Carolina Press, 2004.

Storhoff, Gary and John Whalen-Bridge. Introduction. *American Buddhism as a Way of Life*, ed. Gary Storhoff and John Whalen-Bridge. State University of New York Press, 2010, pp. 1–12.

Studholme, Alexander. *The Origins of* Om Mani Padme Hum: *A Study of the* Karandavyuha Sutra. State University of New York Press, 2002.

Summerell, Orrin F. Introduction. *The Otherness of God*, ed. Orrin F. Summerell. University Press of Virginia, 1998, pp. 1–13.

Suzuki, D. T. *Essays in Zen Buddhism*. Grove Press, 1949.

———. Foreword. *Zen in the Art of Archery*, Eugen Herrigel, pp. 9–13.

Sweet, David LeHardy. *Avant-Garde Orientalism: The Eastern 'Other' in Twentieth-Century Travel Narrative and Poetry*. eBook, Palgrave Macmillan, 2017.

Tan, Amy. *The Joy Luck Club*. Penguin Books, 1989.

Tan, Joan Qiongling. *Han Shan, Chan Buddhism and Gary Snyder's Ecopoetic Way*. Sussex Academic Press, 2009.

Tanaka, Kenneth. "Dramatic Growth of American Buddhism: An Overview." *Dharma World*, vol. 38, July 2011, http://www.rk-world.org/dharmaworld/dw_2011julyseptdramaticgrowth.aspx. Accessed 11 June 2013.

Tapia, Elena. "Symmetry as Conceptual Metaphor in Walker's *The Color Purple*." *International Journal of English Studies*, vol. 3, no. 1, 2003, http://revistas.um.es/ijes/issue/view/4621, pp. 29–44. Accessed 24 Apr. 2018.

Taylor, Charles. *A Secular Age*. Harvard University Press, 2007.

"The Technique." *The Transcendental Meditation Program*, http://www.tm.org/meditation-techniques#technique-top. Accessed 7 July 2013.

Teenage Mutant Ninja Turtles. Dir. Steve Barron. Perf. Judith Hoag, Elias Koteas. 888 Productions, 1990.

Terry, Megan. *Viet Rock: A Folk War Movie*. 1965. Simon & Schuster, 1967.

Thanissaro Bhikkhu. "Romancing the Buddha." *Tricycle*, Winter 2002, http://www.tricycle.com/feature/romancing-buddha. Accessed 7 June 2013.

Thoreau, Henry David. *Walden, or Life in the Woods*, ed. Jeffrey S. Cramer. Yale University Press, 2004.

———. "Walking." *The Atlantic*, May 1862, https://www.theatlantic.com/magazine/archive/1862/06/walking/304674. Accessed 3 Oct. 2016.

Tillich, Paul. *The Courage to Be*. Yale University Press, 1952.

Tomiki, Kenji. "Ninjutsu." *Kodansha Encyclopedia of Japan*, Vol. 6. Kodanshi International, 1983, pp. 6–7.

Trigilio, Tony. *Allen Ginsberg's Buddhist Poetics*. Southern Illinois University Press, 2007.

Truman, Greg. "Herbie Hancock Unplugged." *The Sydney Morning Herald*, 2 July 2010, http://www.smh.com.au/entertainment/music/herbie-hancock-unplugged-20100702-ztm5.html. Accessed 7 July 2013.

Turner, Frederick Jackson. *The Frontier in American History*. Henry Holt, 1921. *Project Gutenberg*, http://www.gutenberg.org/files/22994/22994-h/22994-h.htm. Accessed 25 Nov. 2016.

Turner, Jack. "American Individualism and Structural Injustice: Tocqueville, Gender, and Race." *Polity*, vol. 40, no. 2, 2008, pp. 197–215. *JSTOR*, www.jstor.org/stable/40213468. Accessed 15 Aug. 2016.

Turse, Nick. *Kill Anything That Moves: The Real American War in Vietnam*. Metropolitan Books, 2013.

Tweed, Thomas A. *The American Encounter with Buddhism 1844–1912: Victorian Culture and the Limits of Dissent*. Indiana University Press, 1992.

U.S. Religious Landscape Survey: Religious Affiliation: Diverse and Dynamic. The Pew Forum on Religion & Public Life, 2008, http://religions.pewforum.org/pdf/report-religious-landscape-study-full.pdf. Accessed 20 May 2013.

Versluis, Arthur. *American Gurus: From American Transcendentalism to New Age Religion*. Oxford University Press, 2014.

———. *American Transcendentalism and Asian Religions*. Oxford University Press, 1993.

Vivekananda, Swami. *The Complete Works of Swami Vivekananda*, vol. 8, Advaita Ashrama, 1971.

———. "Speech Delivered by Swami Vivekananda on September 11, 1893 at the First World's Parliament of Religions in Chicago." *The Art Institute of Chicago*, http://www.artic.edu/aic/resources/resource/1082. Accessed 18 Jan. 2017.

Vonnegut, Kurt. *Slaughterhouse Five*. 1969. Dell Publishing, 1991.

———. "Yes, We Have No Nirvanas." *Esquire*, vol. 69, no. 6, 1968, pp. 78–79, 176–79.

Walker, Alice. *The Color Purple*. Harcourt, 1982.

———. "A Conversation with David Swick from *Shambala Sun*." *The World Has Changed: Conversations with Alice Walker*, ed. Rudolph P. Byrd. The New Press, 2010, pp. 303–10.

———. "The Creative Journey: Artists in Conversation with the Dalai Lama on Spirituality and Creativity." Emory University, 19 Oct. 2010, http://www.youtube.com/watch?v=hSDaSwUUS1I. Accessed 27 May 2013.

———. *The Cushion in the Road: Meditation and Wandering as the Whole World Awakens to Being in Harm's Way*. The New Press, 2013.

———. "Interview with John O'Brien from *Interviews with Black Writers* (1973)." *The World Has Changed: Conversations with Alice Walker*, ed. Rudolph P. Byrd. The New Press, 2010, pp. 35–57.

———. *Now Is the Time to Open Your Heart*. Random House, 2004.

———. "The Only Reason You Want to Go to Heaven Is That You Have Been Driven Out of Your Mind (Off Your Land and Out of Your Lover's Arms)." *On the Issues Magazine*, vol. 6, no. 2, 1997, http://www.ontheissuesmagazine.com/1997spring/sp97walker.php. Accessed 7 July 2013.

———. Public Appearance. Washington, DC: Busboys and Poets, 28 May 2013.

———. *We Are the Ones We Have Been Waiting For*. W. W. Norton, 2006.

Watts, Alan. "Beat Zen, Square Zen, and Zen." *Chicago Review*, vol. 12, no. 2, 1958, pp. 3–11, *JSTOR*, www.jstor.org/stable/25293448. Accessed 26 Apr. 2018.

The Way of a Pilgrim; and, The Pilgrim Continues His Way. Trans. R. M. French. Seabury Press, 1965.

Wei, William. *The Asian American Movement*. Temple University Press, 1993.

West, Harry G. and Todd Sanders, eds. and introd. *Transparency and Conspiracy: Ethnographies of Suspicion in the New World Order.* Duke University Press, 2003.

Whalen-Bridge, John. "Buddhism, the Chinese Religion, and the Ceremony of Writing: An Interview with Maxine Hong Kingston." *The Emergence of Buddhist-American Literature,* ed. John Whalen-Bridge and Gary Storhoff. State University of New York Press, 2011, pp. 177–88.

———. "Shoulder to the Wheel: An Interview with Charles Johnson," ed. Jim McWilliams, *Passing,* pp. 300–316.

———. "Waking Cain: The Poetics of Integration in Charles Johnson's *Dreamer.*" *Callaloo,* vol. 26, no. 2, 2003, pp. 504–21.

Whalen-Bridge, John and Gary Storhoff, eds. *The Emergence of Buddhist-American Literature.* State University of New York Press, 2009.

Wheeler, Kate, ed. "*Nixon under the Bodhi Tree* and Other Works of Buddhist Fiction. Wisdom Publications, 2004.

White, Evelyn. *Alice Walker: A Life.* W. W. Norton, 2004.

Whitfield, Stephen J. "Cherished and Cursed: Toward a Social History of *The Catcher in the Rye.*" *The New England Quarterly,* vol. 70, no. 4, 1997, pp. 567–600. *JSTOR,* www.jstor.org/stable/366646. Accessed 1 June 2016.

Whitman, Walt. "A Passage to India." *Leaves of Grass.* 1892. Modern Library, 1934, pp. 321–29.

———. *Democratic Vistas: And Other Papers.* 1871. London: W.J. Gage & Co., 1888. *HathiTrust Digital Library.* Accessed 8 Aug. 2018.

Williams, R. John. *The Buddha in the Machine: Art, Technology, and the Meeting of East and West.* Yale University Press, 2014.

Williamson, Lola. *Transcendent in America: Hindu-Inspired Meditation Movements as New Religion.* New York University Press, 2010.

Wilson, Jeff. *Mindful America: The Mutual Transformation of Buddhist Meditation and American Culture.* Oxford University Press, 2014.

Wise, Tim. *Colorblind: The Rise of Post-Racial Politics and the Retreat from Racial Equality.* City Lights Books, 2010.

Wu, Jean Yu-wen Shen and Thomas C. Chen. Introduction. *Asian American Studies Now: A Critical Reader,* ed. Jean Yu-wen Wu and Thomas C. Chen. Rutgers University Press, 2010, pp. xiii–xviii.

Wu, Jean Yu-wen Shen and Min Song. Introduction. *Asian American Studies: A Reader,* ed. Jean Yu-wen Wu and Ming Song. Rutgers University Press, 2000, pp. xiii–xxiv.

Yoo, David K. Introduction. *New Spiritual Homes: Religion and Asian Americans,* ed. David K. Yoo. University of Hawai'i Press, 1999, pp. 1–18.

Zakaria, Fareed. *The Post-American World: Release 2.0.* 2nd ed. W. W. Norton, 2011.

Zhou, Xiaojing. Introduction. *Form and Transformation in Asian American Literature,* ed. Xiaojing Zhou and Samin Najmi. University of Washington Press, 2005.

Zuo, Xin S. *Generic Weaving, Comic Fantasy, and Buddhism in Maxine Hong Kingston's* Tripmaster Monkey. Dissertation. Lubbock: Texas Tech University, 2001. *ProQuest Dissertations and Theses,* http://search.proquest.com/docview/54235029. Accessed abstract 7 July 2013.

INDEX

activism, 17, 26, 32, 40, 42, 45–46, 63, 65, 67, 86, 119, 122, 138, 144–45, 148, 151–52, 155–57, 160, 169–75, 177, 182
adaptation, cross-cultural, 5, 17, 26, 30–31, 42–45, 51, 58–59, 98–102, 118, 148, 179, 186
aesthetic(s), 20, 23, 32
Alpert, Richard, 132. *See also* Ram Dass
Amazon (River), 12, 130–31, 133
American Gurus: From Transcendentalism to New Age Religion (Versluis), 4
American identity, 3–4, 21–22, 24, 75; and African American identity, 26, 130, 137, 153; and Asian American identity, 26, 154–78; and Christianity, 48, 183
American Individualism (Hoover), 3
Americana (DeLillo), 105
Amerindians/Amerindian, 119, 121, 127–28, 130–36
anātman, 156. *See also* nonself
ancestor(s)/ancestry/ancestral, 23, 26, 54, 58, 116, 118–53, 159–60, 167, 169, 172–74, 178
Anglo-American, 5, 11, 14, 18, 21
appropriation/appropriate(s), 4, 30, 35–36, 48, 50–51, 54, 82, 93, 100, 136, 160, 171, 179–80
Aristotle, 81
Arnold, Edwin, 14
Asian American(s), 13, 21–23, 26–27, 60, 154–78; literary movement, 155; Chinese American, 170–72; Vietnamese American, 156, 159–60; Japanese American, 20, 52, 174

Asian American Studies: A Reader (Wu and Song), 156
Asian American Studies Now: A Critical Reader (Wu and Chen), 156
Asian mysticism, 4, 52, 71, 94, 182
Asian religion(s). *See* Buddhism, Confucianism, Daoism, Hinduism, Shinto
Astin, Alexander and Helen, 8
Austin, Mary, 17
authenticity: and African American identity, 26, 118–53; countercultural rhetorics of, 86; Orientalist idea of Asian, 18; Buddhist, 31; personal, 12, 63–64, 67–68, 73, 183
authoritarianism, 5, 92
authority, 12–13, 57, 64, 82, 89, 97, 99, 133
Avalokitesvara, 34, 37–38
awakening, 4, 55, 113, 125. *See also bodhi*
Axial religions, 55; pre-Axial religions, 55
Ayesha: The Return of She (Haggard), 14

Baraka, Amiri, 138
Baker Roshi, Richard, 90
Bardo, 113–14, 179
Bardo Thodol, 113–14. *See also Tibetan Book of the Dead*
Barth, John, 87
Beat: Buddhism, 23, 28–62, 66, 86, 119, 169, 172; Generation, 21, 30–31, 36–37, 42, 61; Zen, 30, 42, 48, 61
"Beheadings" (Salak), 180
Bellow, Saul, 76

Bhagavad-Gita, 1–2, 11, 20, 66, 69, 72, 74
Bible, 1, 2
Bill of Rights, 176–77
Black Arts Movement, 138
Black Dharma, 119
Black Power Movement, 138
Blavatsky, Helena, 14
bodhi, 4, 35, 132–33, 135 180, 186. *See also* awakening
Bohemianism/bohemian, 28, 47, 64–66, 92
bourgeois, 28–29, 53, 57, 62, 64, 67, 78, 87
Brown, James, 36
Bruce, Lenny, 111–12
Brunk, Conrad G., 4–5
Buddha Bandits Down Highway 99 (Hongo, Lau, and Inada), 155
Buddha in the Attic (Otsuka), 157
Buddhism: engaged, 169, 184; Mahayana, 38, 47, 49–50, 172, 185; Buddhist philosophy, 30–1, 36, 42, 68, 71, 99, 139, 149, 166, 172, 175, 184; Tibetan, 33, 89, 93, 104–8, 113–16, 126, 129–130, 185, 187
Buddhist Churches of America, 61, 155
buffered self, 9, 73, 85, 143, 147–48. *See also* porous self
Byrd, Rudolph, 150

Cabezón, José, 185, 187–88
Campbell, Colin, 8
Campbell, Joseph, 63
Cao, Lan, 19, 23, 26, 154, 157, 159–68
capitalism/capitalist, 25, 47, 64, 102
Carlson, Thomas A., 113
Carus, Paul, 21
Casanova, José, 9
Cassat, Mary, 13
Catcher in the Rye, The (Salinger), 64, 78, 85
Cather, Willa, 18
Catholicism/Catholic, 9, 23, 28, 43, 49, 90, 104–17, 129
celibacy, 66, 115, 183, 185
Chea, Joseph, 118, 158
Chickencoop Chinamen, The (Chin), 155
Chin, Frank, 155
Chin, Marilyn, 157

China/Chinese, 11, 13, 17–18, 20, 36–38, 44, 47, 49, 54, 81–82, 102, 155, 157, 159, 168–73, 177, 180
China Men (Kingston), 170
Chödrön, Pema, 127–28
Christ, 16, 21, 49, 67–72, 124–25, 131
Christianity/Christian, 1–2, 5, 7, 21–22, 25, 29–30, 43, 48–49, 54–55, 62, 67–72, 74, 77, 105, 108–10, 113–14, 116, 121–23, 126–27, 131, 134–35, 137, 141, 144–48, 150, 177, 183
Cioran, Emil, 182
Civil Rights Movement, 137, 150–51, 182
classic, 78–86. *See also* romantic
Cloud of Unknowing, The, 108, 115
Coale, Samuel Chase, 88
Cold Mountain Poems (Snyder), 36–41
Cold War, 106, 113, 115
Collins, Wilkie, 14
Color Purple, The (Walker), 120–26, 130, 133–36, 139–40, 153
Coltrane, John, 119
Commercialization/commercial, 17, 93, 101
Communism, 20, 28
compassion, 9–10, 37, 110, 126–9, 149, 169, 174–76, 186–87
Congress, US, 1, 34, 177, 182
conformity/conformism, 21, 23–24, 28–30, 32, 37, 48, 57, 62, 64–66, 74, 80, 86, 92, 138; anticonformism, 21, 23–24, 30, 53, 66
Confucianism/Confucian, 7, 159–60, 169
Confucius, 11
Connor, Marc, 145
conspiracy/ies, 25, 87–104
consumerism, 3, 5, 23, 31, 37, 43–44, 47, 52, 63, 76, 92, 101
contemplation/contemplative, 67, 69, 110, 116, 122, 147, 156, 159, 164–67, 182
conversion, 9, 17–18, 22, 145, 158
"Conversion of Ah Lew Sing, The" (Austin), 17–18
"Conversion of Sum Loo, The" (Cather), 18
Corelli, Mary, 14
counterculture/countercultural, 3, 8, 15, 21–25, 28–68, 75–104, 119, 122, 132, 138, 157, 159–60, 163, 169–75, 180
crazy wisdom, 22–23, 53, 55, 57, 62

creativity/creative, 3, 5, 12–13, 22, 29, 31–32, 36, 38, 44, 59, 78, 80, 102, 148, 153, 160, 162, 170, 180, 184, 187–88
cross-pressures, 9, 91, 112

Dalai Lama, H. H. the 14th, 9, 110, 130
Daoism, 7, 41, 55, 82, 169, 177
Dark Princess (DuBois), 18
Declaration of Independence, 145
Degas, Edgar, 14
DeLillo, Don, 23–24, 87–88, 104–117
Deming, W. Edwards, 101
democracy, 3–4, 15–16, 33–34, 44, 154, 181
Democratic Vistas (Whitman), 33
Depression (the Great), 3
desire(s), 19, 31, 46, 56, 66, 73, 107, 110, 130, 138, 157, 163, 184, 186
devotion(s), 5, 13, 21, 29, 63, 90–91, 93–98, 127, 146, 158, 163, 167–80
Dhammapada, 12
dharma/dharmic, 7, 41, 44, 47–48, 119, 128, 139, 141, 148
Dharma Academy of North America, 7
Dharma Bums, The (Kerouac), 43, 46–50, 52–53, 66–67, 159, 171
Dharmapala, 158
Dial, The, 11
Diamond Sutra, The, 68
disenchantment/disenchanted, 5, 15, 65, 153, 158
dissent, 32, 35, 60–61, 92
Donner, Frank J., 97
Dreamer (Johnson), 120, 138–39, 144–53, 168
Dreiser, Theodore, 20
Du Bois, W. E. B., 18
Duc, Thich Quang, 160, 163

East/Eastern: culture, 17; religion(s), 15, 47, 51, 54–55, 68, 104–5, 120; spirituality, 122; and West, 20, 25, 50, 52, 69, 177. See also West/Western
Eburne, Jonathan, 29–30
Eckhart, Meister, 68
ecstasy, 12, 113
Eliot, T. S., 18–19, 160, 162
Emerson, Ralph Waldo, 6, 11–13

emptiness, 6, 18–19, 21, 23, 32–35, 37, 42, 44, 50, 53, 110, 120, 141, 145, 147, 149, 152, 159, 166, 169, 172, 185–86. See also *sunyata*
End of the Road, The (Barth), 87
engaged Buddhism: See Buddhism
enlightened individualism, 3–10; and abstraction, 25, 70; and Christianity, 21–22, 62; and colorblindness, 152; and countercultures, 15, 21–22, 31–32, 157, 163; and Orientalism, 4–5, 44, 50, 179
Enlightenment: American, 117, 182; European, 3, 181–82; liberalism, 32, 176, 182–83; Western, 169, 188. See also liberalism
enlightenment: Asian, 3, 25, 168. See also *bodhi, moksa*, nirvana
environmentalism, 38, 41, 62
epiphany, 12, 50, 56, 71, 73, 139, 142–43, 146–47, 165, 168, 172
esotericism/esoteric, 89–91, 97–98, 106, 114, 117. See also secrecy
ethics, 5, 9, 26, 35, 52, 60, 121, 148, 162, 174, 179
"Ethnical Scriptures" (Emerson and Thoreau), 11
Ethnocentrism/ethnocentric, 5
"Etiquette of Freedom, The" (Snyder), 41–42
Europe/European: art, 13, 18; corruption, 19; scholarship, 10–11. See also Enlightenment (European)
Evans-Wentz, Walter, 20
Even Cowgirls Get the Blues (Robbins), 51–58, 120
exotic/exoticize/exoticizing, 5, 12, 14, 18, 25, 29–30, 34, 39, 47–52, 61, 72, 81–82, 101, 105, 110–11, 120, 160, 163–64, 181

fairness, 3
fanaticism/fanatic, 67, 90, 105
Federalist Papers, The, 181
Fenollosa, Ernest, 14, 18
Fields, Rick, 118
Fifth Book of Peace, The, 26, 154, 157, 170–78
Fire Sermon, The, 19, 163–66
First Amendment, 176–77
fixed self, 10, 23
Forster, E. M., 18
Franny and Zooey (Salinger), 24, 61–74, 76–77, 80, 85–86

freedom, 3–4, 23–25, 28–60, 66, 72–73, 83, 91, 97–108, 117, 121, 124, 126, 133, 139, 141, 145, 149, 160, 166–68, 178–79, 183–84. *See also* liberty
Freemasonry, 90
Freud, Sigmund, 106
frontier, 35, 56, 84, 105, 107–8, 117

Gabbard, Tulsi, 1–2
Gaddis, William, 87–88
Gampopa, 187
Gandhi, Mahatma, 145, 148
Ganges (River), 11–12, 38–39
Giamo, Benedict, 31
Giles, Todd, 6
Ginsberg, Allen, 23, 28–35, 46, 51, 76, 90, 122, 129, 133, 163, 169, 171
God, 7, 9–10, 15–16, 29, 45, 63, 68, 70, 77, 83, 108–11, 114, 116, 122–27, 134, 145–47, 183
Goddard, Dwight, 11, 19, 45
Good Sex (Jung et al.), 184
Gospel of Sri Ramakrishna (Gupta), 63, 70–71
Grace, Nancy, 31, 43
grand narratives, 87–88
Griswold, Jerry, 30
guru(s), 4, 9, 53, 57, 70, 76, 90–91, 93–94, 129

Haggard, H. Rider, 14
Hall, Stuart, 10
Han Shan, 36–42, 47
Hancock, Herbie, 119
Hartmann, Sadakichi, 14
Hawkes, John, 88
He, Yuemin, 30
Hearn, Lafcadio, 14
Heart Sutra, 34, 175
hedonism/hedonistic, 10, 181
Herberg, Will, 28
Hergesheimer, Joseph, 18
Herrigel, Eugen, 29, 75, 81–82, 94, 99
Hick, John, 63
Hilton, James, 18
Hinduism/Hindu: metaphysics, 6, 21, 71, 121, 125–26, 148; scripture(s), 1, 11, 66; teaching(s), 4, 11, 18, 26, 46, 52; ritual(s), 14; mysticism, 18; mantra(s), 21

hippie: activism, 64; counterculture, 28, 38, 41, 53, 62, 163, 169, 175. *See also* counterculture(s)
Hirono, Mazie, 1–2
holiness, 6, 23, 53
homosexuality, 46
Hong Kinston, Maxine, 23, 26, 154–57, 168–78
Hoover, Herbert, 3
Human Be-In, 40, 122
Humanism, 9–10, 158
Huxley, Aldous, 62–63

identity. *See* American identity
illusion/illusory, 7, 27, 55, 76, 114, 145, 147, 149, 151–52, 157, 165, 177
imagery, 11, 20, 22, 39, 43, 57, 68, 117, 133–35, 168
immanence, 95, 103, 112
immanent frame, 9–10, 15, 91, 103, 143, 158, 177
immigration/immigrant(s), 13, 17, 26, 86, 118, 132, 154, 157, 159, 178
imperialism, 6
impermanence/impermanent, 7, 19, 37, 42
impersonal, 5, 10, 15–16, 123–26
inauthenticity. *See* authenticity
India, 11, 13, 15–16, 20, 36–38, 44, 46, 76–77, 105, 141, 145, 172, 180
individualism: American, 3–4, 8–10, 15, 23–27, 34, 50, 75, 84–85, 88–89, 97, 105, 108, 117, 124, 154, 168, 188 (*see also* American identity, enlightened individualism); frontier, 84, 108; US, 21, 48, 103, 107, 116; Western, 31, 168
injustice, 3, 150
interdependence, 10, 18, 103, 107, 143, 148, 150
introspection, 10, 62, 67, 82, 148
Isis Unveiled (Blavatsky), 14
Islam, 2, 116
Iwamura, Jane Naomi, 7

Jack Kerouac School of Disembodied Poetics, 35, 45
Jackson, Carl, 30
James, William, 16, 63
Janette, Michelle, 156

Japan/Japanese, 11, 13–14, 20, 29, 35–36, 38, 47, 51, 53, 58, 74, 81–82, 90, 94, 97–103, 138, 149, 154–55, 173–74, 180
Jarman, Joseph, 119
Java Head (Hergesheimer), 18
Jefferson, Thomas, 1
Jesus. *See* Christ
Jew(s)/Judaism/Jewish, 2, 23, 28, 127, 135
John of the Cross, St., 109–11
Johnson, Charles, 23, 26, 118–20, 137–53, 181
Jones, Sir William, 11
Joy of Living, The (Mingyur), 185–86
Joy Luck Club, The (Tan), 157

Kant, Immanuel, 81
Karate Kid, The, 101
karma/karmic, 7, 73–74, 76, 99–101, 114, 140–41, 159–68
Kerouac, Jack, 11, 23, 28–35, 42–52, 163, 169
Kim (Kipling), 18
King, Rev. Dr. Martin Luther, 138–39, 144–53, 181
Kingston, Maxine Hong, 23, 26, 154–57, 168–78
Kipling, Rudyard, 18
koan(s), 49–50, 55–56, 69. *See also* Zen
Koestler, Arthur, 182
Kohn, Robert, 104
Konstantinou, Lee, vii, 32

landscape(s), 2, 8, 102–4, 107–8, 120, 164
Lauret, Maria, 132
law(s), 10, 16, 45, 177
Leary, Timothy, 76, 87, 132
Lennon, John, 76
Leong, Russell, 157
LGBTQ, 182, 185. *See also* homosexuality
liberalism, 3, 8, 17, 32, 103, 138, 176, 181–84
liberty, 12, 16, 56
Light of Asia, The (Arnold), 14
Lincoln in the Bardo (Saunders), 179
Lion's Roar, 119. See also *Shambhala Sun*
Locke, John, 73
Lost Horizon (Hilton), 18–19
Lott, Deshae, 30

Lowe, Lisa, 156
Lowell, Amy, 18
Luminarium (Shakar), 179
Lustbader, Eric Van, 100

Madison, James, 181
Mahesh Yogi, Maharishi, 9, 76, 122–23
mainstream, 8, 21–25, 28–30, 41, 46–47, 61–90, 104, 106–7, 137–38, 188
mantra(s), 32, 34–35, 40, 72, 74, 109–16, 122, 161, 171
Mao II (DeLillo), 105
martial arts, 93, 101–3
materiality, 25, 27, 127, 169, 174
McClure, John, 88, 91, 100
McMahan, David L., 113
meditation: analytical, 158; breathing, 174; Buddhist, 17, 130–33; Christian, 108; eating, 174; seated, 5; secular, 17; solitary, 159; walking, 174; writing, 174 (*see also* Spirit Rock Meditation Center, TM, Transcendental Meditation, *tonglen*)
Meeting of East and West, The (Northrop), 20
memory/memories, 59, 79, 129, 146, 164–66
metaphysics/metaphysical, 6, 10, 21, 23, 25, 33, 71, 74, 76, 79, 82, 121, 125–26, 140, 148, 152, 158, 162, 172, 185
Mexico City Blues (Kerouac), 43
Middle Passage (Johnson), 120, 139–44, 147, 151, 153, 159
Militarism, 5
Mill, John Stuart, 34
Mindful Nation, A (Ryan), 182
Mindfulness, 17, 99–100, 174, 182
Mindfulness-Based Stress Reduction (MBSR), 17
Mingyur Rinpoche, Yongey, 185–88
miracle(s), 5, 151
Mississippi (River), 12, 38
Mitchell, W. J. T., 152
Modernism, 2, 18–19, 157, 160
Moksa, 31, 181
monastic(s) 8, 44, 95, 183
Monet, Claude, 13
Monkey Bridge (Cao), 26, 154, 157, 159–68, 178
Moonstone, The (Collins), 14

Mori, Toshio, 155
Morinaga, Maki Isaka, 97–98
Mormonism/Mormon, 9, 90
Morrison, Toni, 169
Mr. Sammler's Planet (Bellow), 76
My Chinese Marriage (Porter), 18
mystery/mysterious, 6, 14, 34, 53, 55, 94, 101, 105, 107–8, 111
mystic(al)/mysticism, 4, 17–19, 23–24, 39, 44, 52, 58, 61–86
mythology/myth, 9, 12, 47, 49, 107, 132, 136, 156, 160, 170, 177

Names, The (DeLillo), 105
Naropa University, 129. See also *Jack Kerouac School of Disembodied Poetics*
Nash, William, 145
nature/natural, 103, 120, 124, 130, 131–35
New Age, 4, 8, 175
Newton, Isaac, 81
Nguyen, Viet Thanh, 157
Nicene Creed, 70
Nile (River), 12
Ninjutsu, 25, 93, 96–104
nirvana, 160, 164–68, 181
Nixon under the Bodhi Tree, 180
No No Boy (Okada), 155
nonattachment, 3, 44, 48, 75, 187
nonduality/nondual, 6, 10, 21, 26, 29, 38–39, 69, 78, 82–86, 107, 111–12, 117, 119–21, 129, 134, 137–47, 152–53, 159, 180–83, 185, 187–88
nonself, 23, 26, 33, 38, 44, 143, 147, 150, 154–78
nontheistic, 10
normative, 24, 68, 86
Northrop, W. F. C., 20, 79
nova effect, 2
Now is the Time to Open Your Heart (Walker), 120–21, 126–28, 130–37, 152–53

oath(s), 1
Obama, Barack, 152
Odin, Steve, 81
Okada, John, 155
Olcott, Henry Steel, 14, 118
Oppenheimer, J. Robert, 20
opportunity, 3

Orientalism/Orientalist, 4–6, 14, 17–19, 21–23, 30, 37, 43, 47–56, 79–80, 155, 157, 164, 175, 179
Orinoco (River), 12
orthodoxy/orthodox, 12, 68, 70–71, 81, 138, 183
otherness, 29, 105, 107, 181
Otsuka, Julie, 157
Oxherding Tale (Johnson), 138
Ozeki, Ruth, 157

Paganism/pagan, 54–55, 58, 121, 124, 127
paranoia/paranoid, 25, 64, 88–97, 106–17, 161, 174
Park, Josephine, 18, 155, 160
Passage to India, A (Forster), 18
"Passage to India" (Whitman), 172
Passionate Buddha, The (Sachs), 187
patriotism, 3, 17, 23–24, 32
Pentagon, 40, 122
Perennial Philosophy, The (Huxley), 62–63
perennialism/perennial philosophy, 62–63, 68
"Perfect Day for Bananafish, A" (Salinger), 64–65
Pew Forum on Religion & Public Life, 8
Phoenix Eyes (Leong), 157
Pirsig, Robert, 20, 23–24, 61–62, 75–87, 131, 138, 171
Plate (River), 12
Plato, 81, 83
porous self, 10, 143, 148. See also buffered self
Porter, Katherine Anne, 18
postmodernism/postmodern, 24–25, 60, 86–88, 101, 104, 115–17
postsecular, 2, 167
Pound, Ezra, 18
Prabhupada, A. C. Bhakdivedanta Swami, 76
Prajnaparamita Heart Sutra. See Heart Sutra
prophecy, 32
Protestantism/Protestant, 1, 8, 23, 28, 158
Prothero, Stephen, 1, 10, 31, 118
Psychedelic Experience, The (Leary et al.), 132–33
Pynchon, Thomas, 23–24, 87–88, 91–92

quality, 56, 80–85, 97

racism/racist, 3, 5, 26, 54, 119–20, 129, 139, 149–50, 152, 158
radicalism/radical, 24–25, 29, 60, 67, 75, 87, 91, 93–97, 171, 188
Rajneesh, 90
Ram Dass, 76, 132. *See also* Alpert, Richard
Ramakrishna, 61, 63, 70–71, 74, 158
Ranchan, Som P., 74
rationality, 8–9, 80, 83
Reagan, Ronald, 93, 95
Recognitions, The (Gaddis), 87
Revolutionary War, 11
reincarnation, 7, 57, 73–74
renunciation, 4, 13, 46, 67, 181, 184, 186
Revenge of the Mooncake Vixen (Chin), 157
rights, 176–78; human rights, 153; individual rights, 3–4, 16, 92, 117, 181
Riprap (Snyder), 36–42
ritual(s), 8, 13–15, 23, 25, 39–40, 88, 105, 107, 127, 154–59, 165–69, 173
Robbins, Tom, 23, 28, 32, 51–60
Romance of Two Worlds, A (Corelli), 14
romantic, 78–86. *See also* classic
Romantic/Romanticism, 12, 33
rugged, 3, 12, 85, 117
Running Dog (DeLillo), 105
Ryan, Tim, 182

Sachs, Robert, 187
Salak, Kira, 180
Salinger, J. D., 61, 63–75, 77–78, 85–86, 131, 138, 171
Salzberg, Sharon, 186
San Francisco Zen Center, 35
Sanskrit, 6, 39–40, 45, 70, 73, 81, 93, 110, 115–16, 132, 145, 152, 157, 166
Satha-Anand, Suwanna, 184
satori, 58–59
Saunders, George, 179
Savvas, Theophilus, 88
Schmidt, Leigh, 8
Schueller, Malini Johar, 6
Schultz, Bud and Ruth, 97
science, 14, 161–64, 167
Science of Being and Art of Living (Maharishi Mahesh Yogi), 123

scripture(s), 1–2, 11, 19, 34, 43, 66, 149, 163
Scripture of the Golden Eternity, The (Kerouac), 43
Secrecy, 88–117. *See also* esotericism
Secular Age, A (Taylor), 2, 9
secularity/secular, 2, 7, 9–10, 17, 53, 155, 158, 167, 177, 181–82
Self-Realization Fellowship, 89
self-reliance, 13, 36, 84
Self-Reliance (Emerson), 12
selfless(ness), 1, 151–52, 170, 173
Selzer, Linda, 119, 131
Senzaki, Nyogen, 29
Sermons of a Buddhist Abbot (Soyen), 16
sexuality, 30, 32, 37–38, 44, 46, 57, 66, 183–87; homosexuality, 46; liberation, 53, 105; sexual misconduct, 88–89, 94, 112, 176
"Seymour—An Introduction" (Salinger), 74–75
Shakar, Alex, 179
Shambhala Sun, 152. *See also* *Lion's Roar*
Shimano Roshi, Eido Tai, 76
Shine (River), 12
Shinto, 7, 20
Shorter, Wayne, 119
Siddha Yoga, 89
Silko, Leslie Marmon, 169
skillful means, 45, 183. *See also* *upaya*
Slaughterhouse Five (Vonnegut), 76
Smith, Huston, 7, 63
"Smoky the Bear Sutra" (Snyder), 38–42
Snyder, Gary, 23, 28–32, 35–42, 51–53, 55–56, 59, 62, 66, 72, 103, 122, 163, 169, 173, 175
social justice, 3, 185
Some of the Dharma (Kerouac), 43–48
Soyen, Shaku, 15–16, 22, 158
Spirit Rock Meditation Center, 35, 128, 130, 136
spirits, 5, 10, 121, 128, 130, 133, 159, 161
spirituality, 6–9; ancestral, 121, 130, 136; Asian-inspired, 24, 88, 125; Buddhist, 135; environmentalist, 41; Hindu, 196
squareness/square, 62, 64, 75, 78–81, 86
Sri Lanka/Sri Lankan, 10, 14
St. Lawrence (River), 12
Stalling, Jonathan, 18
Steele, Ralph, 119

stereotype(s)/stereotyping, 6, 17–18, 21, 30–32, 36, 43, 47–48, 52, 73, 78–80, 90, 101, 113, 155, 170, 180
Stoic, The (Dreiser), 20
Storhoff, Gary, 142, 145
Stride Toward Freedom (M. L. King), 145
suffering/suffer, 13, 35, 49, 58, 81, 114, 126, 129, 132–33, 139, 146, 148, 157, 164–66, 173
suicide, 12, 70, 64–65, 69, 162, 164
sunyata, 6
superstition(s)/superstitious, 5, 10, 13–15, 158
Suzuki, D. T., 11, 14, 16, 19–20, 36, 43, 61, 64, 68, 94
symbol(s)/symbolism, 2, 6, 9, 25, 39–40, 56, 67, 73–74, 110, 135, 140–41, 150, 159, 167
synthesis, 3–4, 10, 20, 23, 32–33, 35, 39–44, 47, 49, 52, 59, 68, 74, 79, 88, 133, 135, 148, 150, 162, 164, 169, 177, 185, 187–88

Tale for the Time Being (Ozeki), 157
tales of imagination, 156, 159
tales of witness, 156, 159
Tan, Amy, 157
Taylor, Charles, 2, 5, 9, 28, 55, 112, 127, 143, 167, 177, 183
technocracy, 44, 77, 87
Teenage Mutant Ninja Turtles, 100
territorial expansion, 3
Terry, Megan, 173
Thailand/Thai, 11, 184
theodicy, 5
theology, 14, 29
Thoreau, Henry David, 11–13
Tibet/Tibetan, 11, 33, 37–38, 51, 53, 56, 89, 93, 104–17, 126–30, 132, 185, 187
Tibetan Book of the Dead, 113. See also *Bardo Thodol*
Tibetan Peach Pie (Robbins), 51, 58–59
Tillich, Paul, 182
TM, 122–26. See also Transcendental Meditation
tonglen meditation, 126–28
transcendence: Asian, 3–10, 103, 185; Buddhist, 49–50; Hindu, 126, 180; spiritual, 23, 121, 127, 140 (see also *bodhi, moksa, nirvana*)
Transcendental Meditation, 9, 76, 89, 122. See also TM

Transcendentalism, 2, 4, 11–13, 31
transnationalism/transnational, 2, 5, 14, 130, 135, 178, 180
transparency, 89–90, 99
Tricycle (magazine), 119
Trigilio, Tony, 31, 33
Tripmaster Monkey (Kingston), 157, 170–71
Trungpa, Chögyam, 33–34, 53, 76, 90, 129
Turner, Frederick Jackson, 84, 108
Turning the Wheel (Johnson), 139
Tweed, Thomas, 4, 10

ultimate reality, 7, 26, 110, 115, 123, 125, 142
uncanny, 91, 106–10, 116
Underworld (DeLillo), 24–25, 87–91, 104–17
undifferentiation/undifferentiated, 7, 15, 26, 114–15, 142, 148
unity, 11, 23, 69, 93, 95, 124–26, 140–44
universalism/universal/universalist, 6, 11, 13–16, 26, 54, 63, 97, 140, 142, 149, 152, 181, 185, 187
Upanishads, 19, 68, 84
upaya, 183. See also skillful means
utopianism/utopian, 87, 94, 122, 144

Varieties of Religious Experience, The (James), 16
Vedanta, 15–16, 19, 74, 172, 183
Versluis, Arthur, 4, 7
Viet Rock (Terry), 173
Vietnam War, 57–58, 77, 86, 88, 111, 115, 122, 157, 159, 162–63, 168–80
Villa Incognito (Robbins), 51, 57–58
Vineland (Pynchon), 24–25, 87–104, 106–7, 116–17
Vivekananda, Swami, 15–16, 21, 61, 63–64, 183
Vonnegut, Kurt, 76, 88

Walden (Thoreau), 11–12
Walker, Alice, 23, 26, 118–41, 153, 184, 188
"Walking" (Thoreau), 12
Washington, George, 1, 16
Waste Land, The (Eliot)
Watts, Alan, 19, 29–30, 36, 42, 48, 61–62, 75
Way of a Pilgrim, The, 68, 70
Weber, Max, 5

West/Western: abstractions, 173; adaptation(s), 5, 160, 178; civilization, 20, 45; culture(s), 2, 30, 32, 44; individualism, 31, 168; religion, 111; science, 161–64. *See also* East/Eastern

Whalen, Philip, 29, 32

Whalen-Bridge, John, 6, 150

Whistler, James, 13

White Noise (DeLillo), 105

Whitfield, Stephen, 64

Whitman, Walt, 6, 32, 171

wild/wildness, 36–42, 52, 57–59, 62, 140

Williams, R. John, 18, 52, 78, 85, 100

Willis, Jan, 119

Wilson, Jeff, 31

wisdom, 5, 11–12, 14, 39, 48, 54–58, 65, 69–70, 72, 89, 102–3, 106–7, 111–12, 115–16, 120, 123, 128, 130, 136, 139–53, 172, 187. *See also* crazy wisdom

Wise, Tim, 152

Woman Warrior, The (Kingston), 169–70

World Parliament of Religions, 13–17, 31, 61–64, 108. *See also* World's Columbian Exposition

World's Columbian Exposition, 14–15, 108. *See also* World Parliament of Religions

WWI, 19, 162

WWII, 4, 11, 20–22, 77, 93

yagé, 131–35

Yokohama, California (Mori), 155

You Are Not Here (Kachtick), 180

Young, James O., 4

Zen, 14–16, 19, 30, 35–36, 38, 47, 53–59, 68, 74–75, 81–82, 94–95, 99–105, 110, 138, 149, 169, 180, 182; Beat Zen, 30, 42, 48; Zen Boom, 22, 61; Zen koan(s), 49–50, 55, 69; Zen Lunatics, 47–48, 53, 62

Zen and the Art of Motorcycle Maintenance (Pirsig), 24, 61–62, 75, 78–86

Zen in the Art of Archery (Herrigel), 75, 81, 94

Zen Mission, 19

LITERATURE, RELIGION, AND POSTSECULAR STUDIES
LORI BRANCH, SERIES EDITOR

Literature, Religion, and Postsecular Studies publishes scholarship on the influence of religion on literature and of literature on religion from the sixteenth century onward. Books in the series include studies of religious rhetoric or allegory; of the secularization of religion, ritual, and religious life; and of the emerging identity of postsecular studies and literary criticism.

Enlightened Individualism: Buddhism and Hinduism in American Literature from the Beats to the Present
  KYLE GARTON-GUNDLING

A Theology of Sense: John Updike, Embodiment, and Late Twentieth-Century American Literature
  SCOTT DILL

Walker Percy, Fyodor Dostoevsky, and the Search for Influence
  JESSICA HOOTEN WILSON

The Religion of Empire: Political Theology in Blake's Prophetic Symbolism
  G. A. ROSSO

Clashing Convictions: Science and Religion in American Fiction
  ALBERT H. TRICOMI

Female Piety and the Invention of American Puritanism
  BRYCE TRAISTER

Secular Scriptures: Modern Theological Poetics in the Wake of Dante
  WILLIAM FRANKE

Imagined Spiritual Communities in Britain's Age of Print
  JOSHUA KING

Conspicuous Bodies: Provincial Belief and the Making of Joyce and Rushdie
  JEAN KANE

Victorian Sacrifice: Ethics and Economics in Mid-Century Novels
  ILANA M. BLUMBERG

Lake Methodism: Polite Literature and Popular Religion in England, 1780–1830
  JASPER CRAGWALL

Hard Sayings: The Rhetoric of Christian Orthodoxy in Late Modern Fiction
  THOMAS F. HADDOX

Preaching and the Rise of the American Novel
  DAWN COLEMAN

Victorian Women Writers, Radical Grandmothers, and the Gendering of God
  GAIL TURLEY HOUSTON

Apocalypse South: Judgment, Cataclysm, and Resistance in the Regional Imaginary
  ANTHONY DYER HOEFER